IN DER FREMDE
Pictures from Home

ROMEO ALAEFF

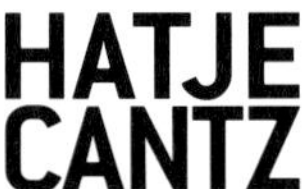

"We began as wanderers, and we are wanderers still."

— Carl Sagan, *Cosmos*

IN DER FREMDE *

Pictures from Home

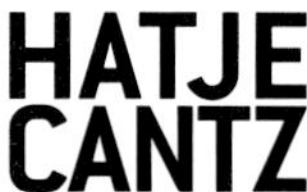

ROMEO ALAEFF

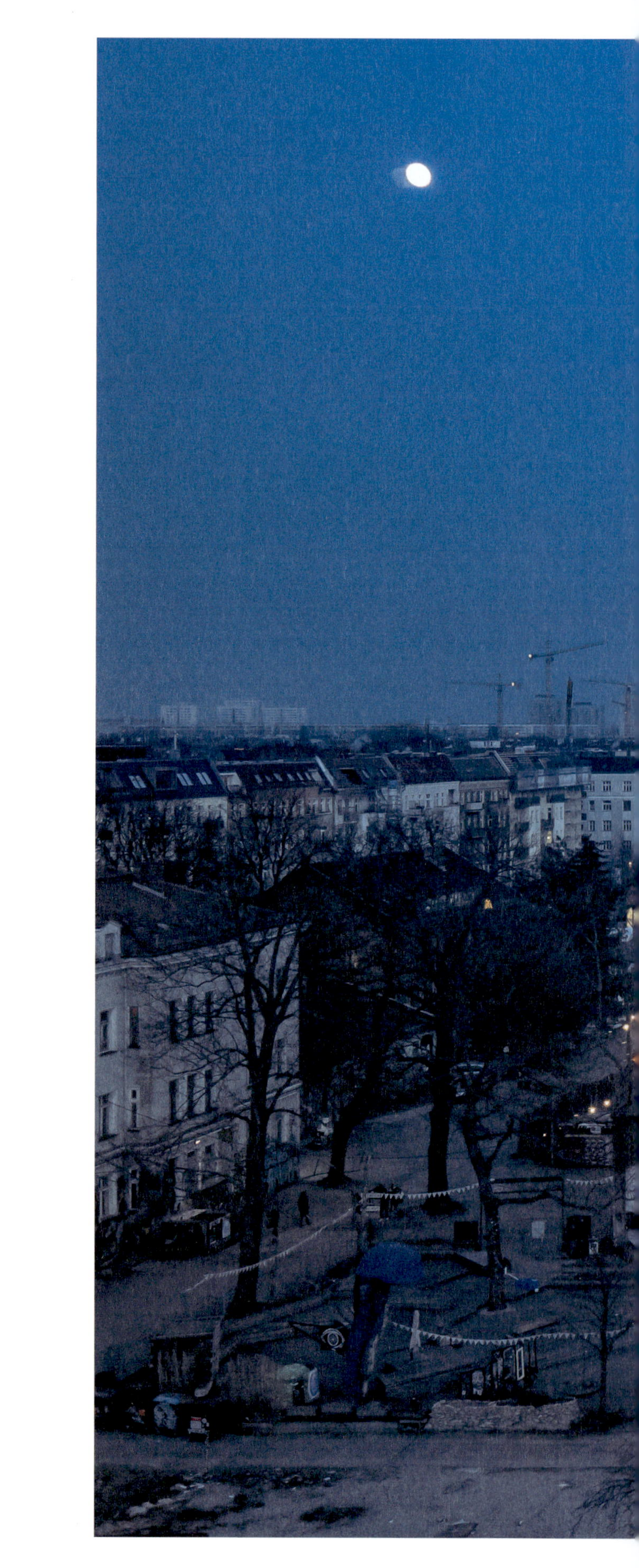

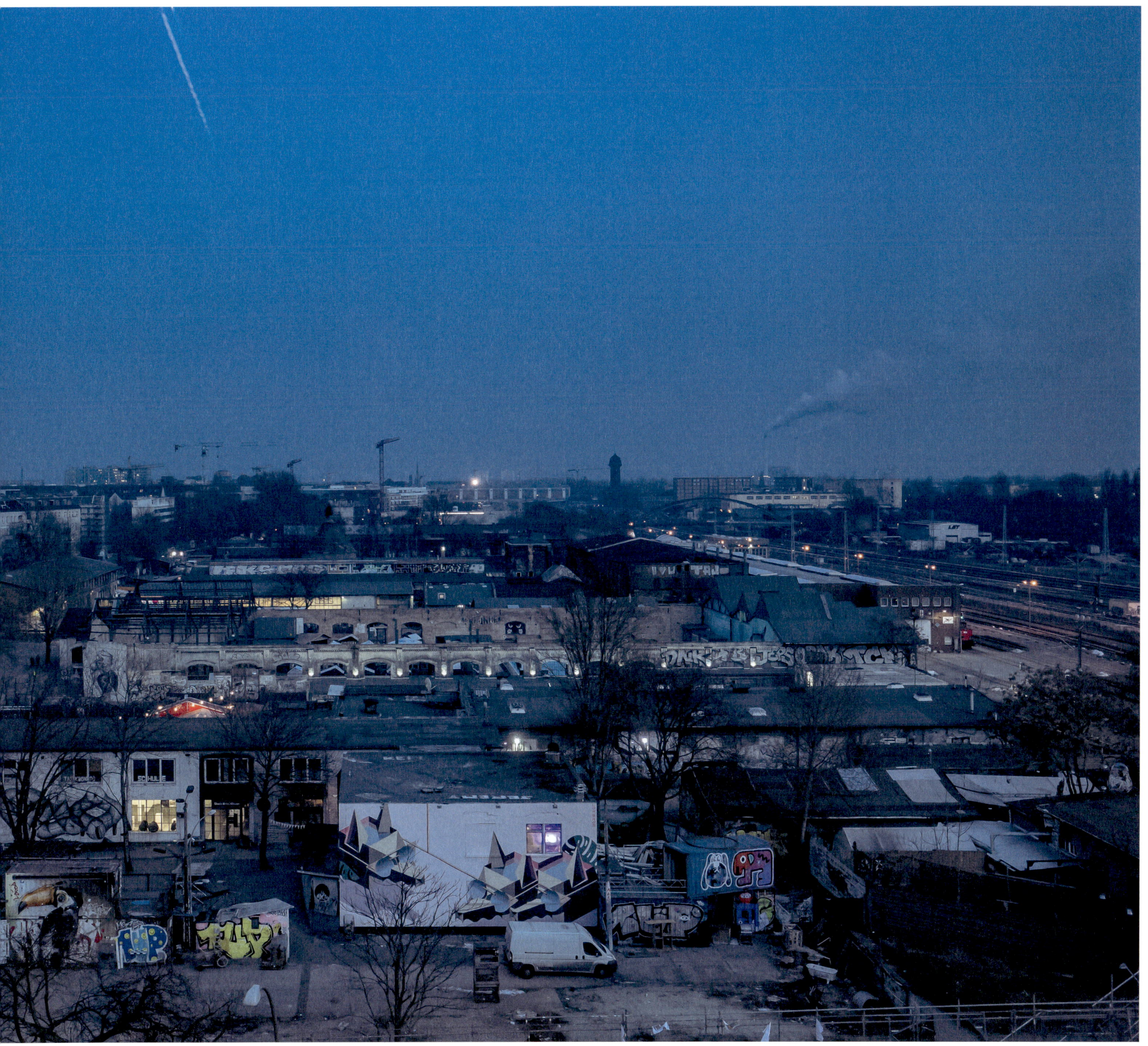

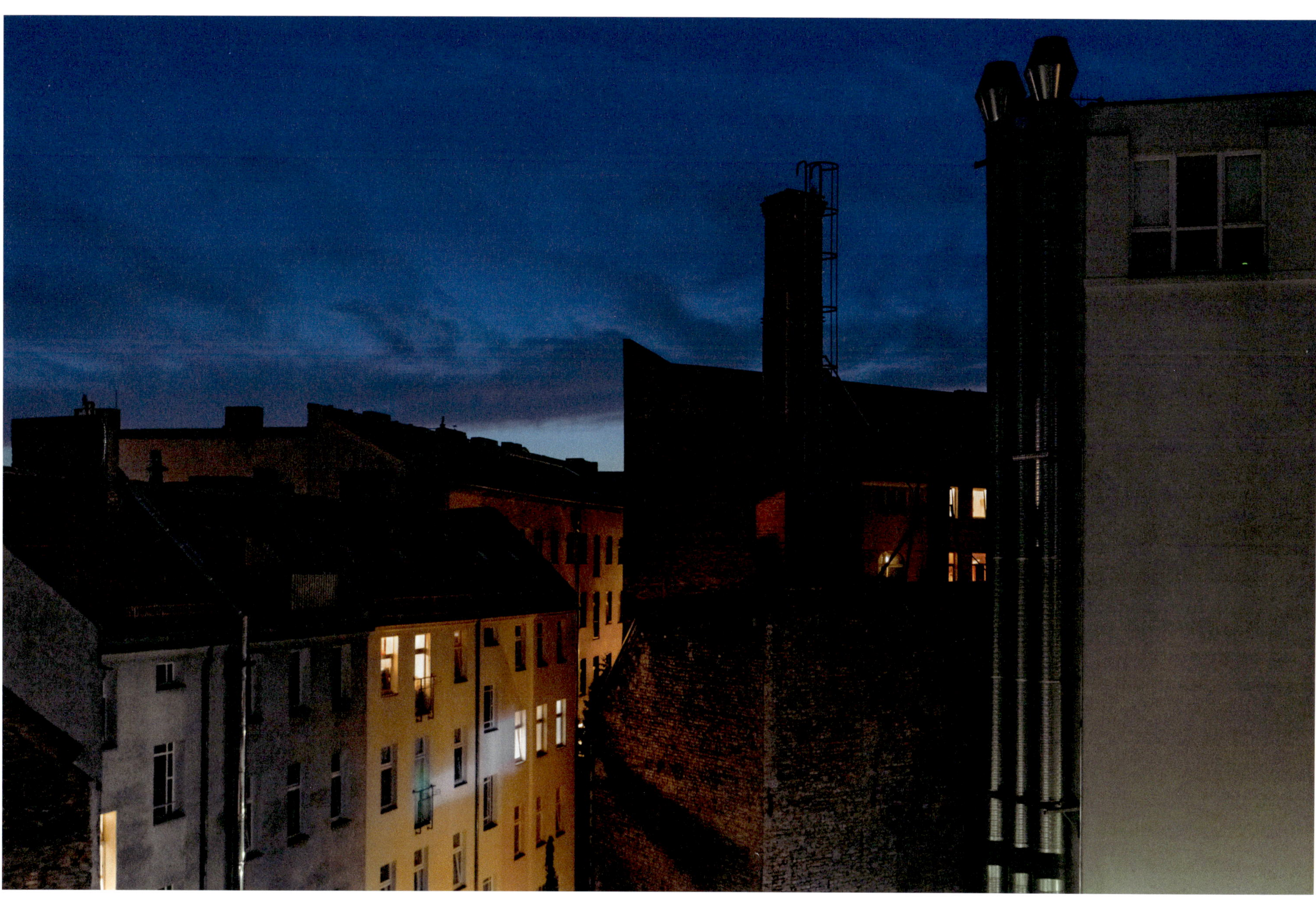

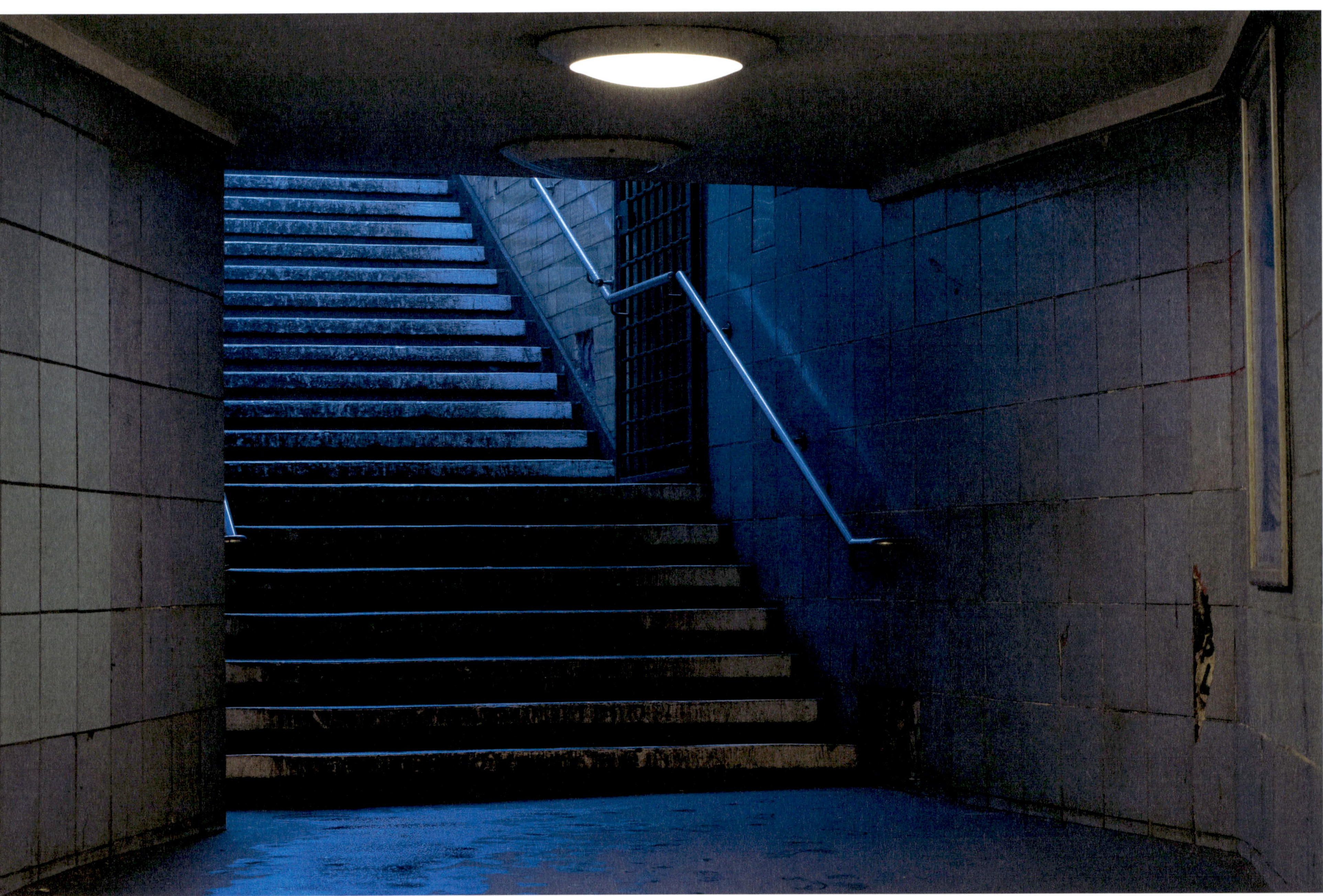

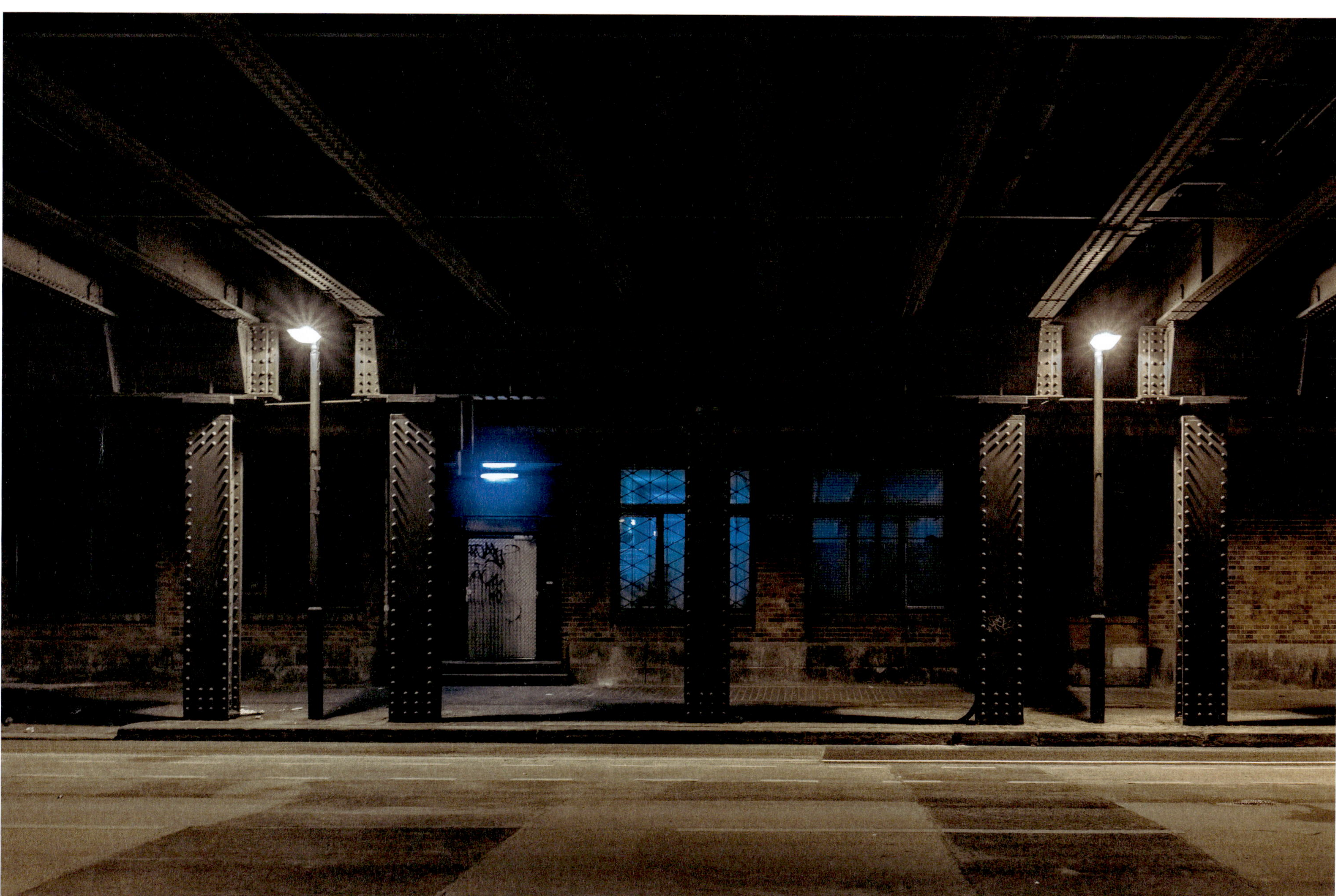

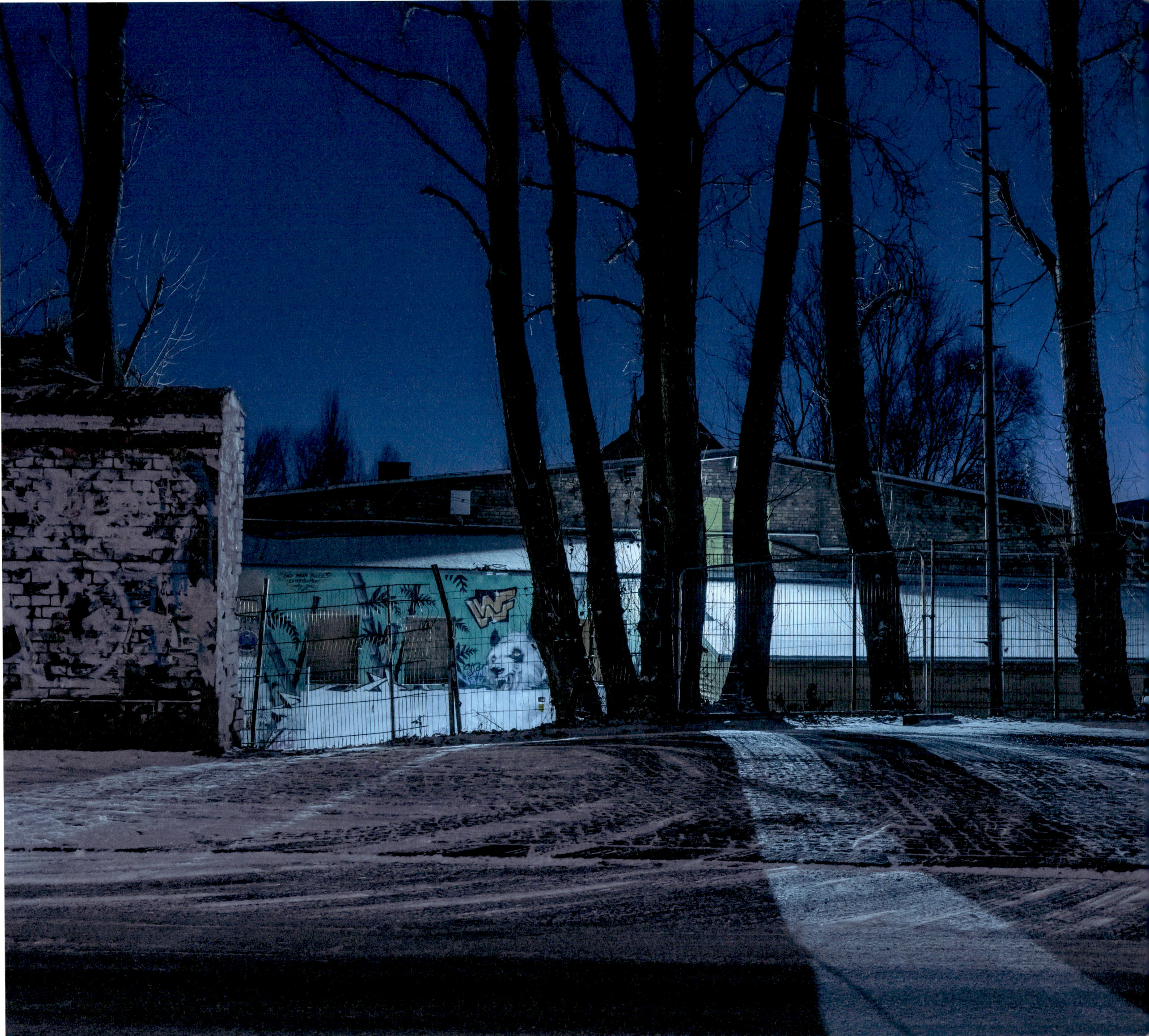

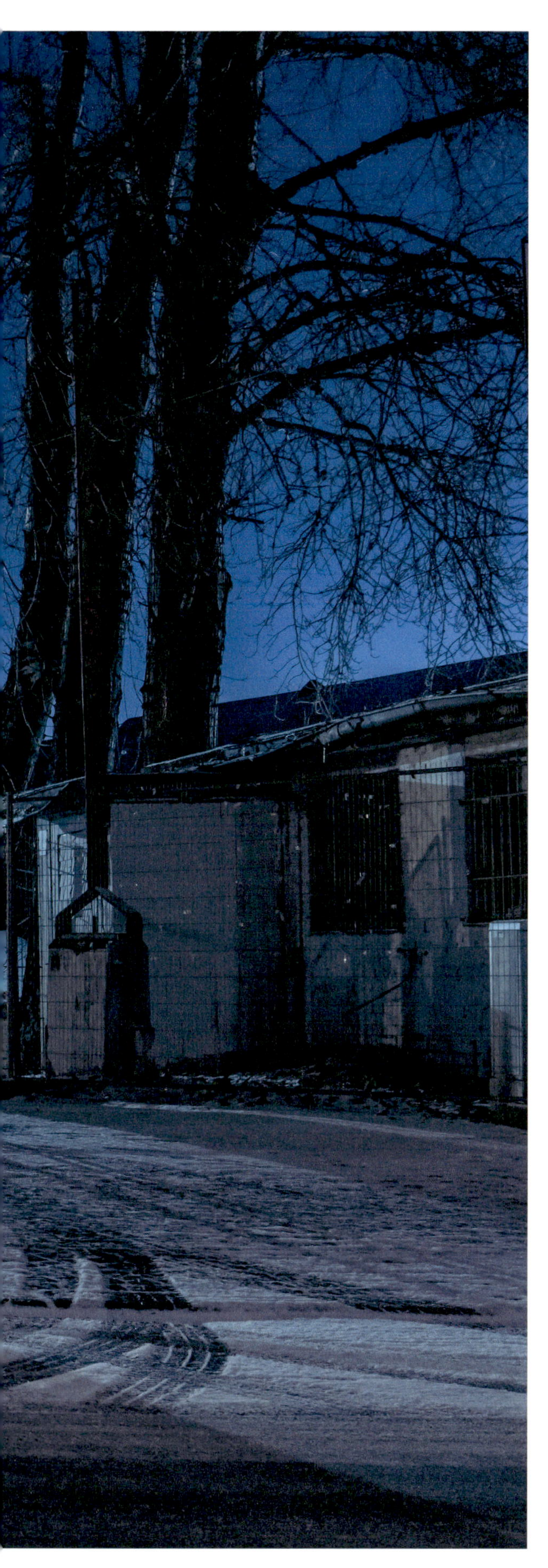

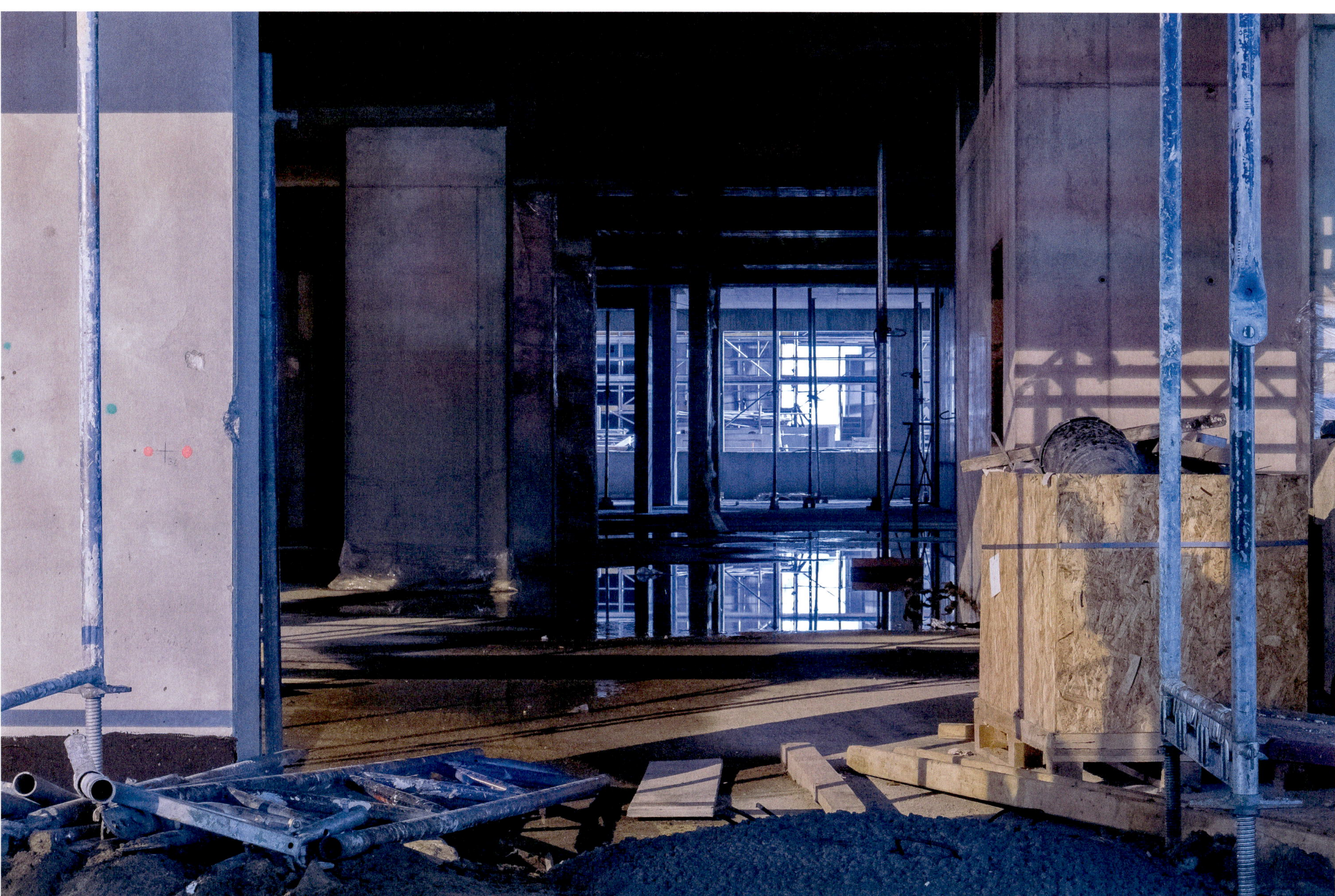

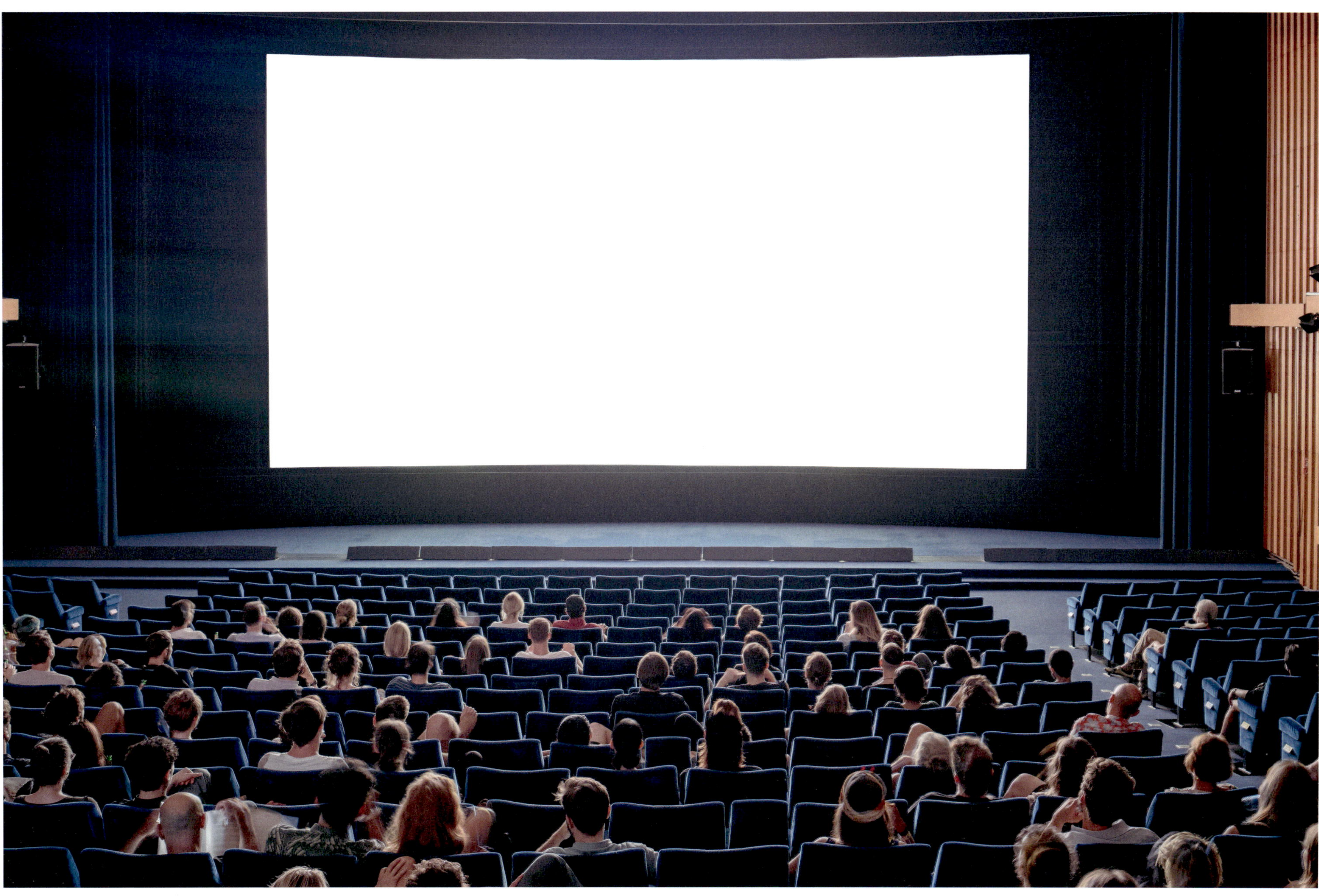

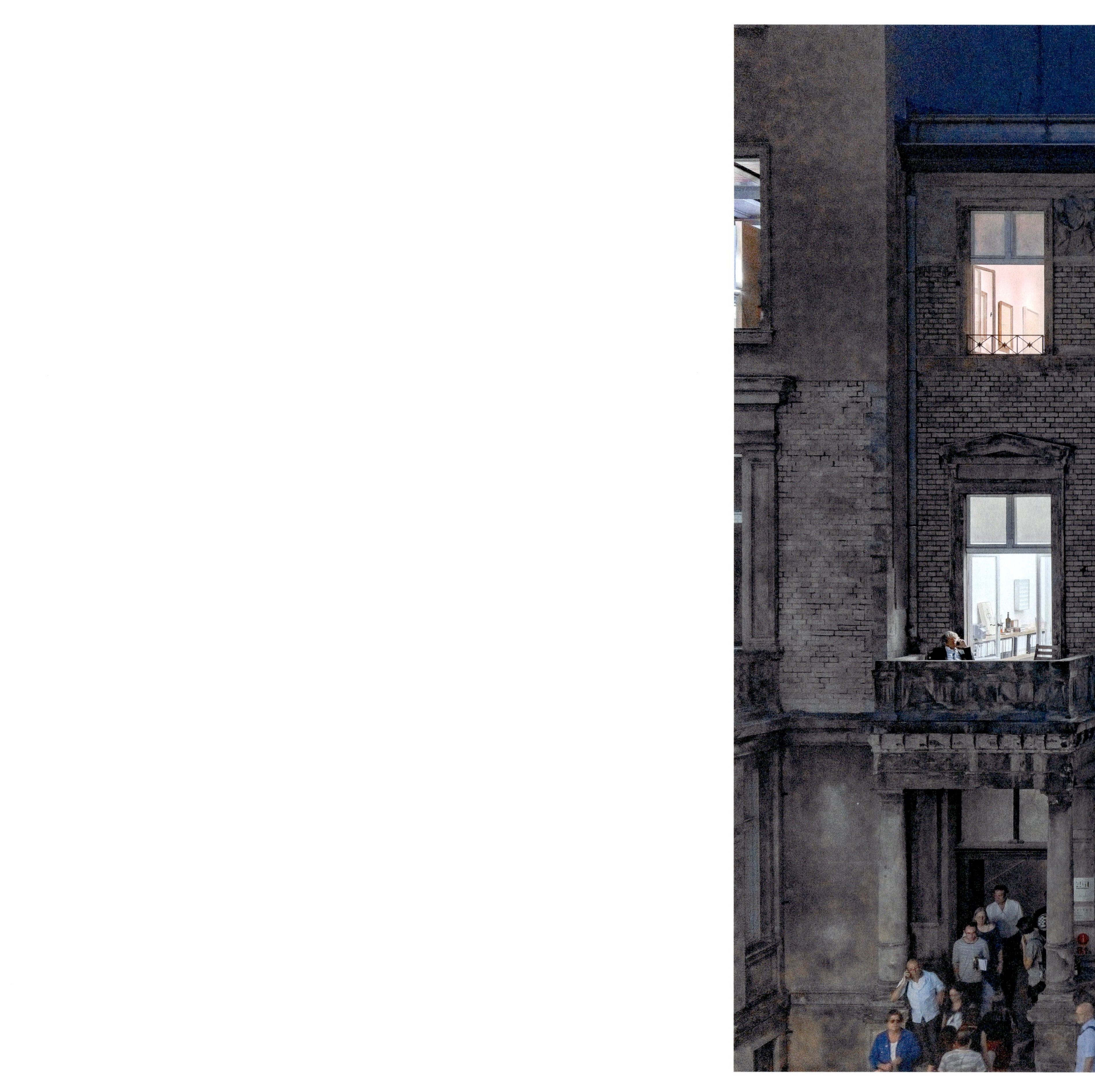

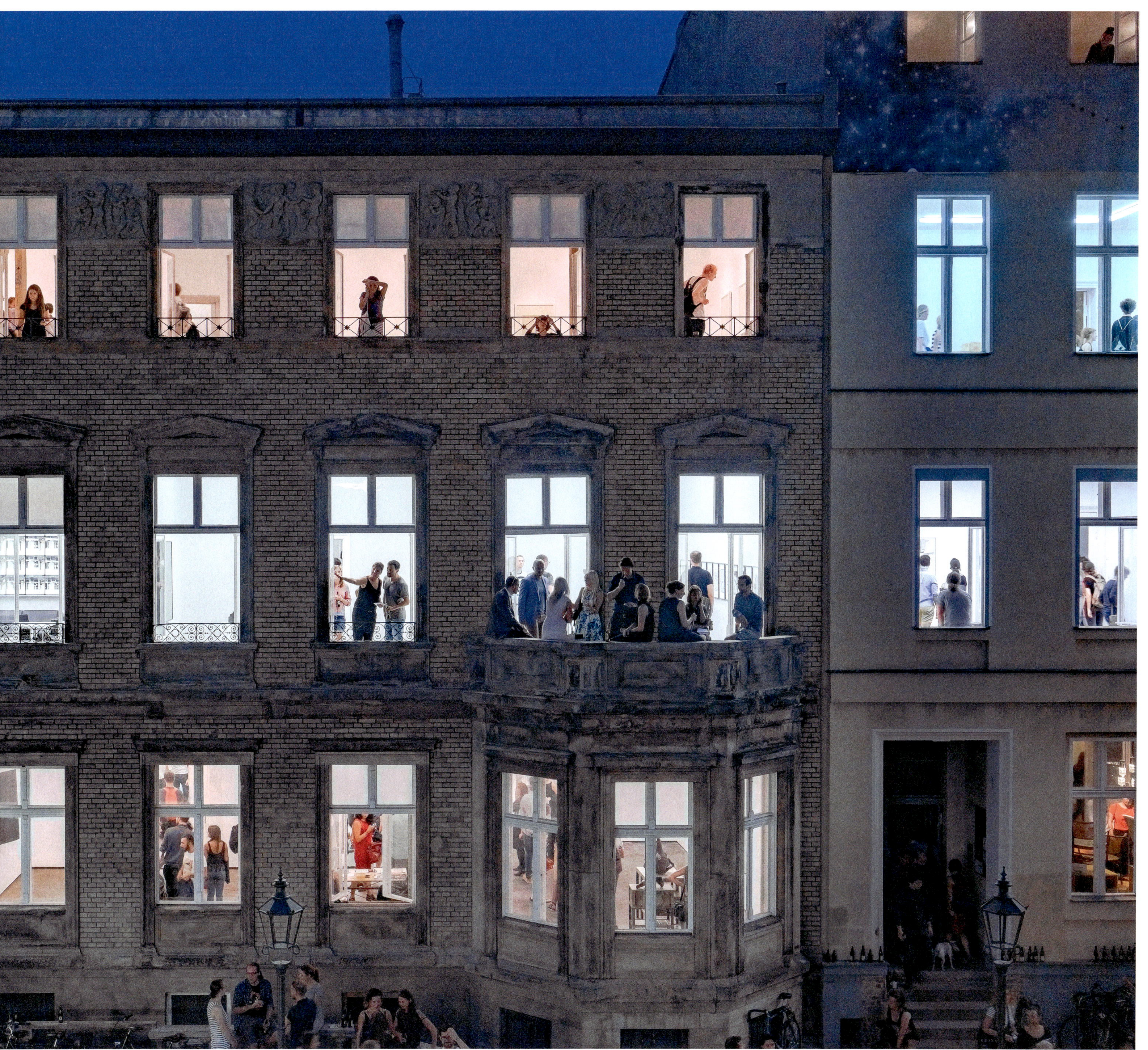

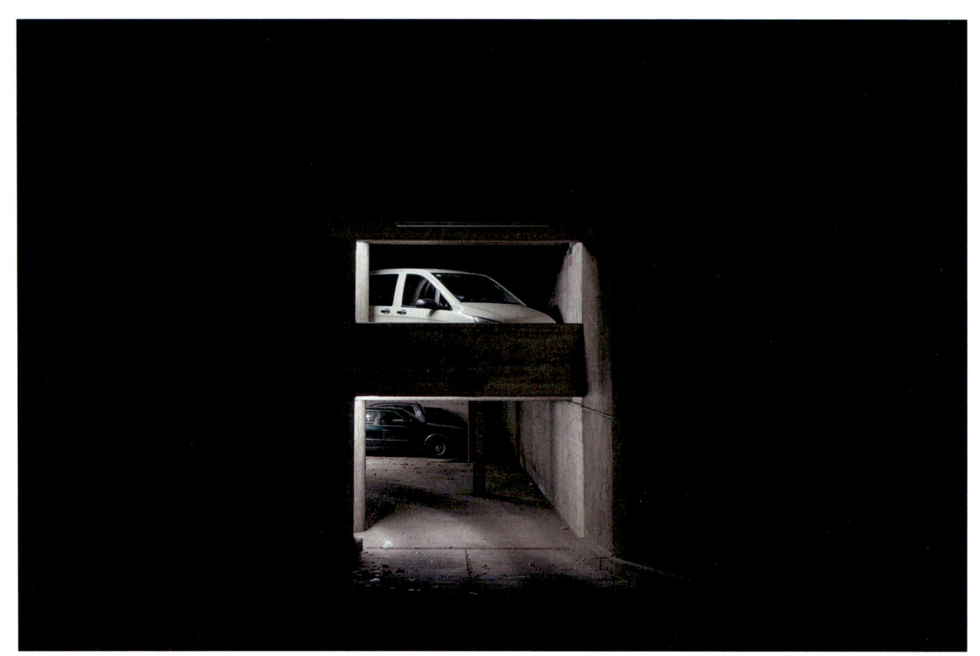

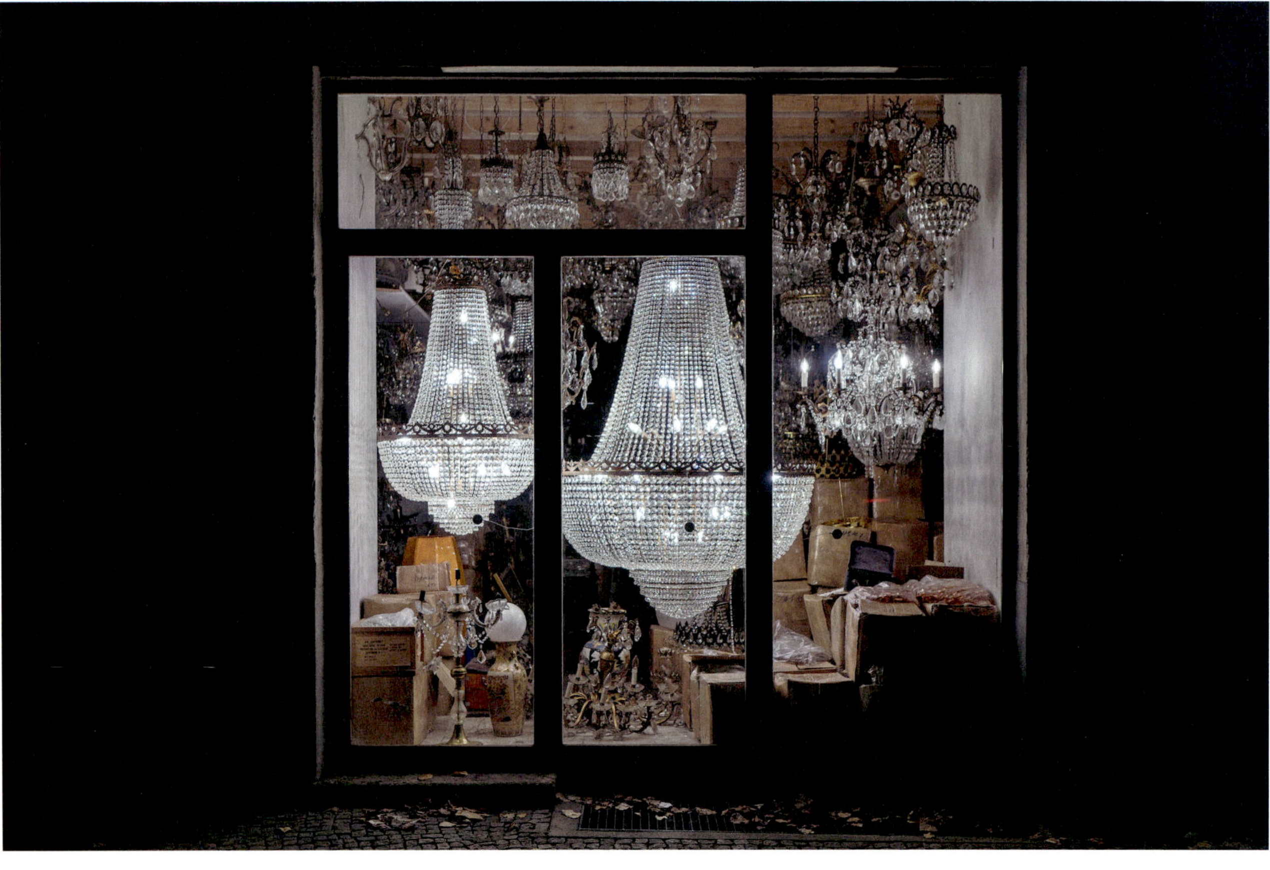

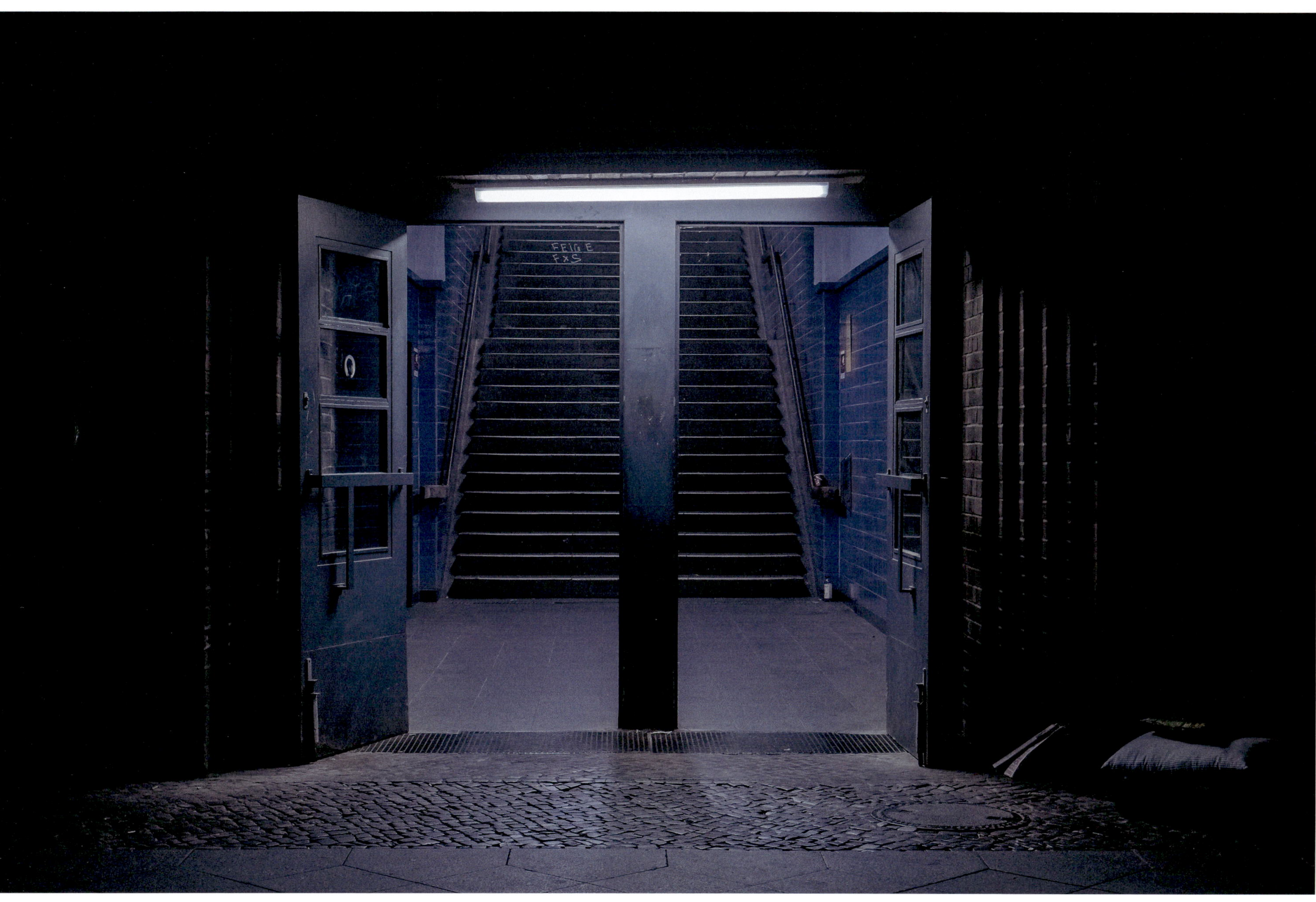

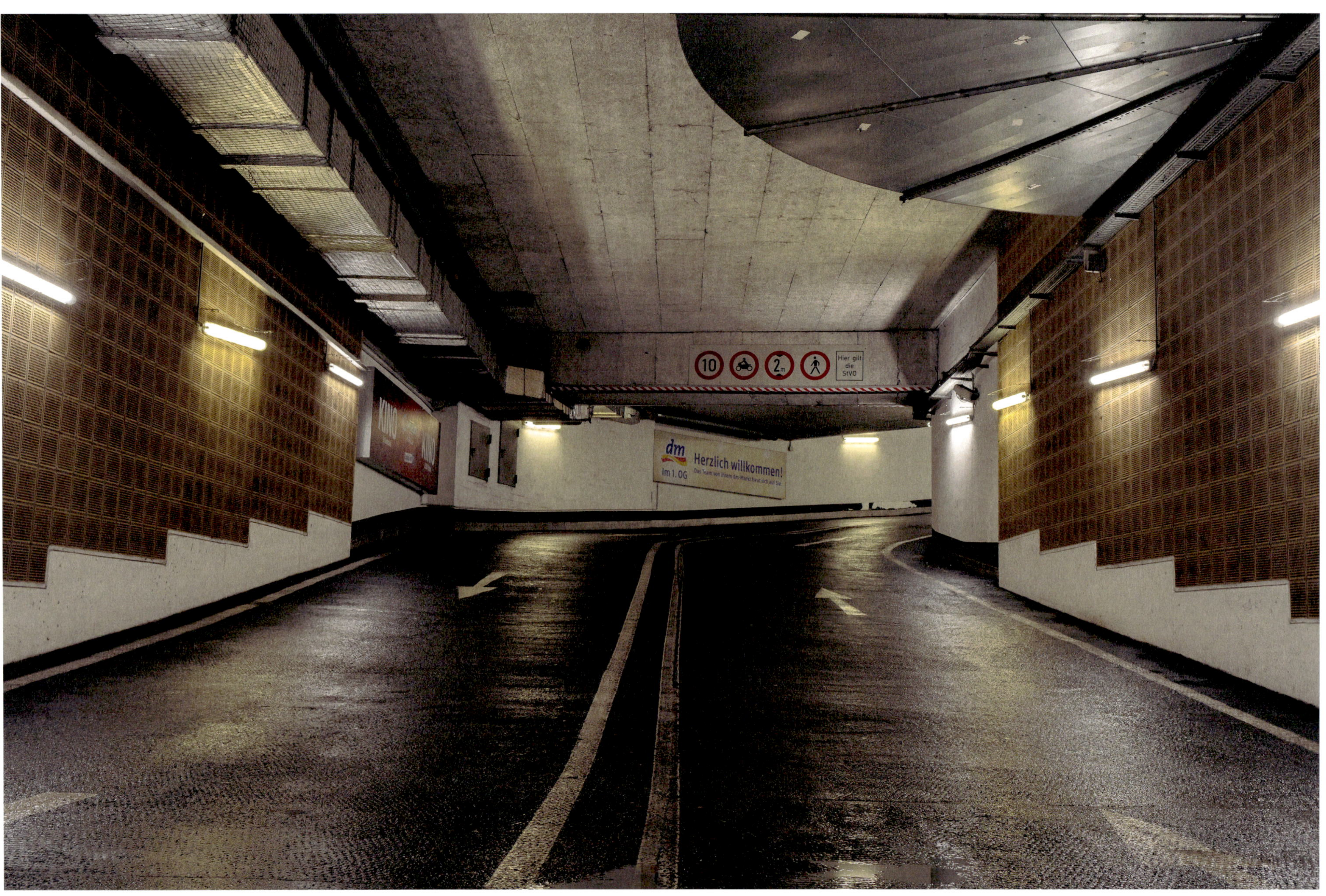
Hier gilt die StVO
dm
im 1.OG
Herzlich willkommen!

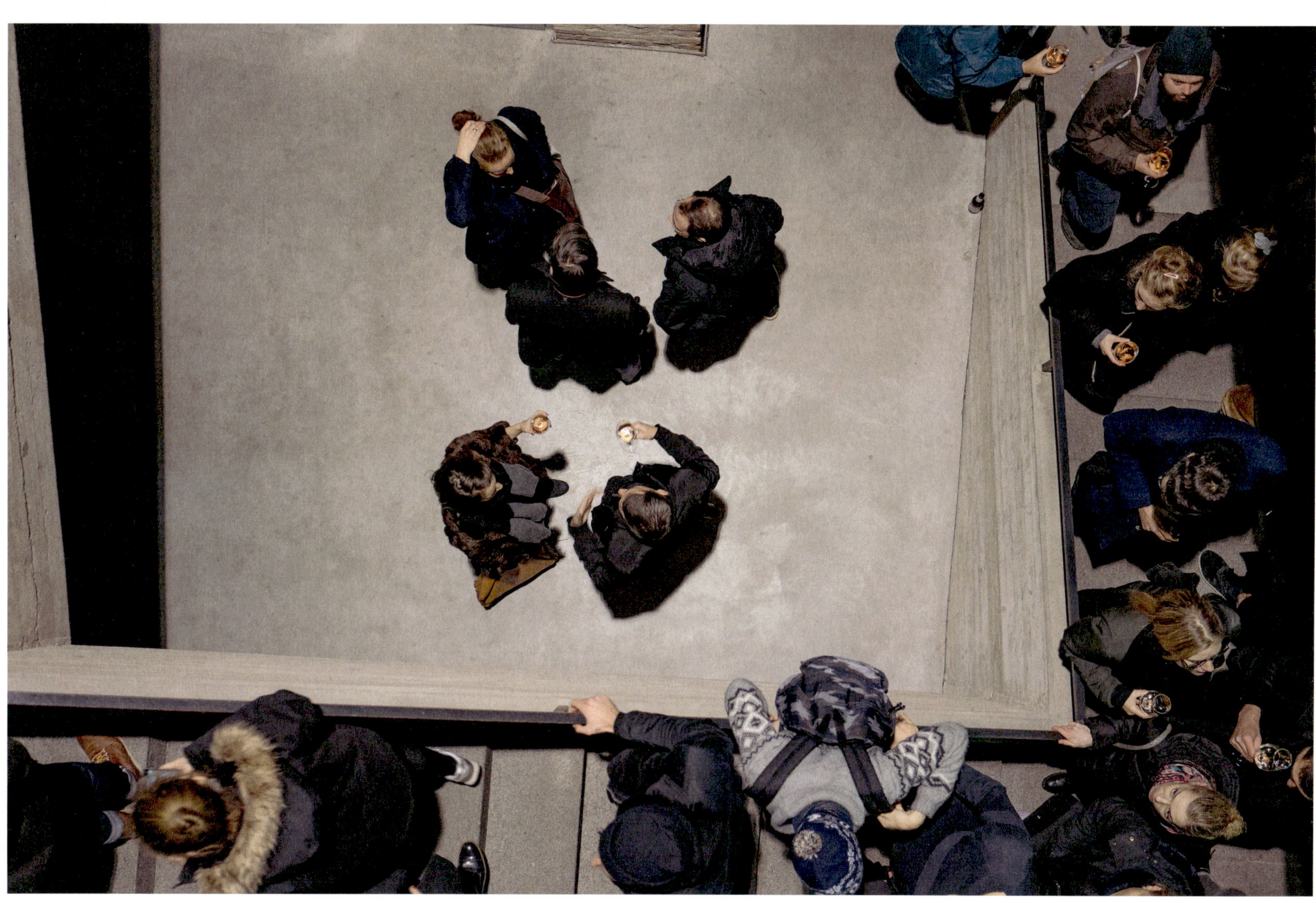

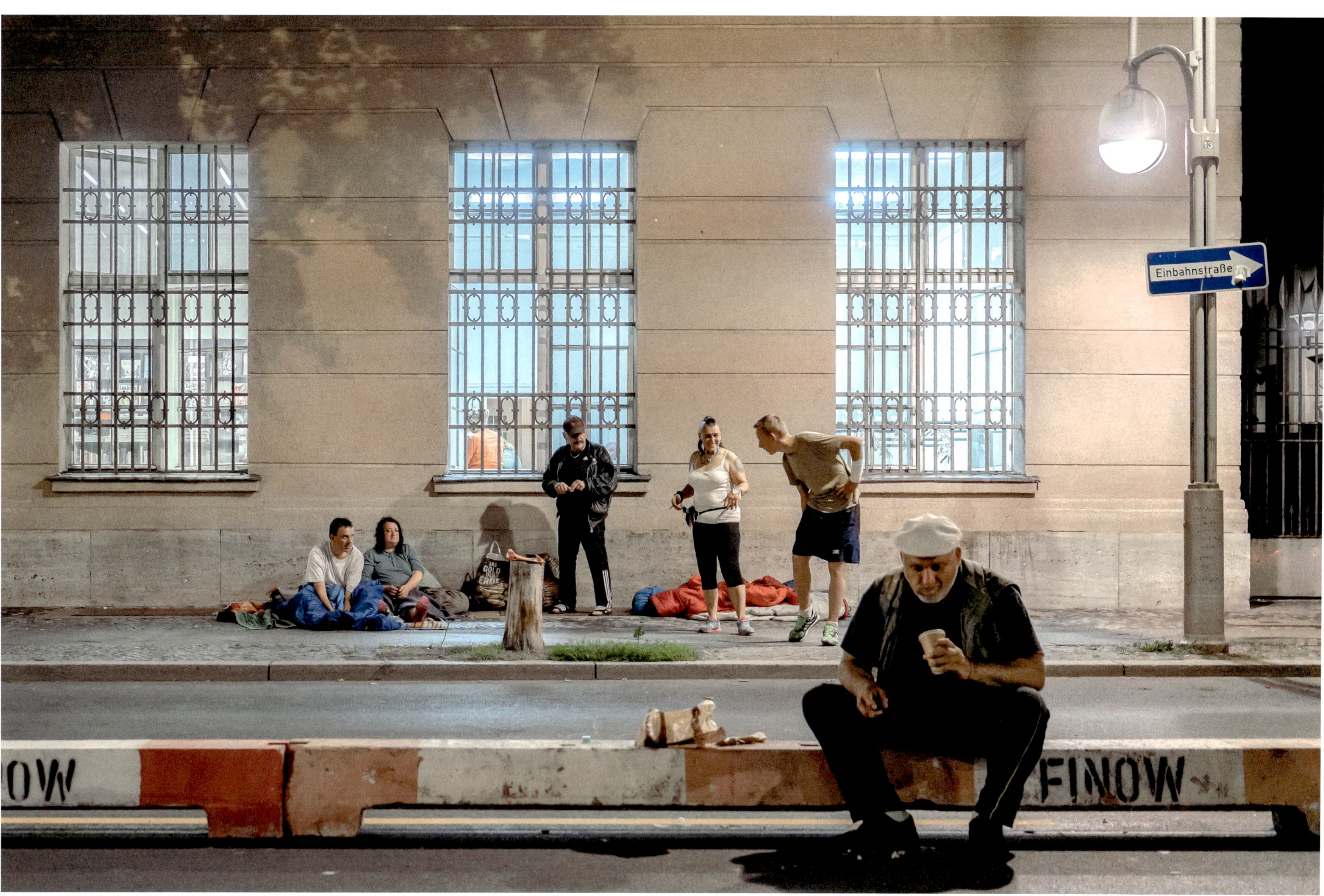

Einbahnstraße
FINOW
NOW

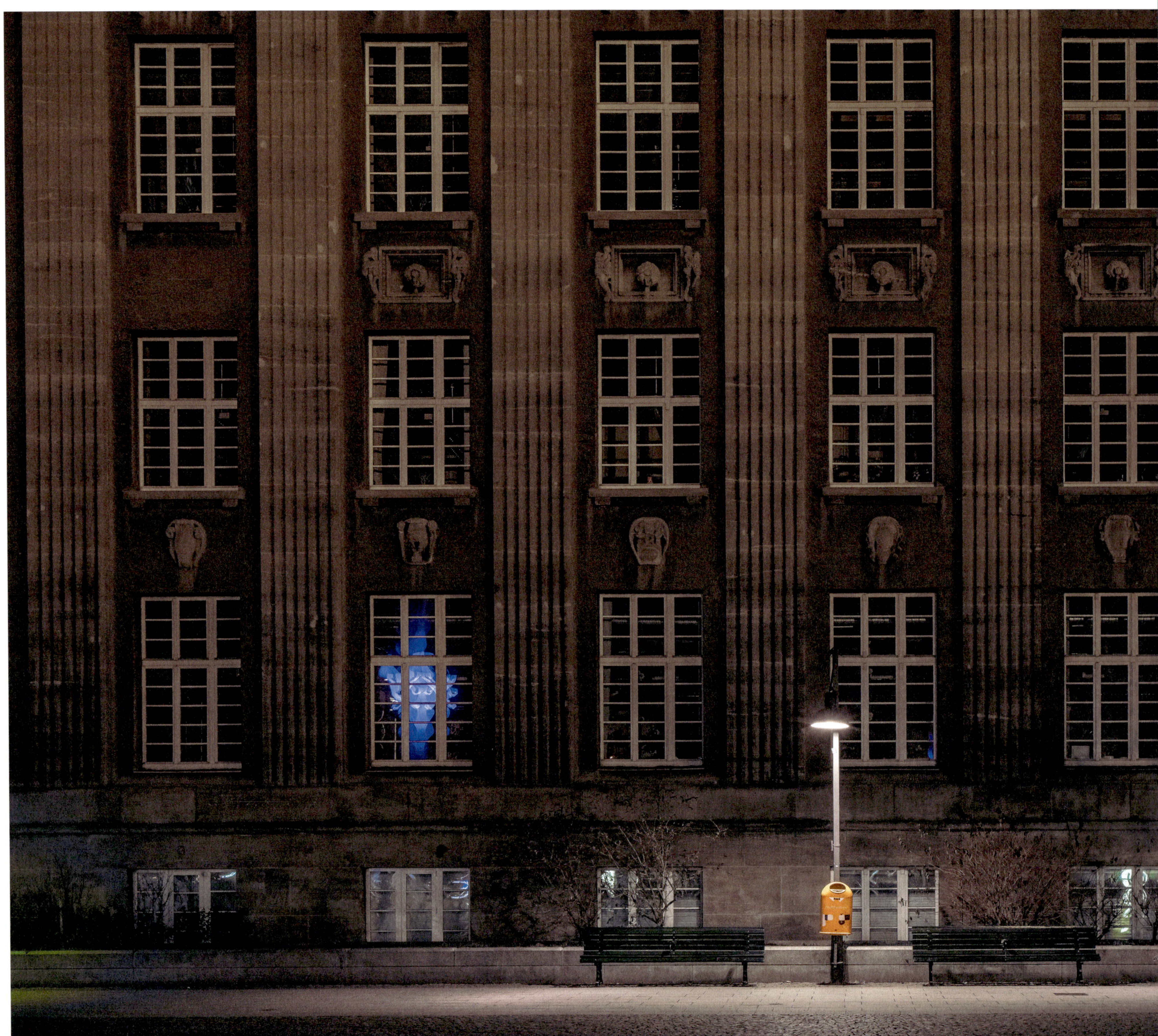

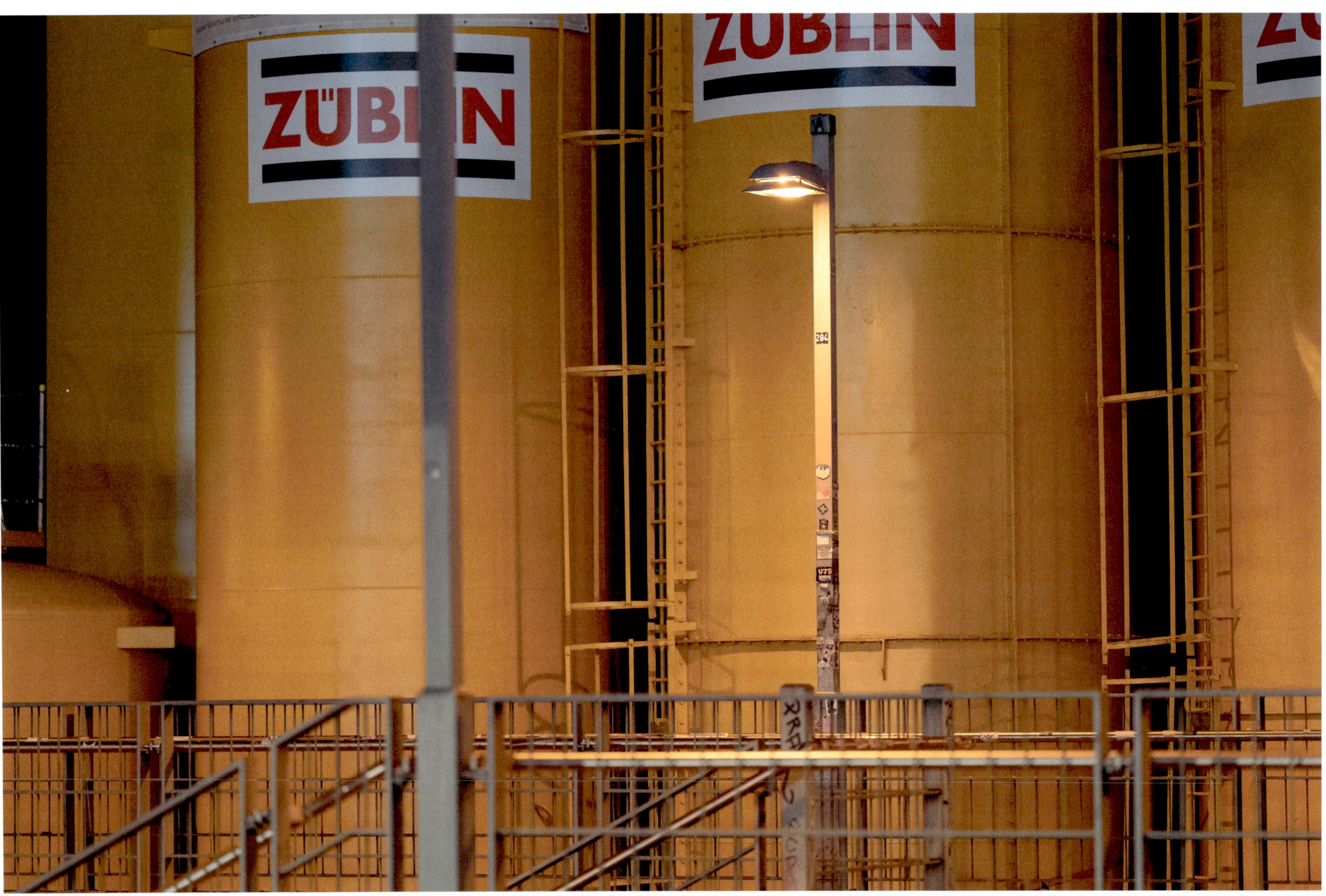

ZÜBLIN
ZÜBLIN

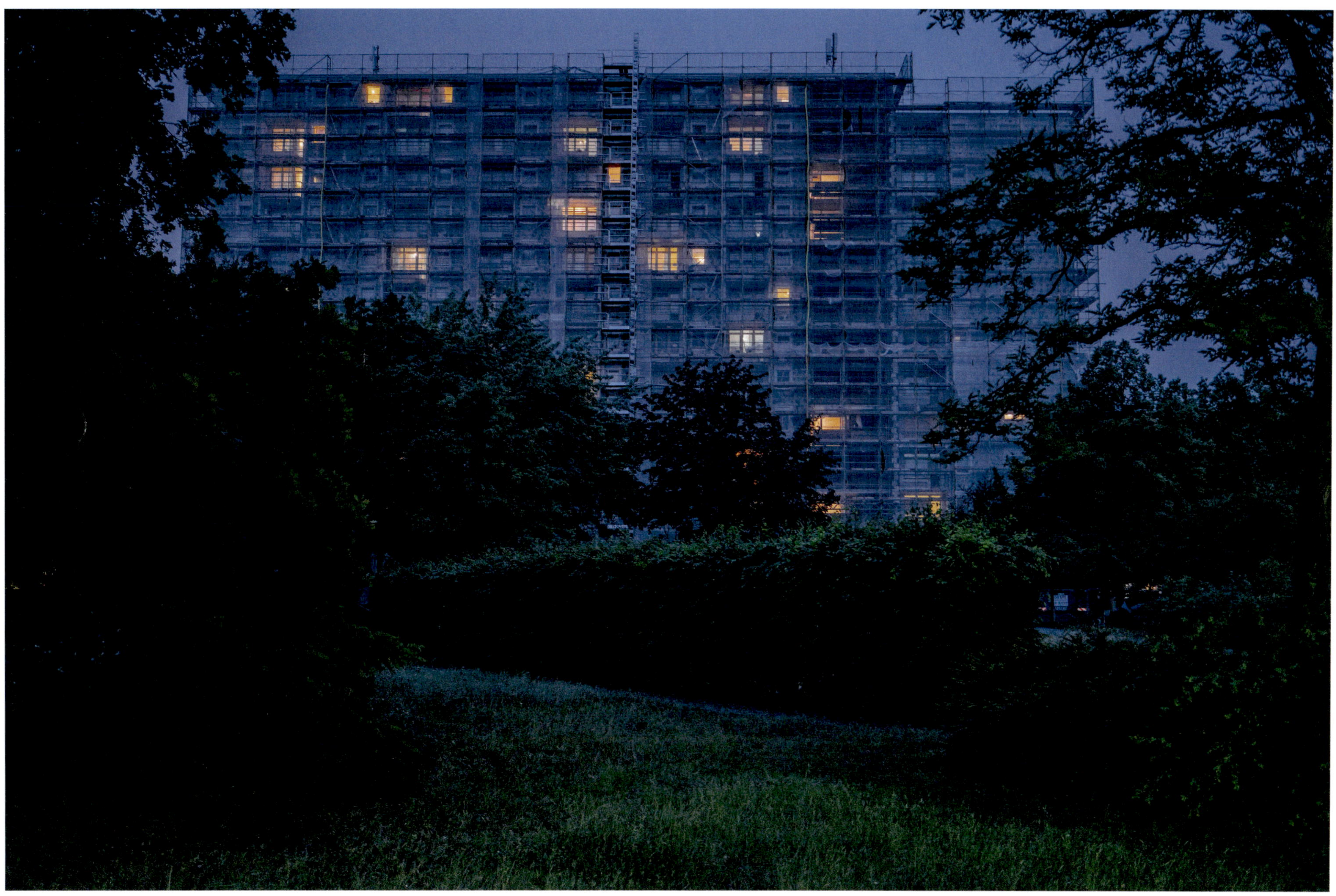

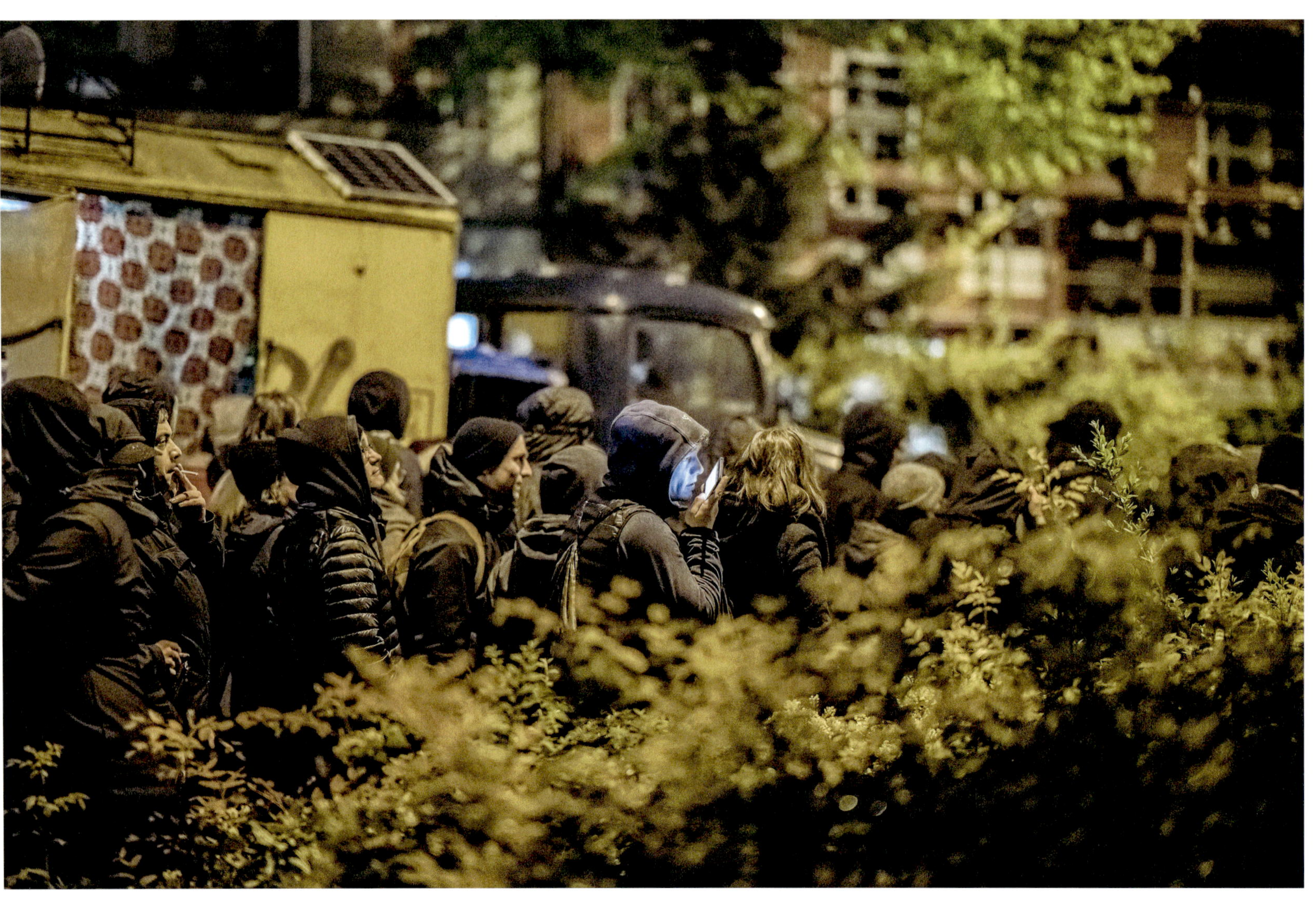

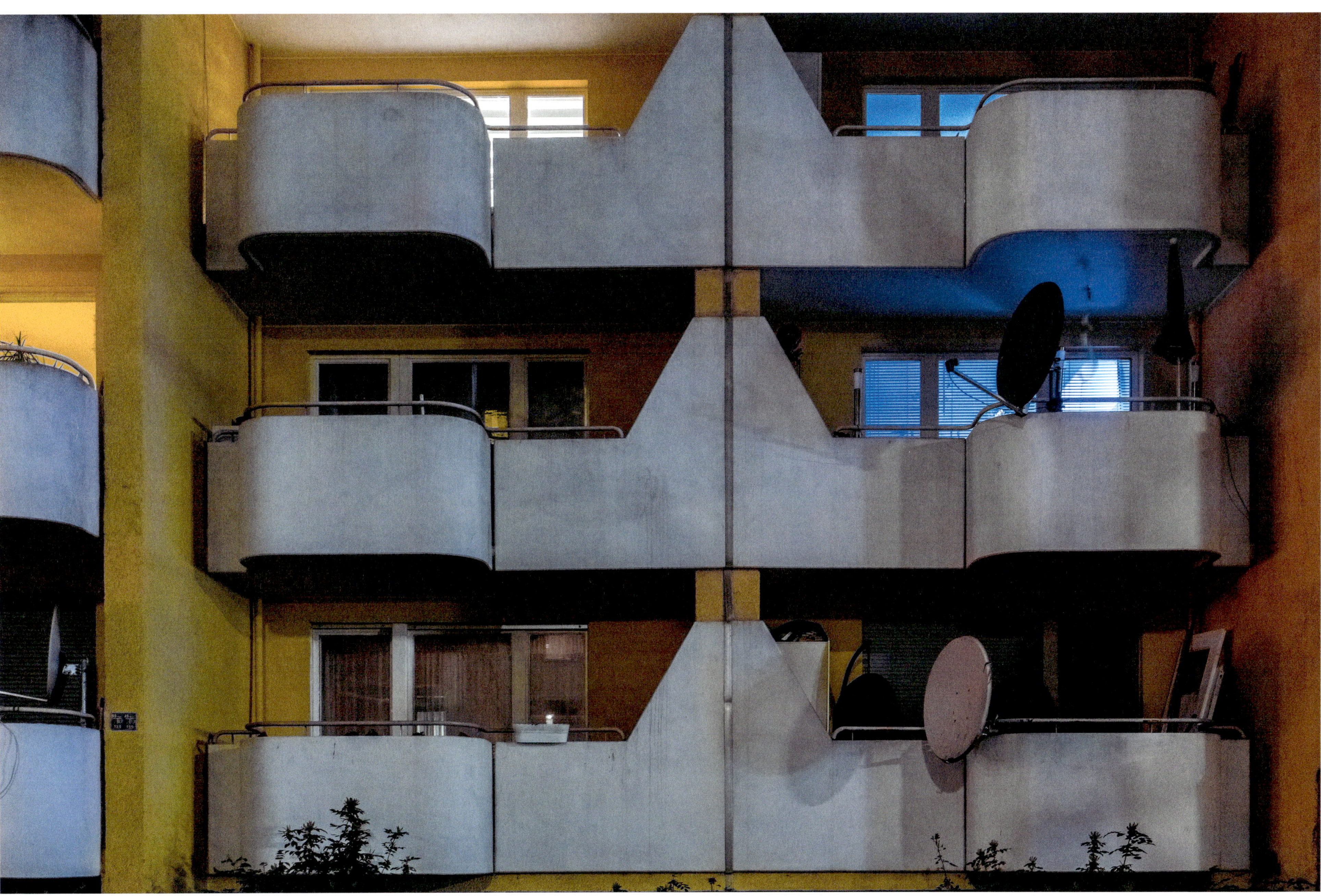

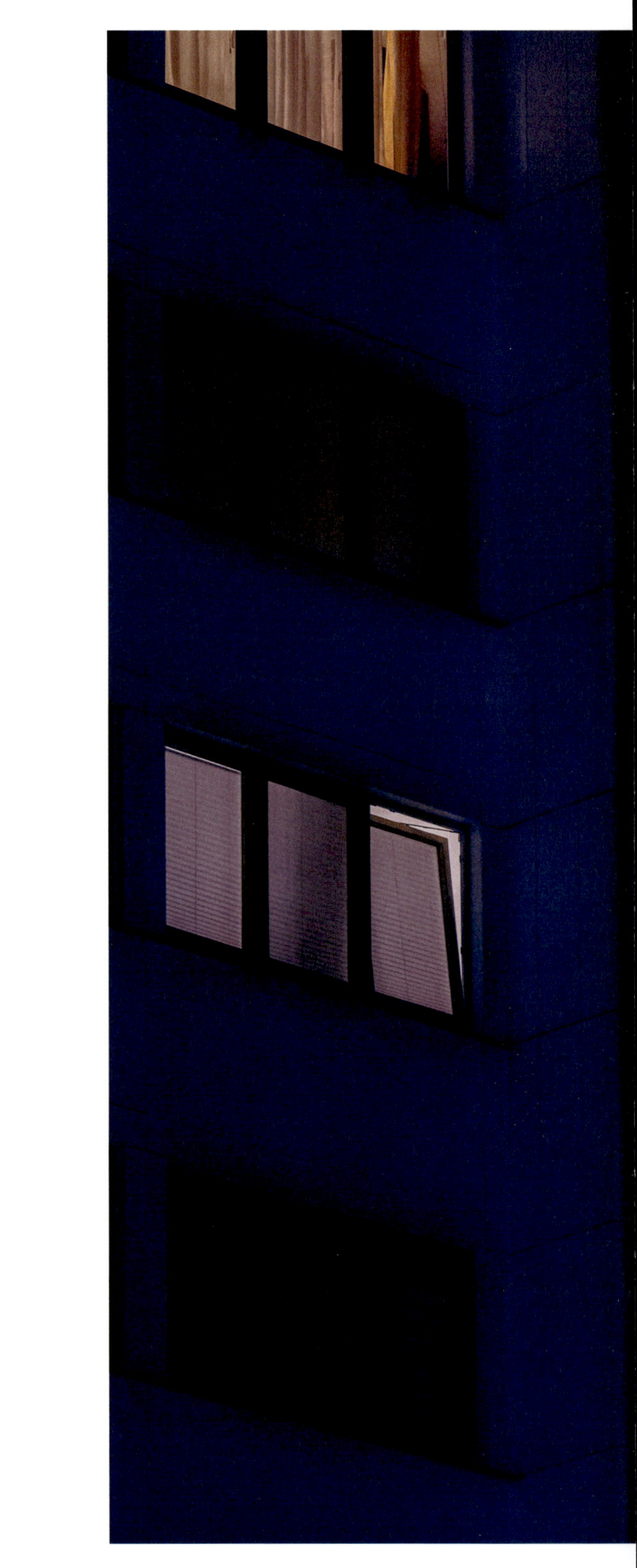

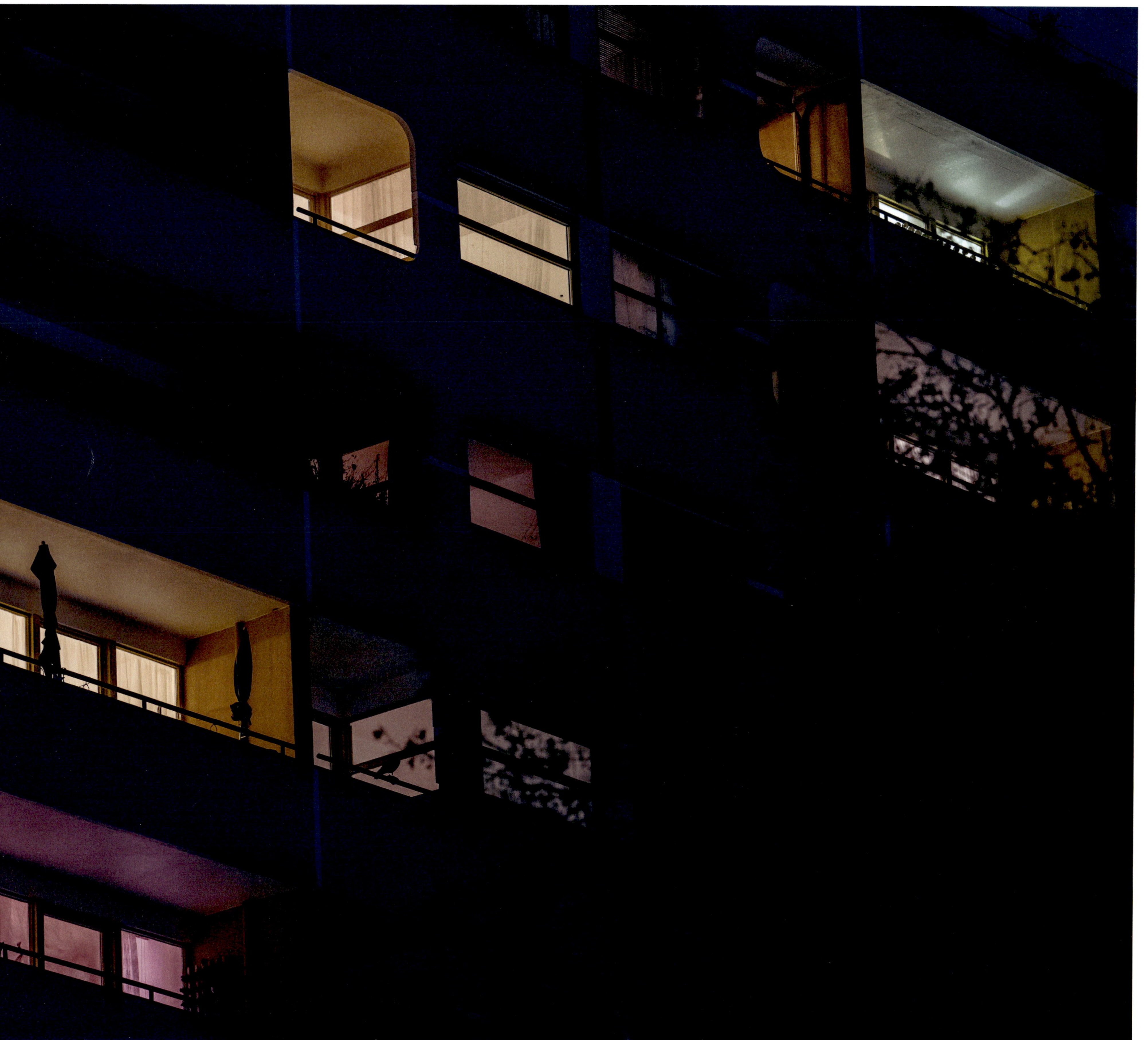

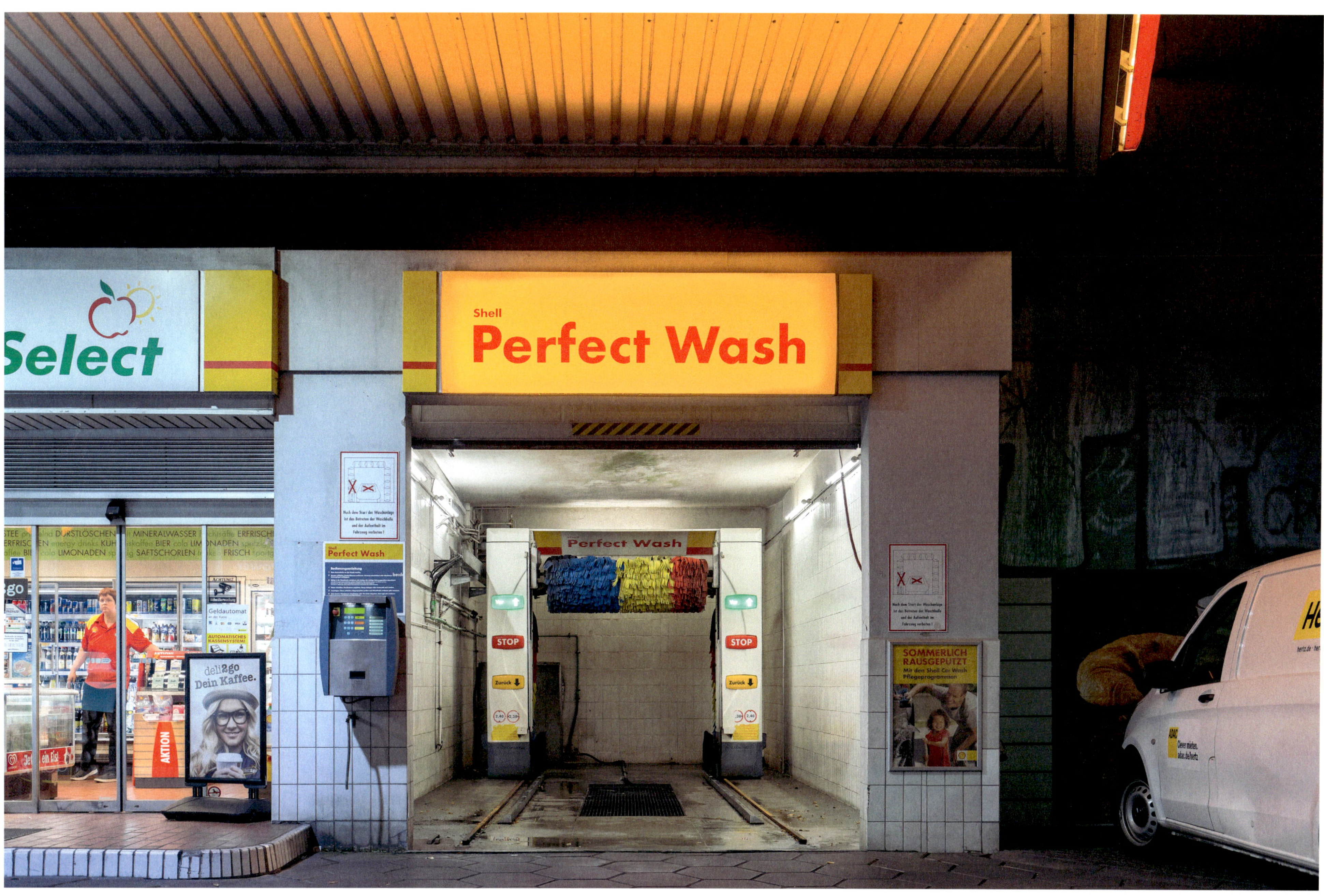

Select
Shell
Perfect Wash
Perfect Wash
STOP
STOP
Zurück
Zurück
deli2go
Dein Kaffee.
AKTION
Geldautomat
SOMMERLICH
RAUSGEPUTZT
Mit dem Shell Car Wash
Pflegeprogrammen

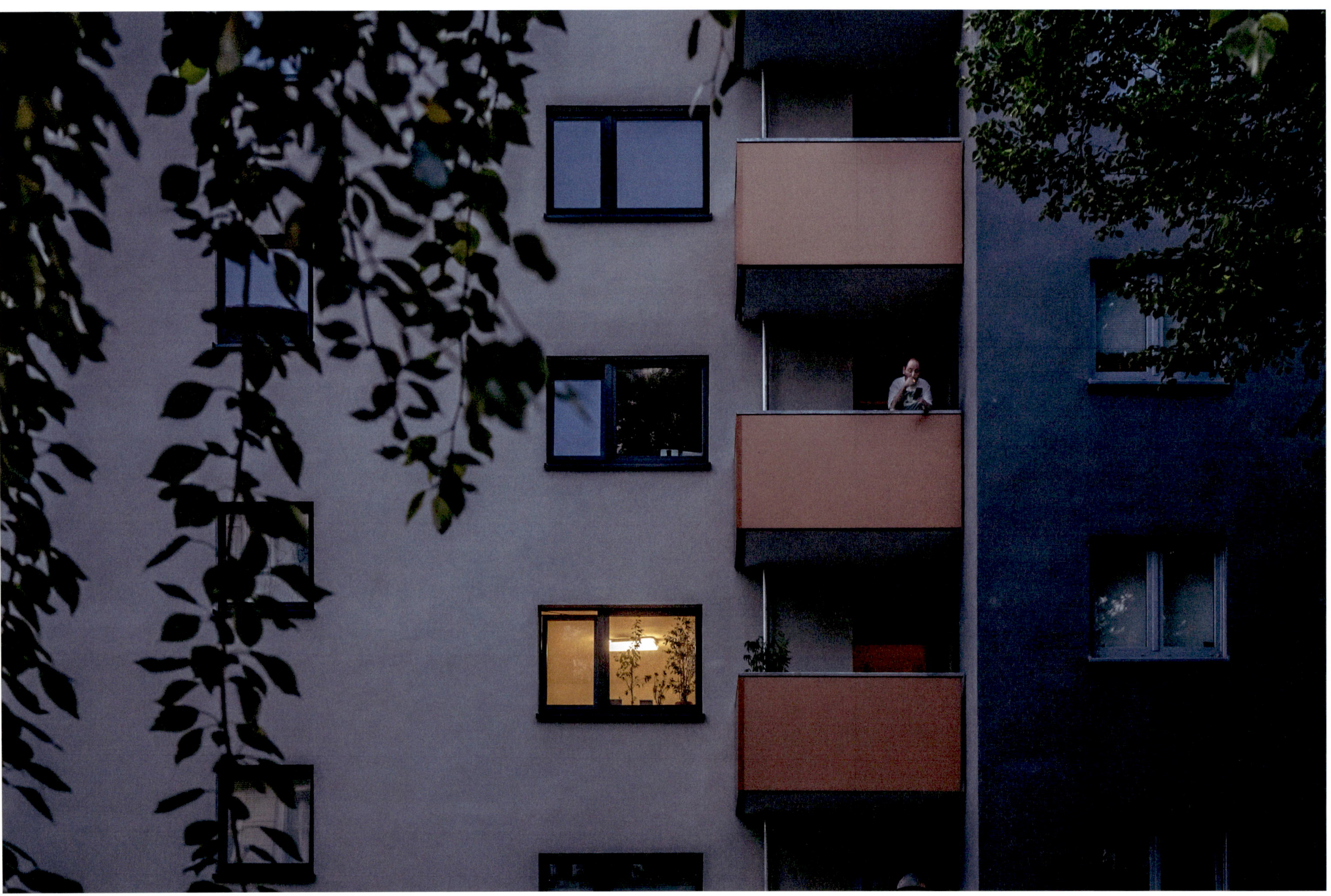

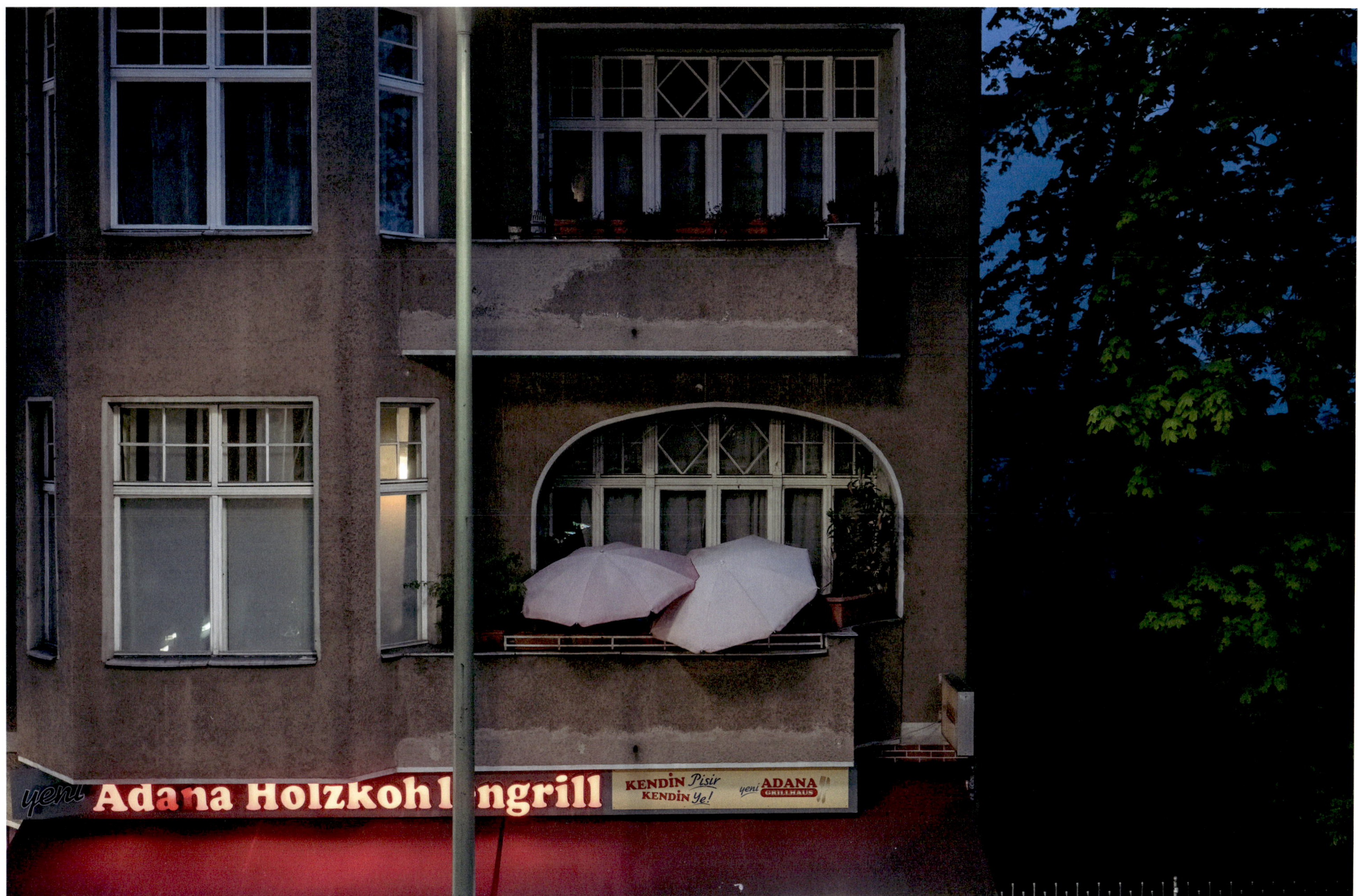

yeni Adana Holzkohlengrill
KENDİN Pişir KENDİN Ye!
yeni ADANA GRILLHAUS

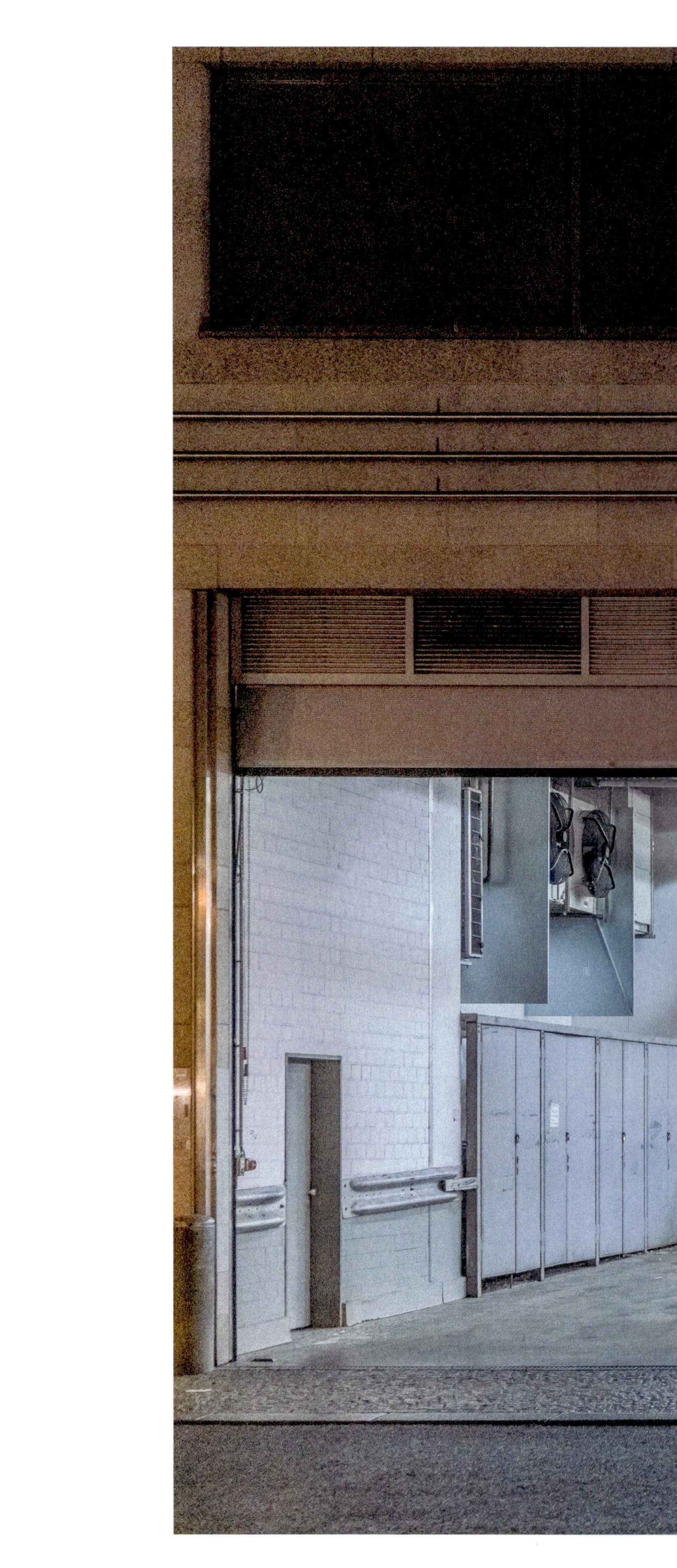

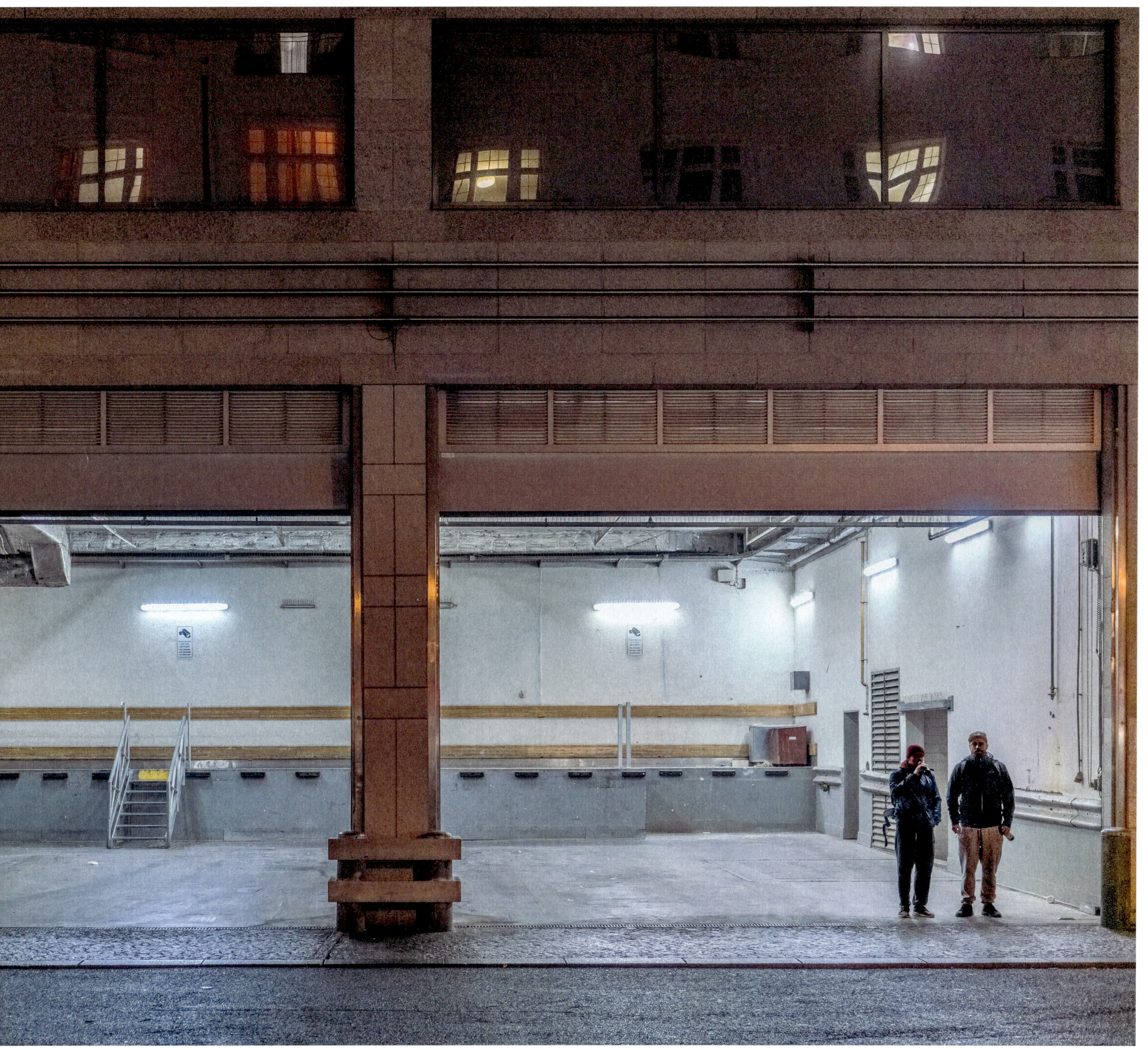

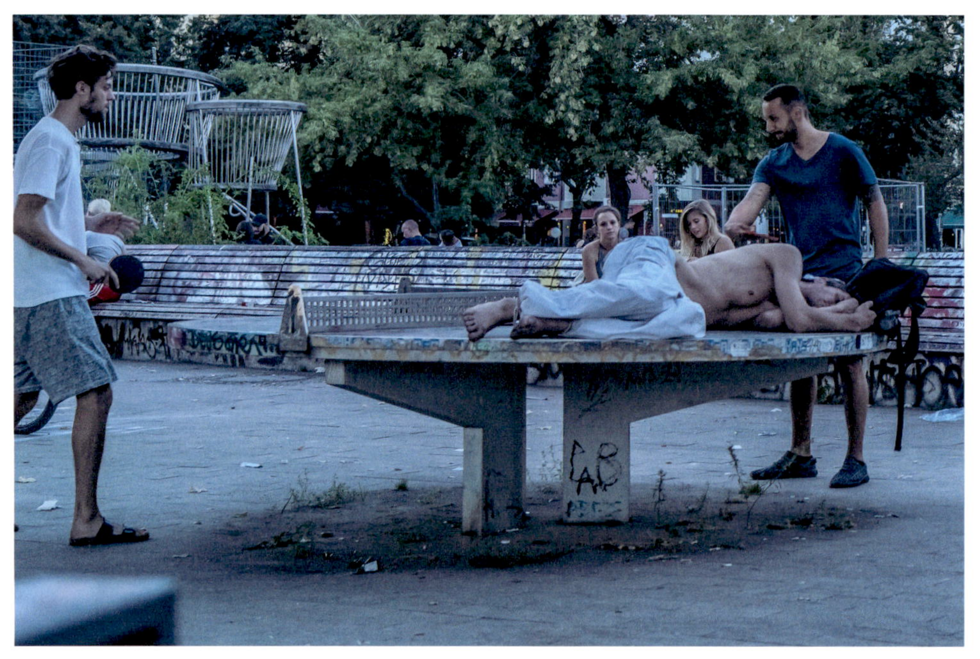

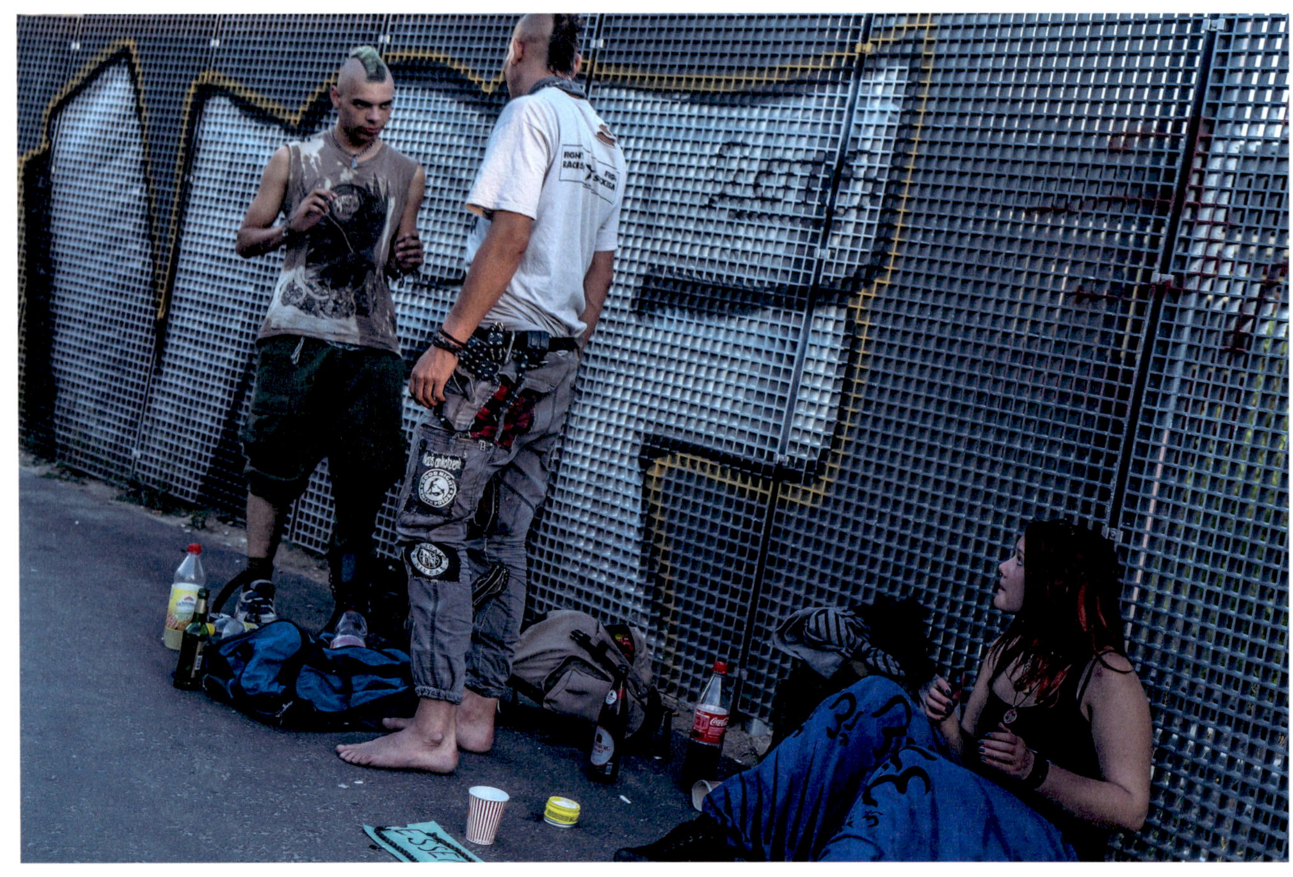

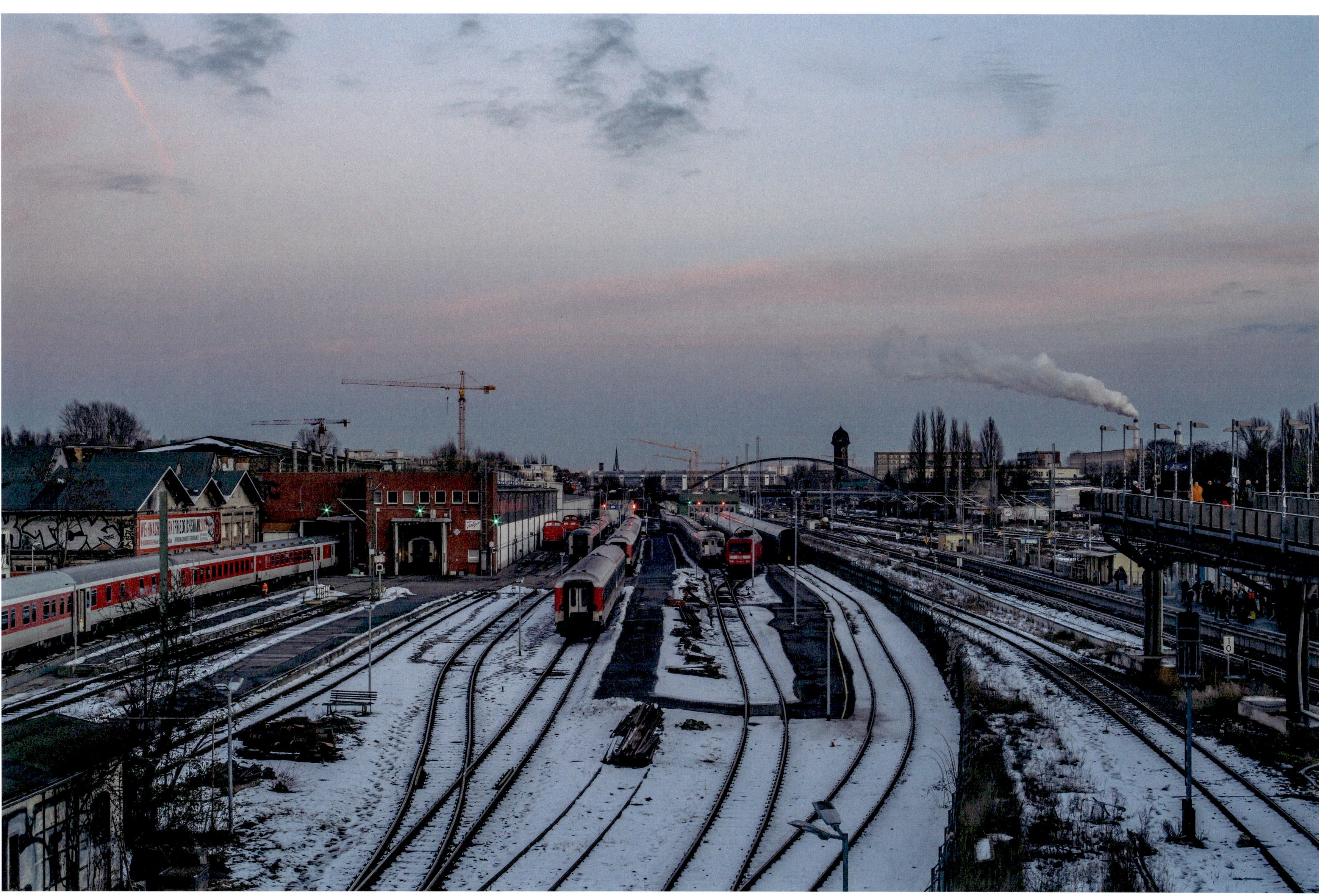

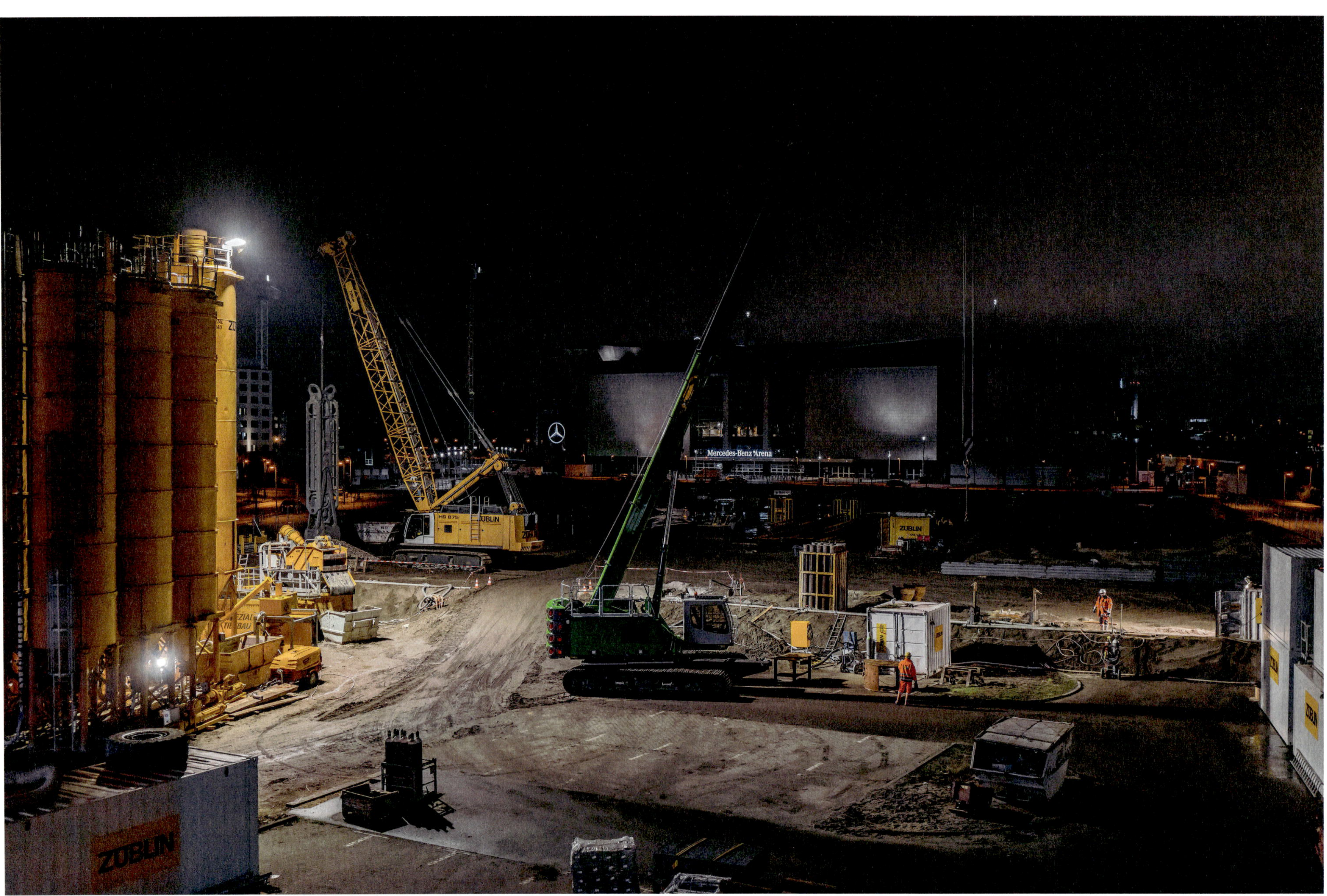

ZÜBLIN
Mercedes-Benz Arena

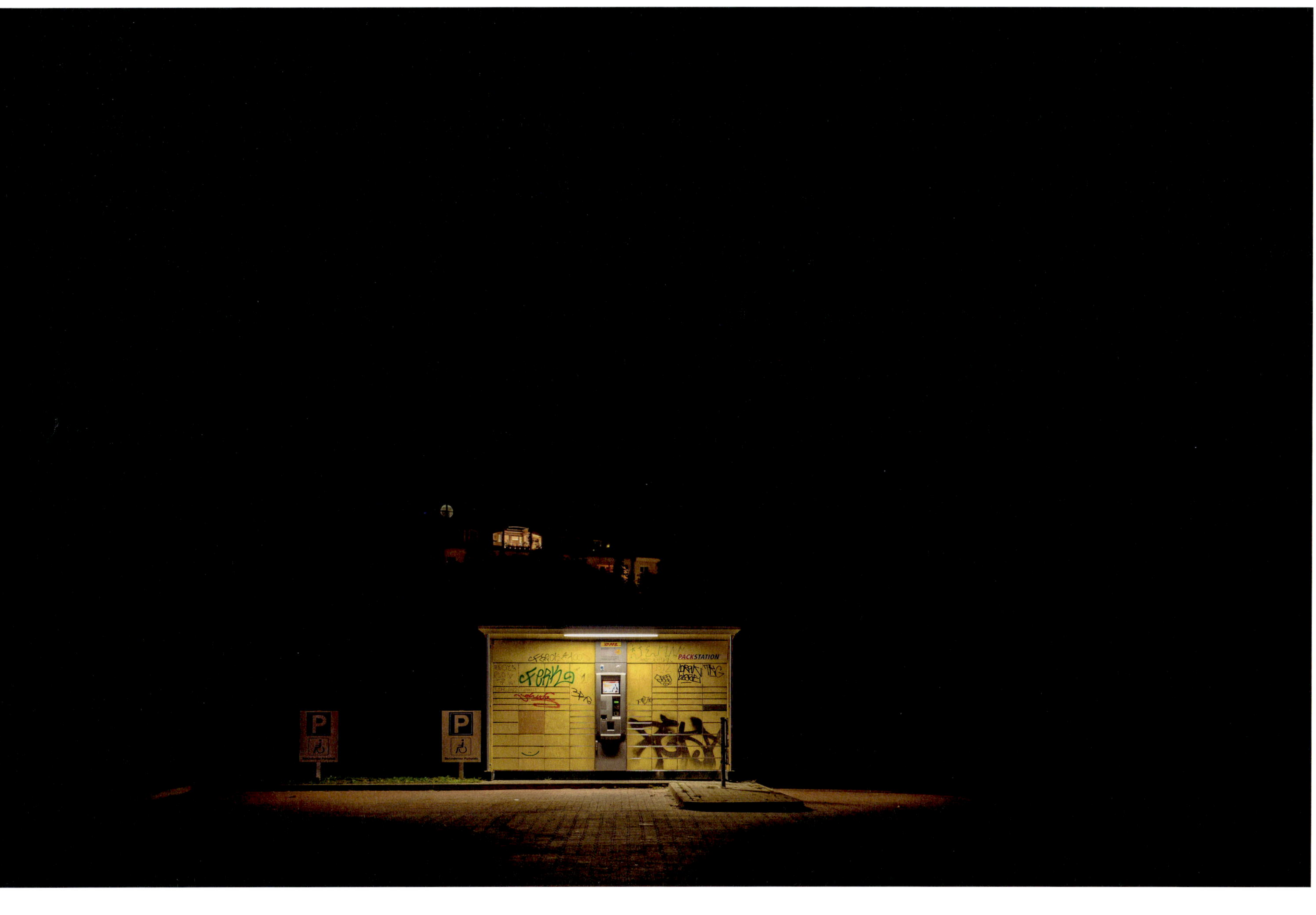

DHL
PACKSTATION
P
P

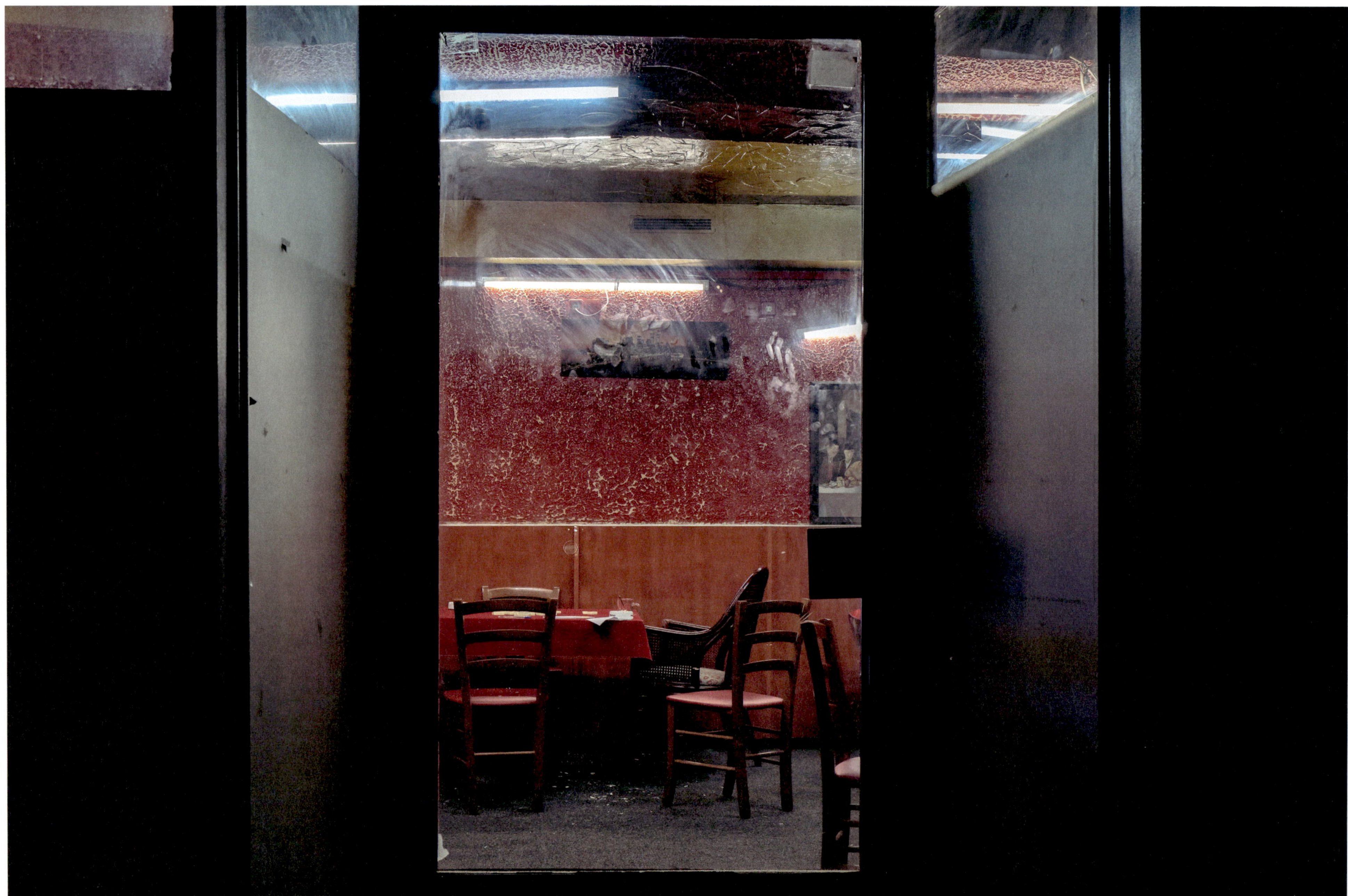

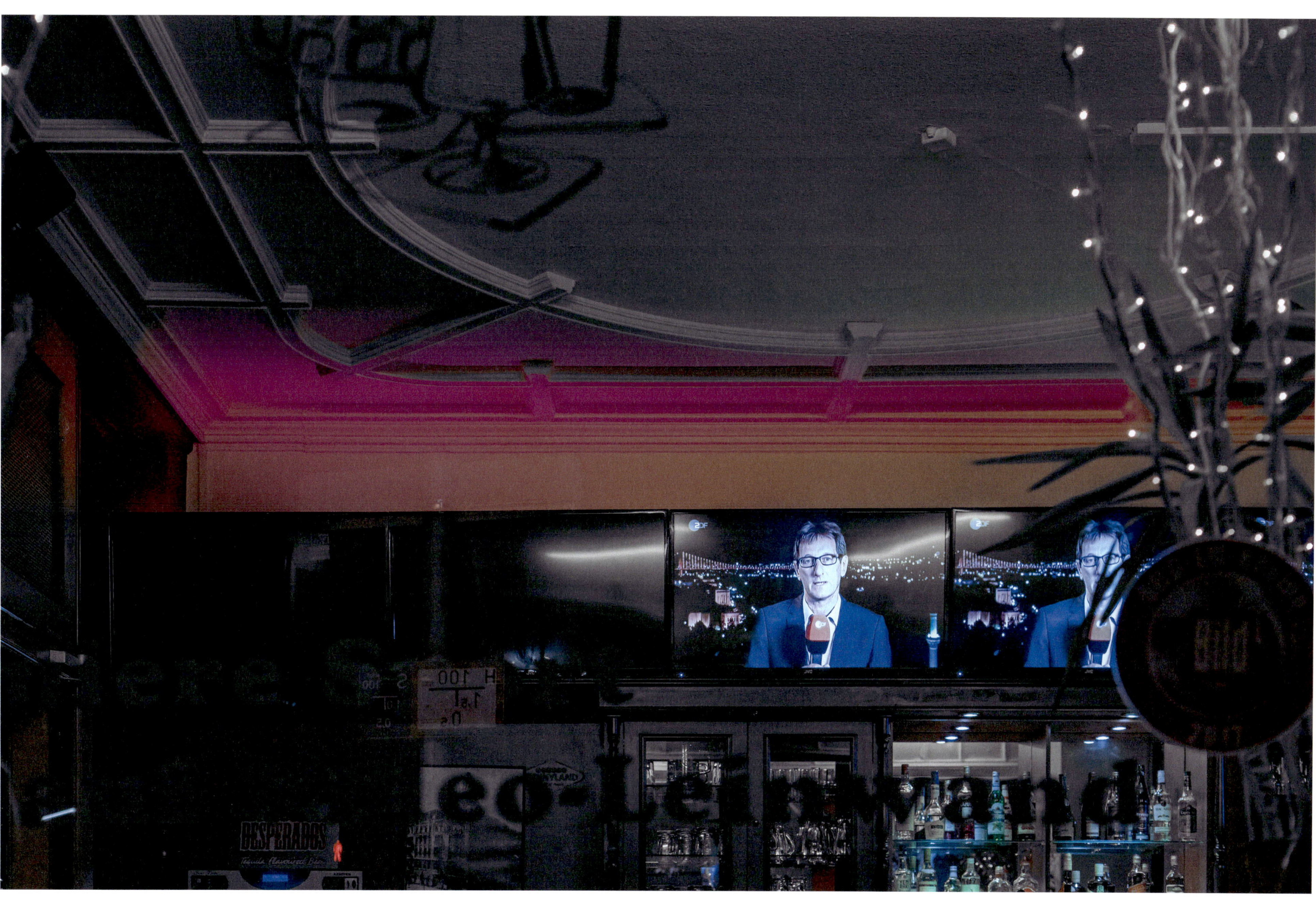

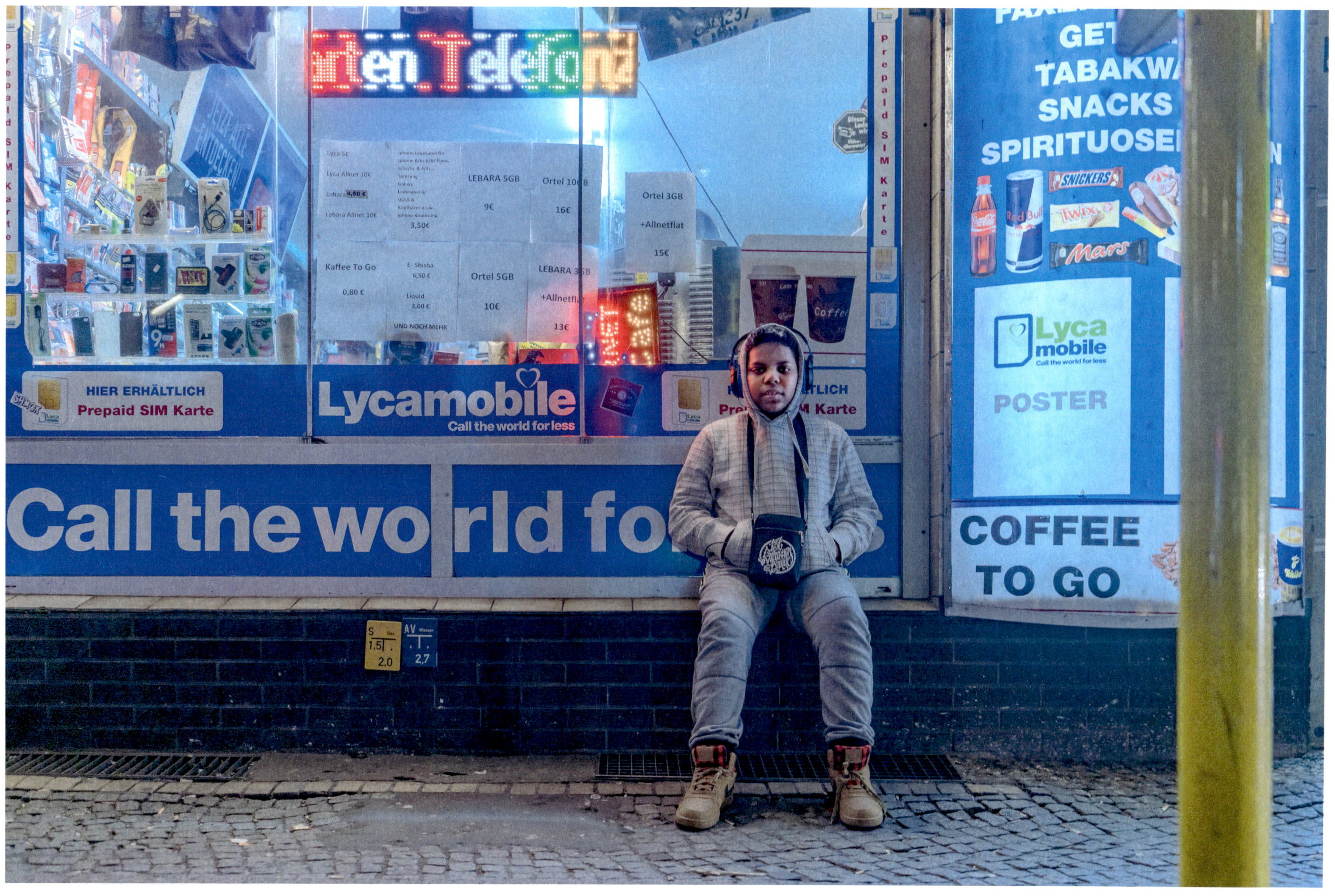
Prepaid SIM Karte
...ten Telefon...
Prepaid SIM Karte
Lyca 5€
Lyca Allnet 10€
Lebara 4,50 €
Lebara Allnet 10€
LEBARA 5GB
9€
Ortel 10GB
16€
Ortel 3GB
+Allnetflat
15€
Kaffee To Go
0,80 €
E-Shisha
6,50 €
Liquid
3,00 €
Ortel 5GB
10€
LEBARA 3GB
+Allnetflat
13€
UND NOCH MEHR
HIER ERHÄLTLICH
Prepaid SIM Karte
Lycamobile
Call the world for less
Call the world fo
PAX
GET
TABAKWA
SNACKS
SPIRITUOSE
SNICKERS
TWIX
Mars
Red Bull
Lyca mobile
Call the world for less
POSTER
COFFEE
TO GO
S
1.5
2.0
A V
2,7

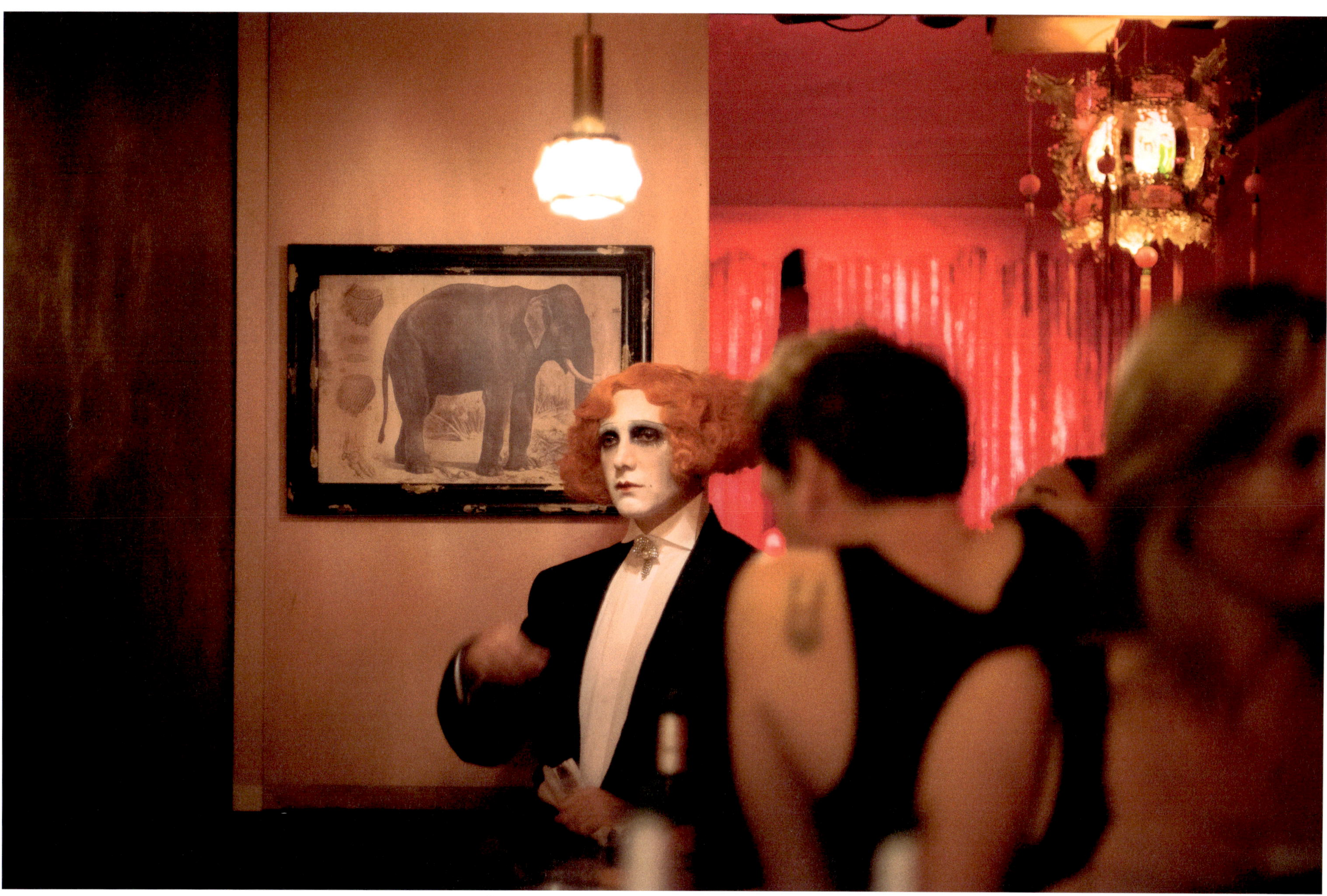

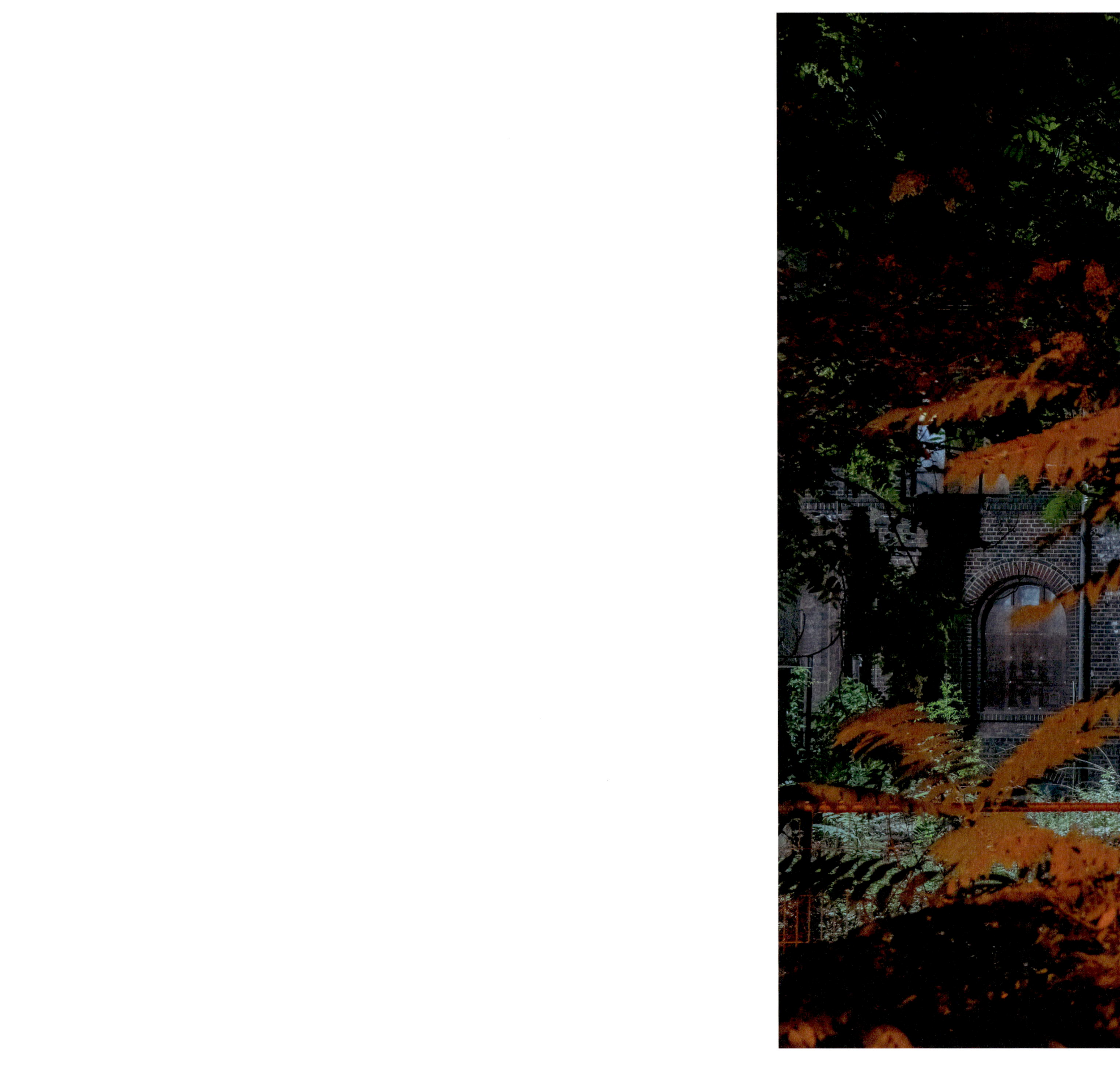

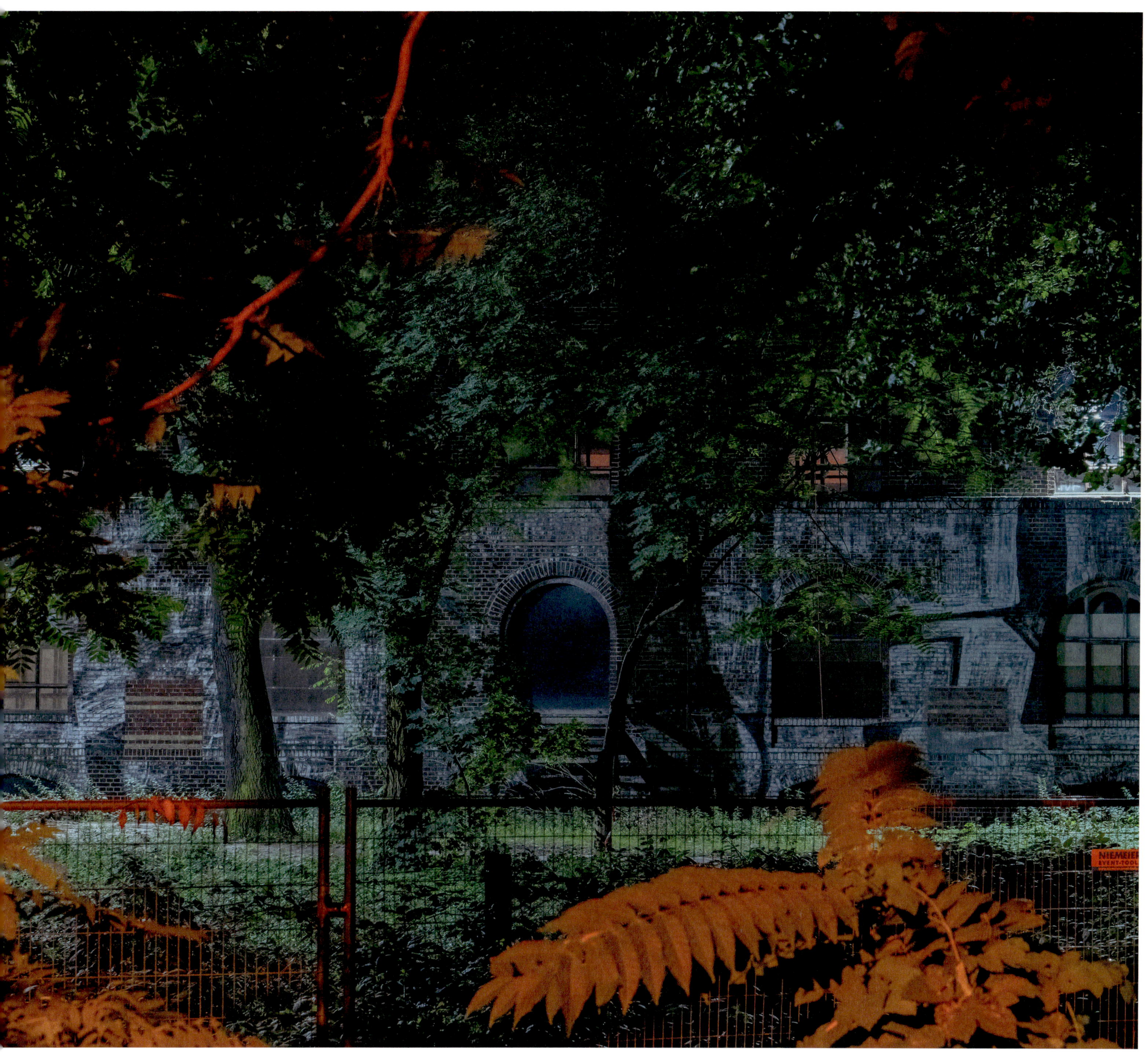
NIEMEIER
EVENT-TOOL

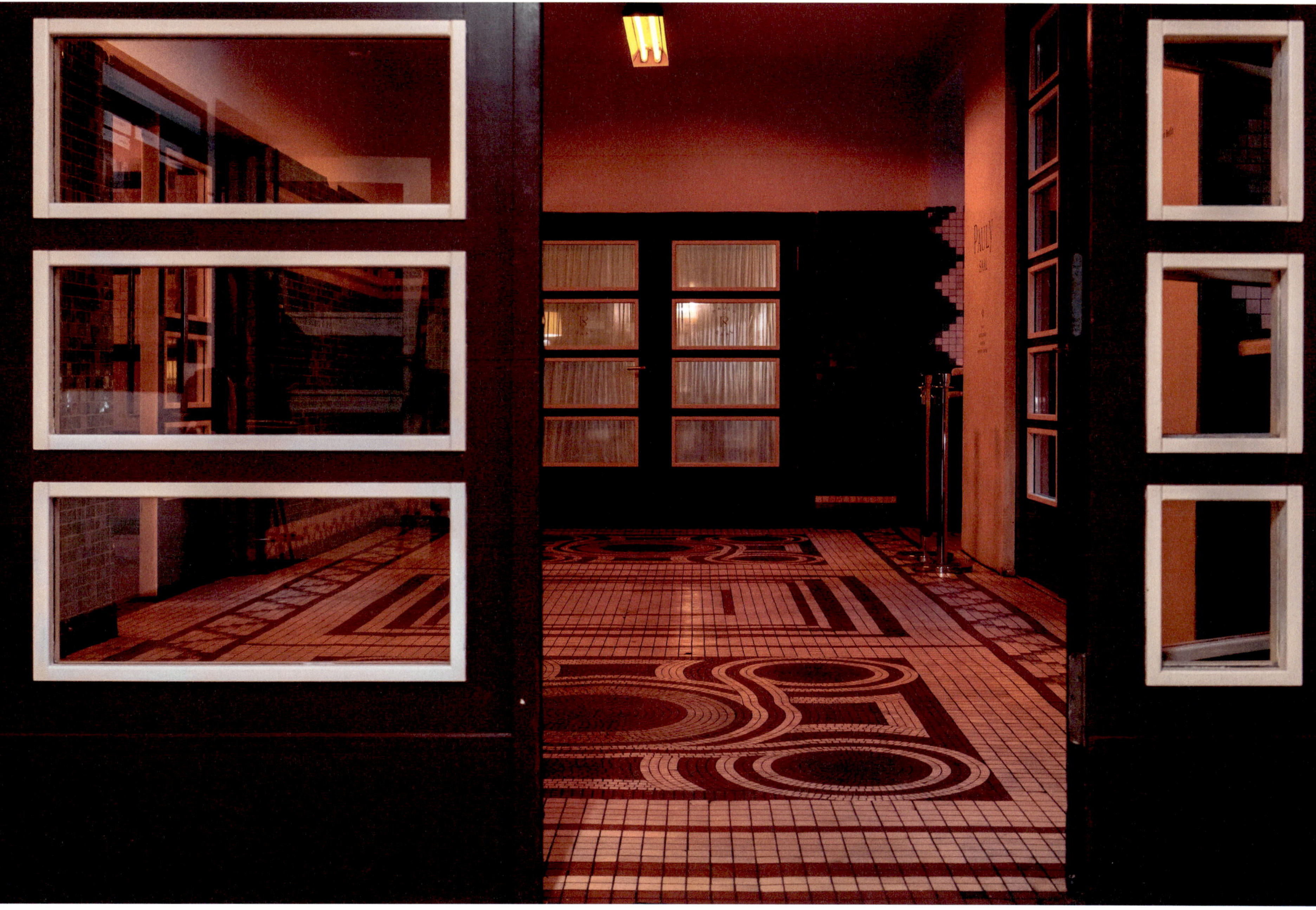

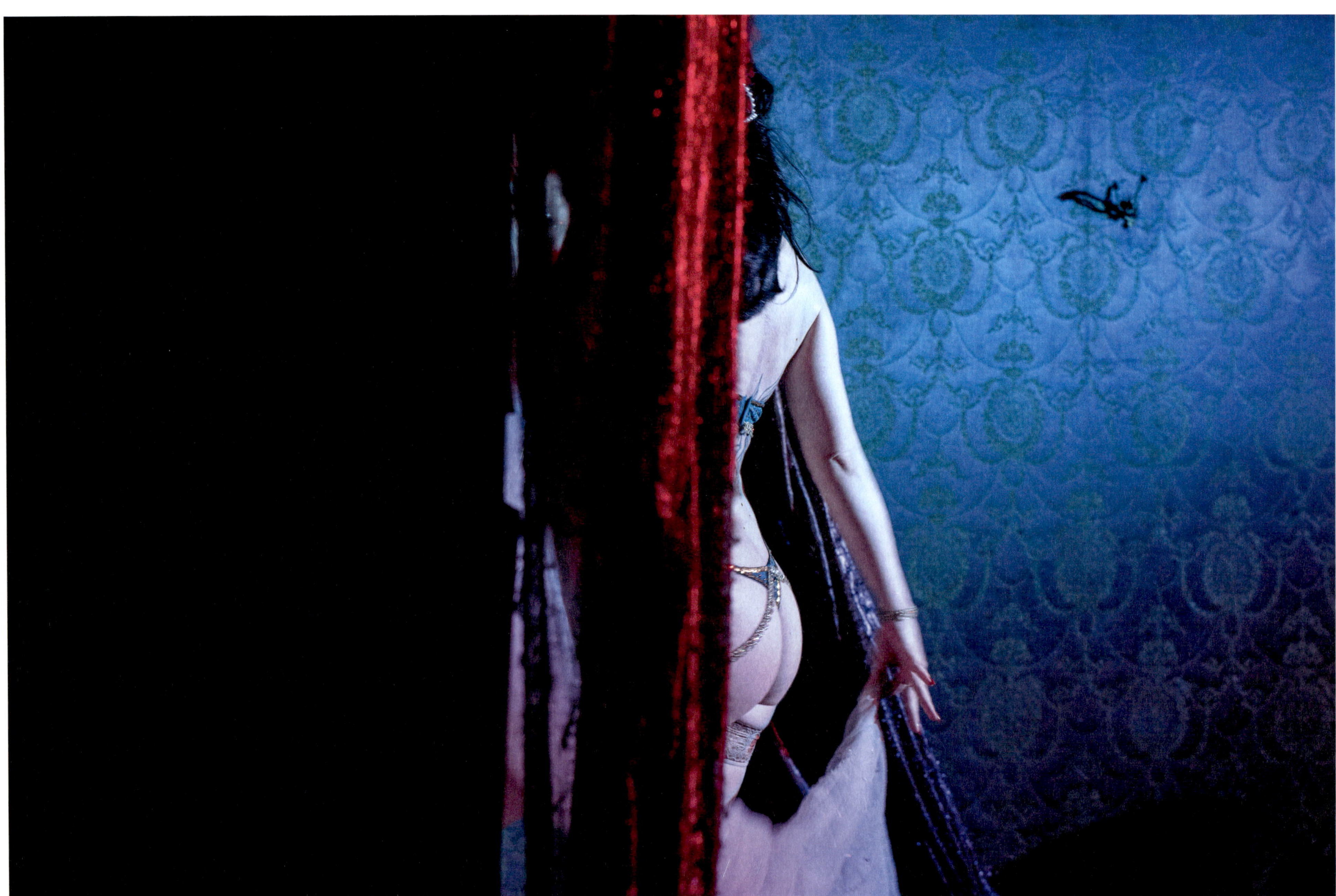

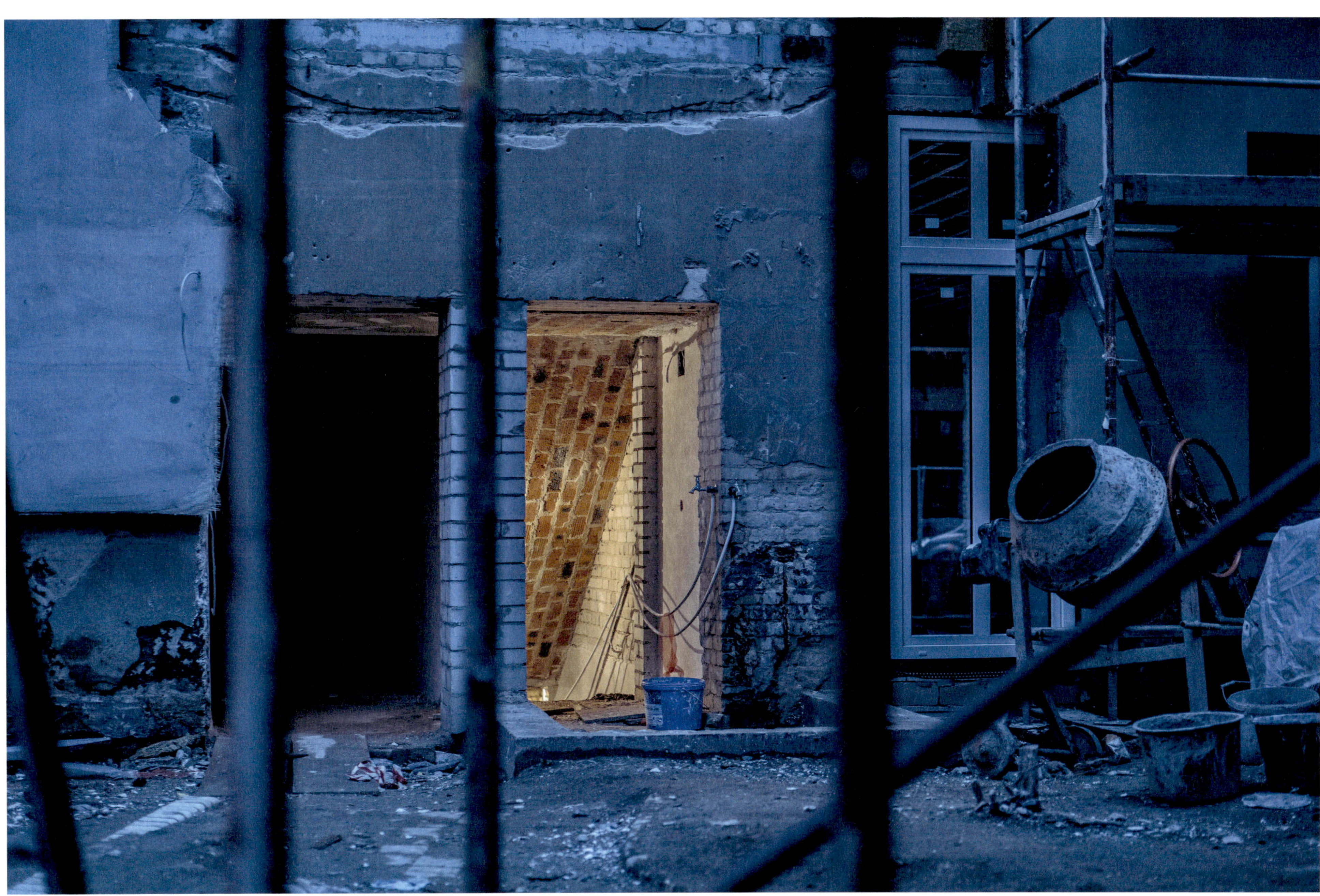

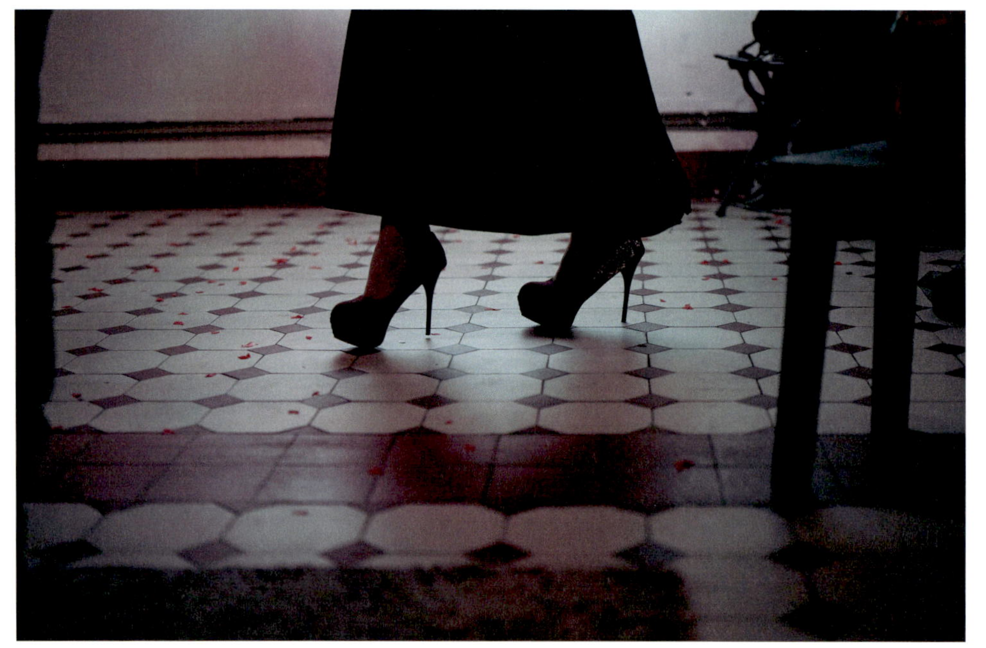

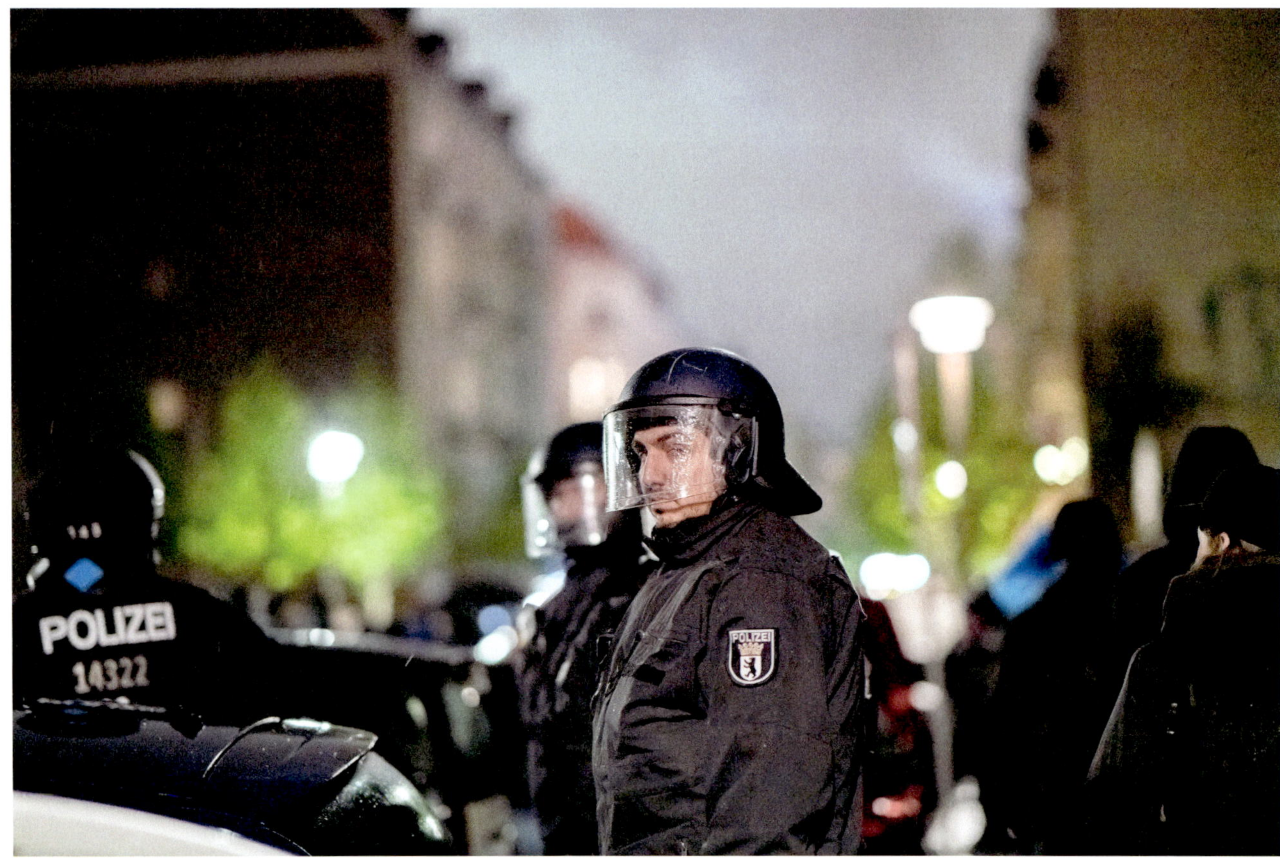

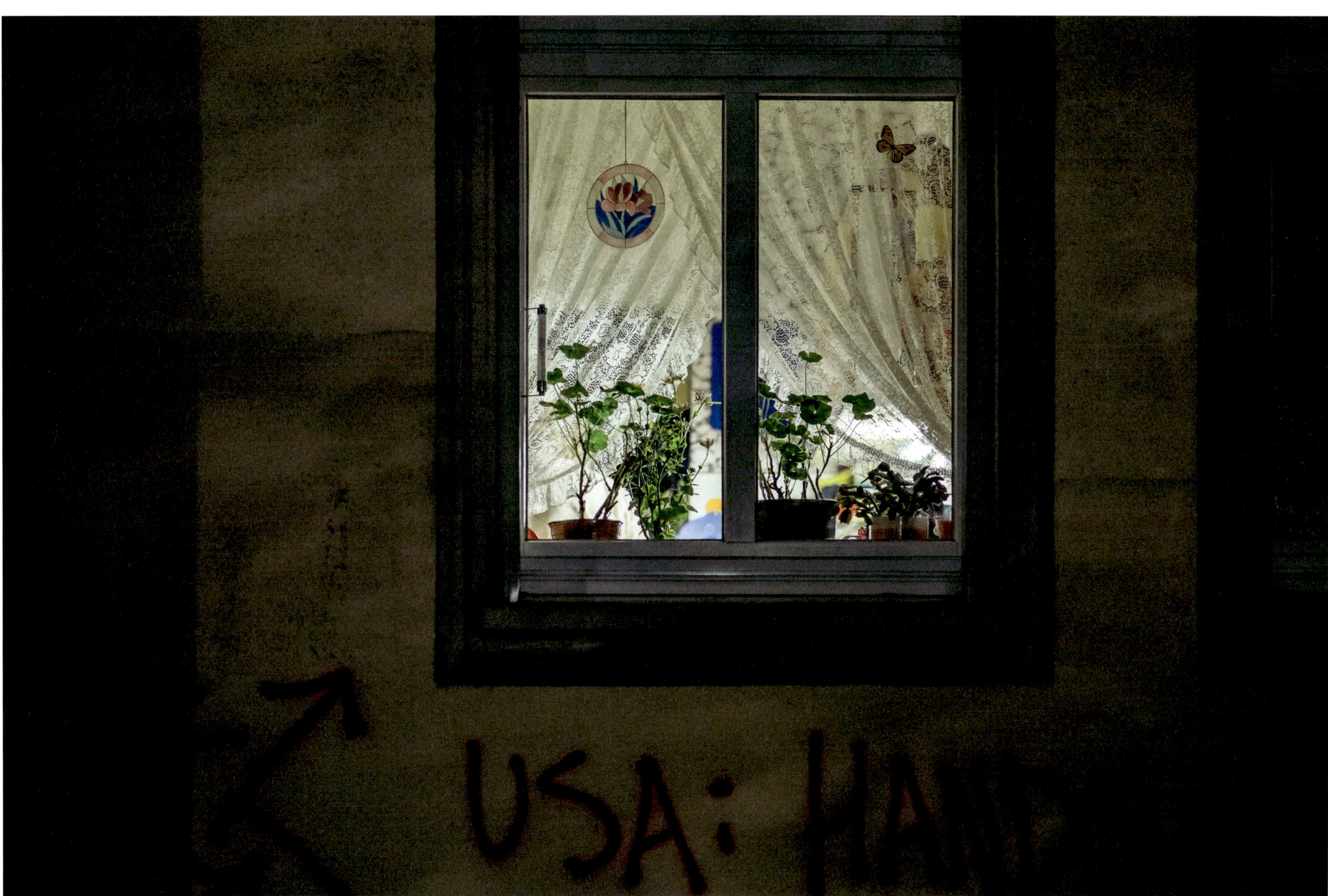

USA: HAN

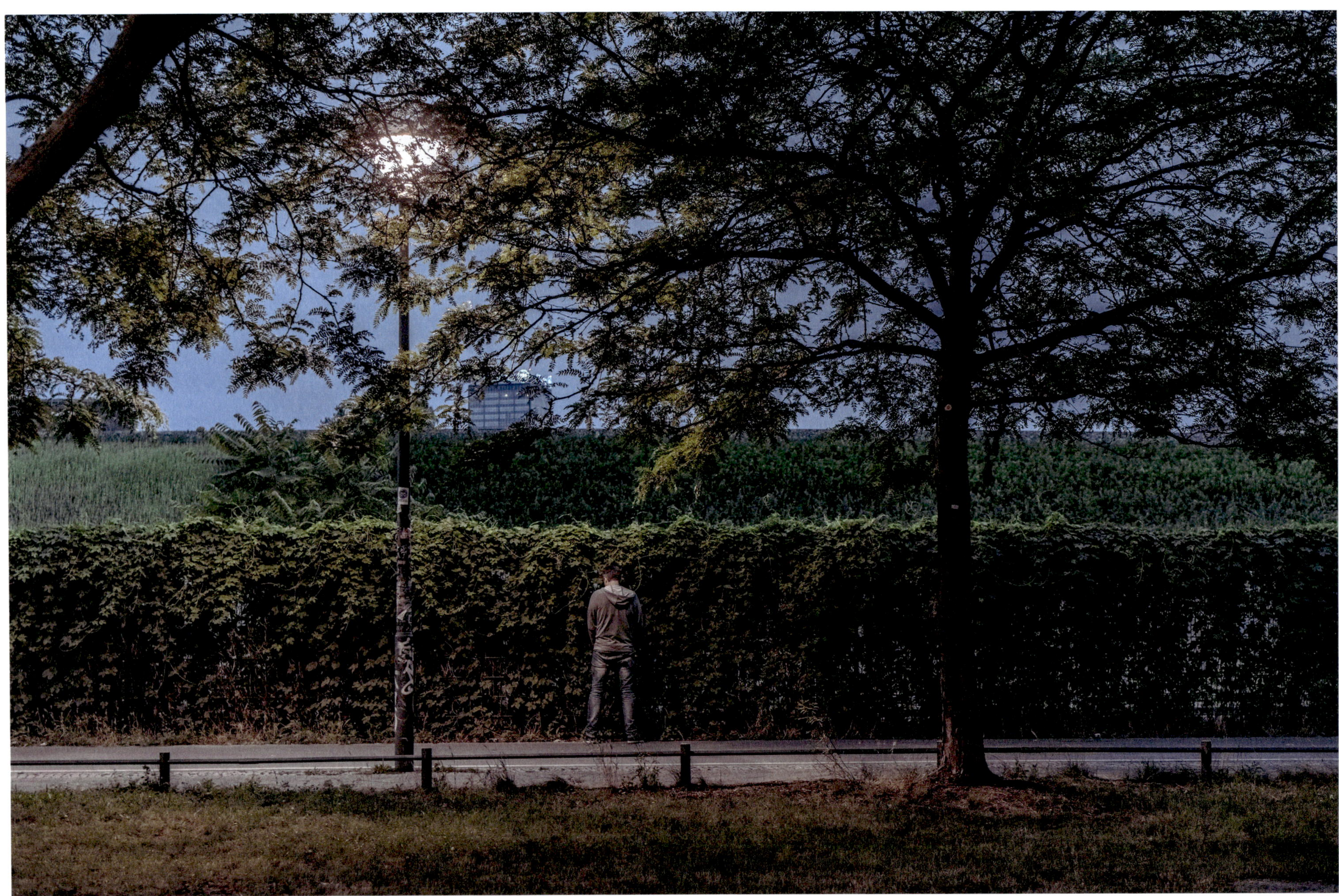

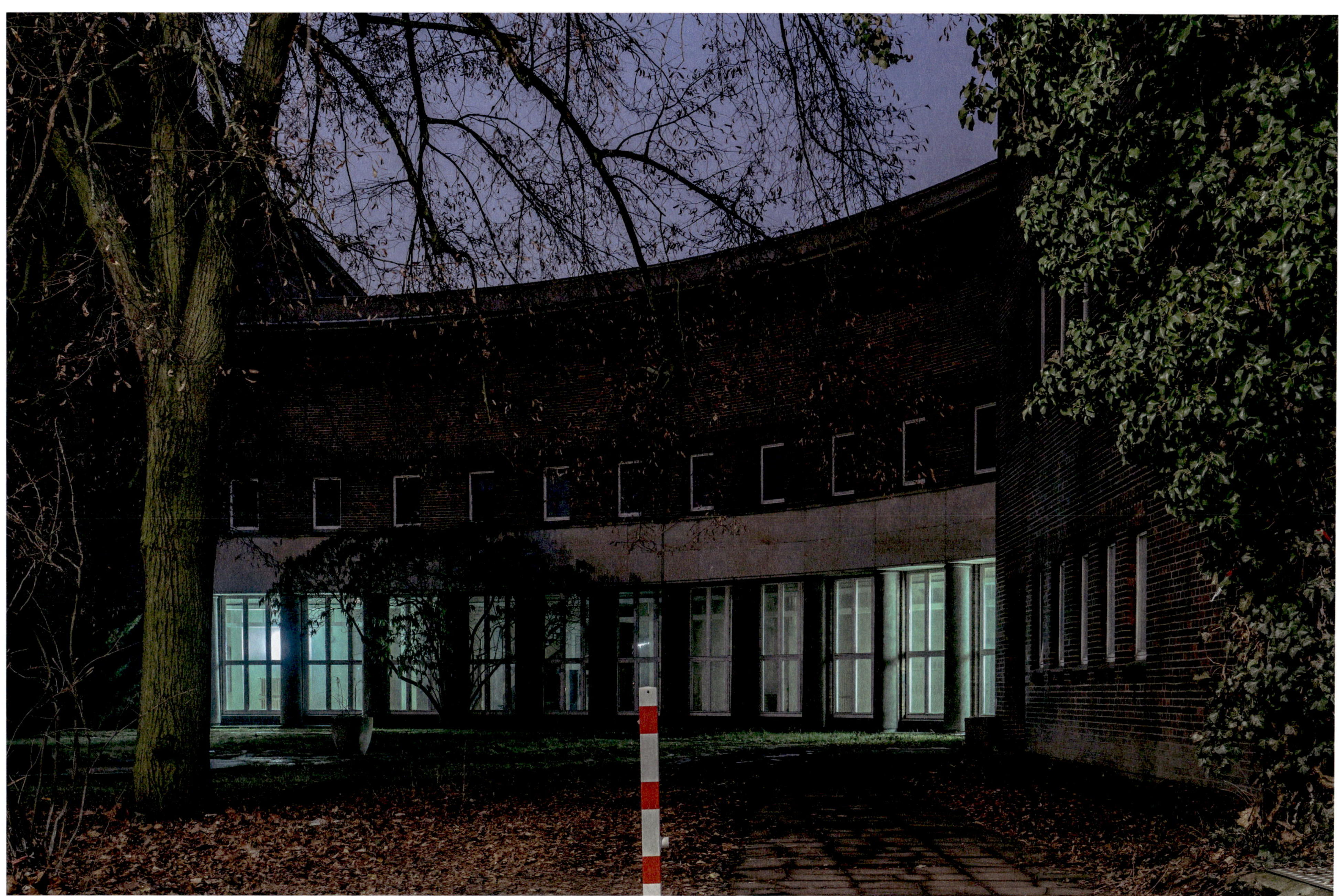

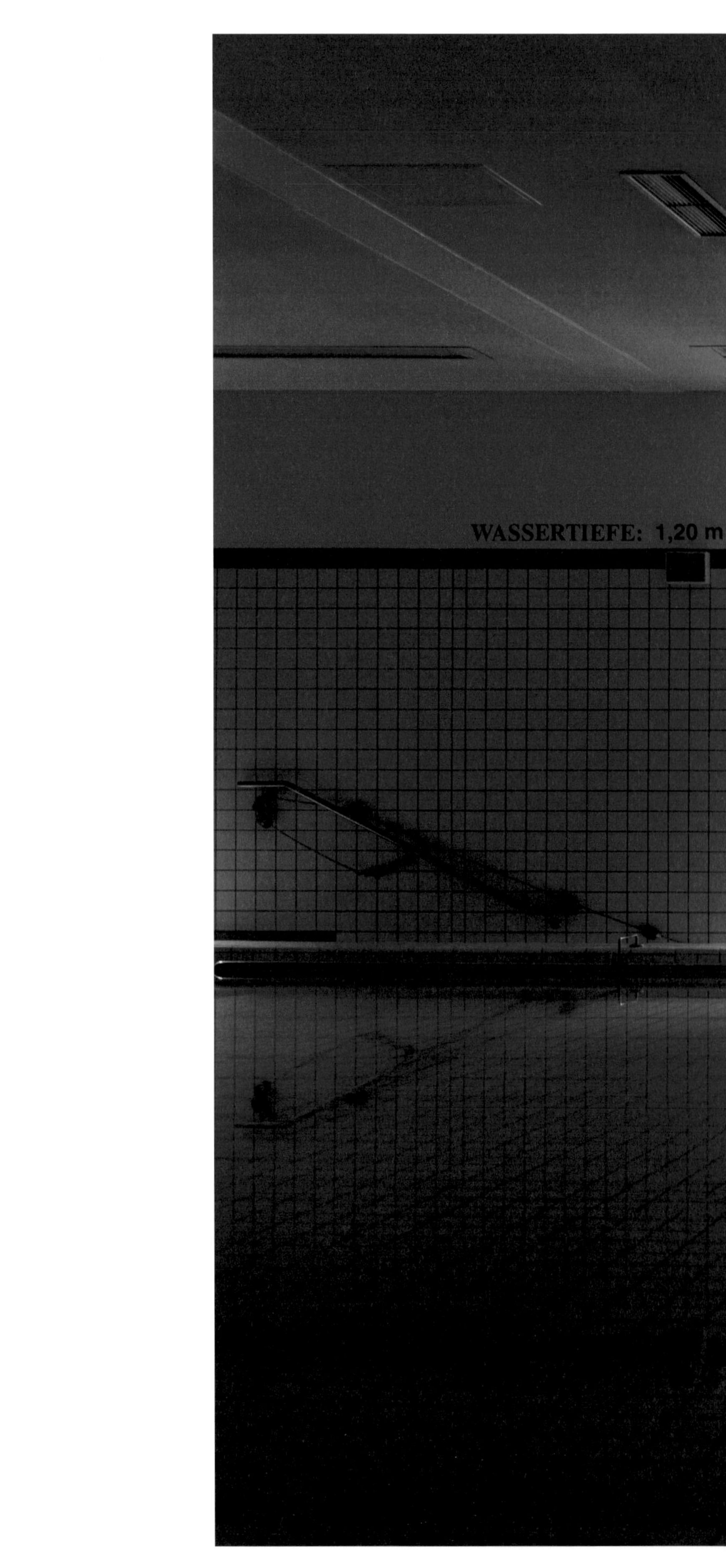

WASSERTIEFE: 1,20 m

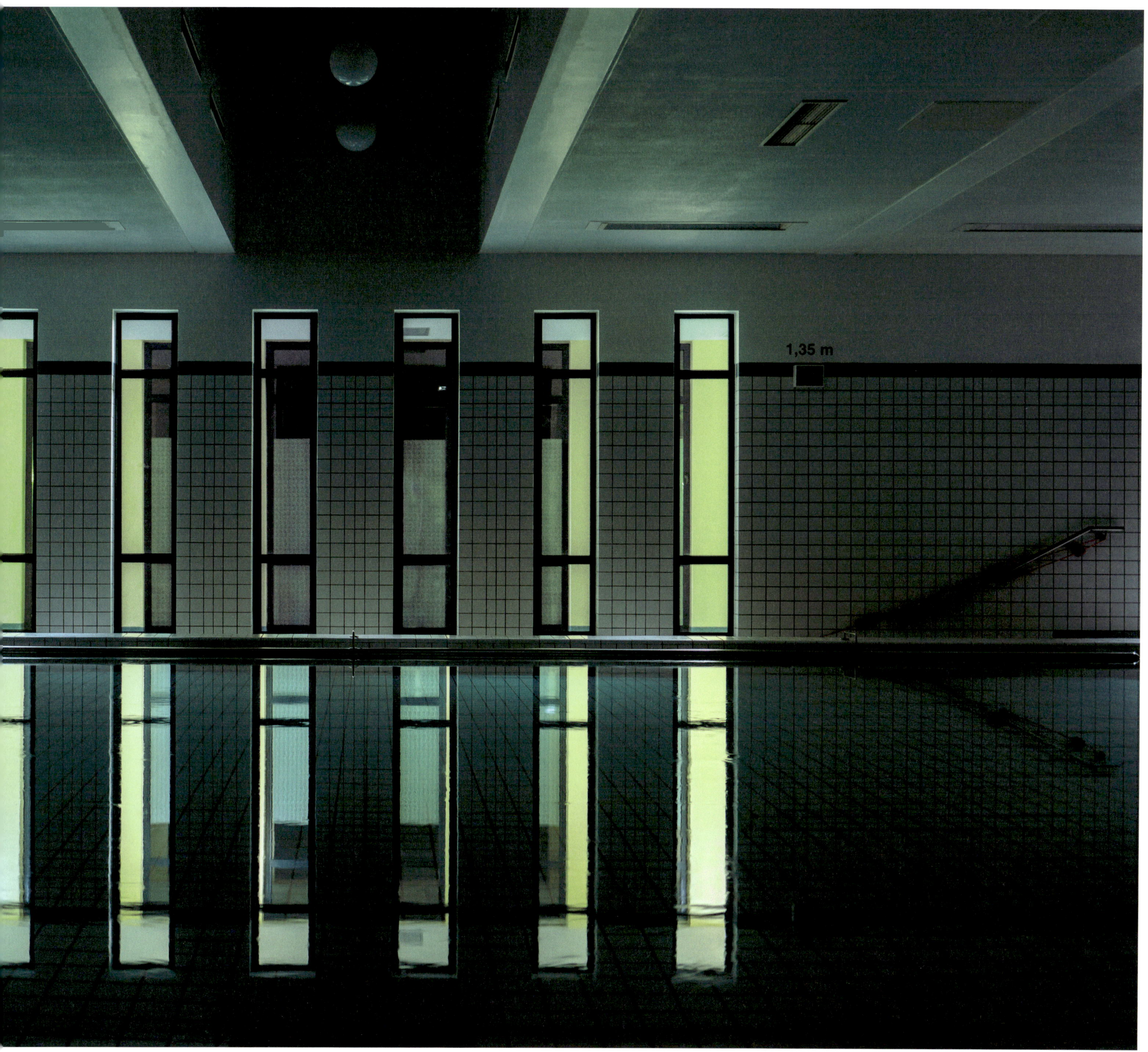
1,35 m

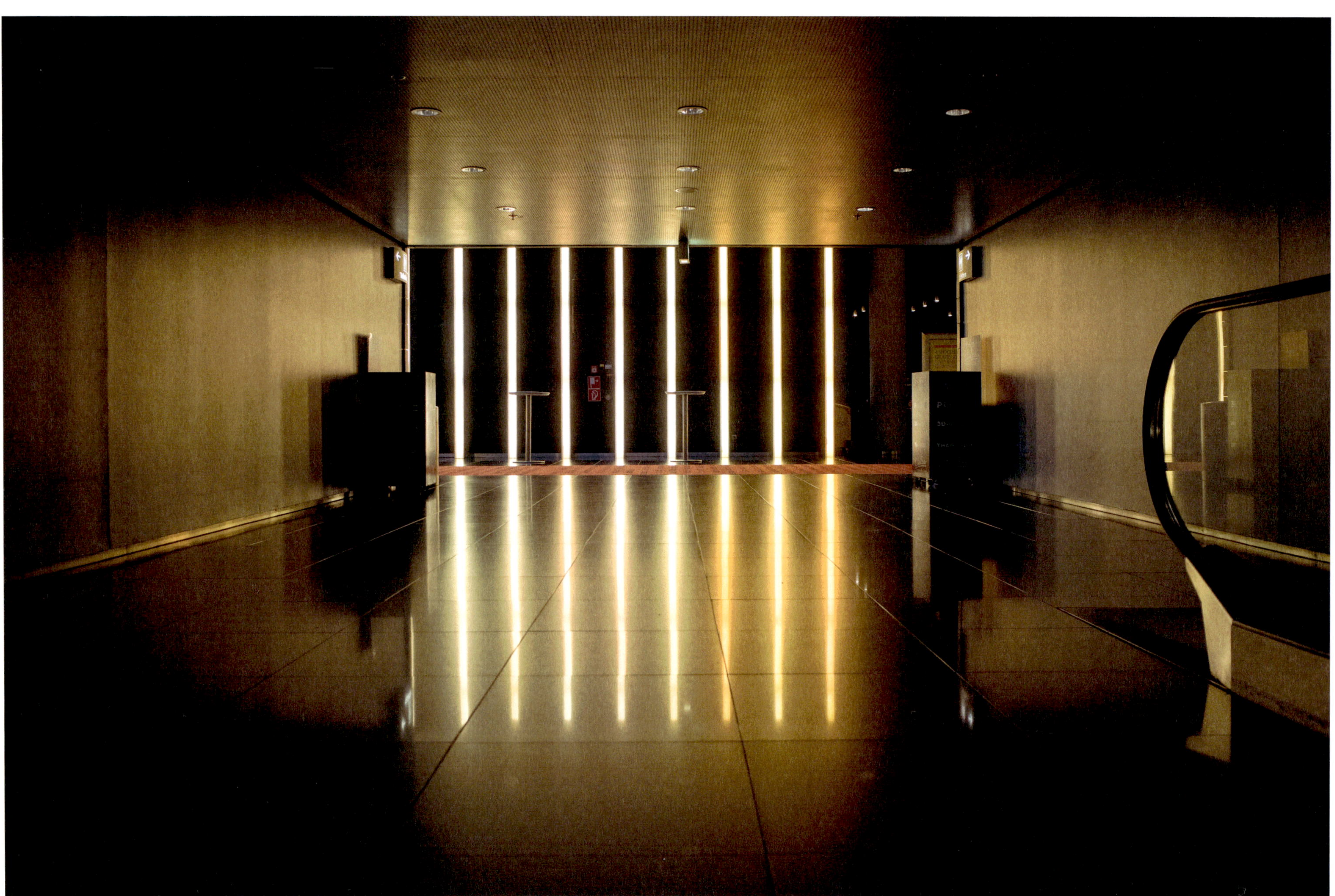

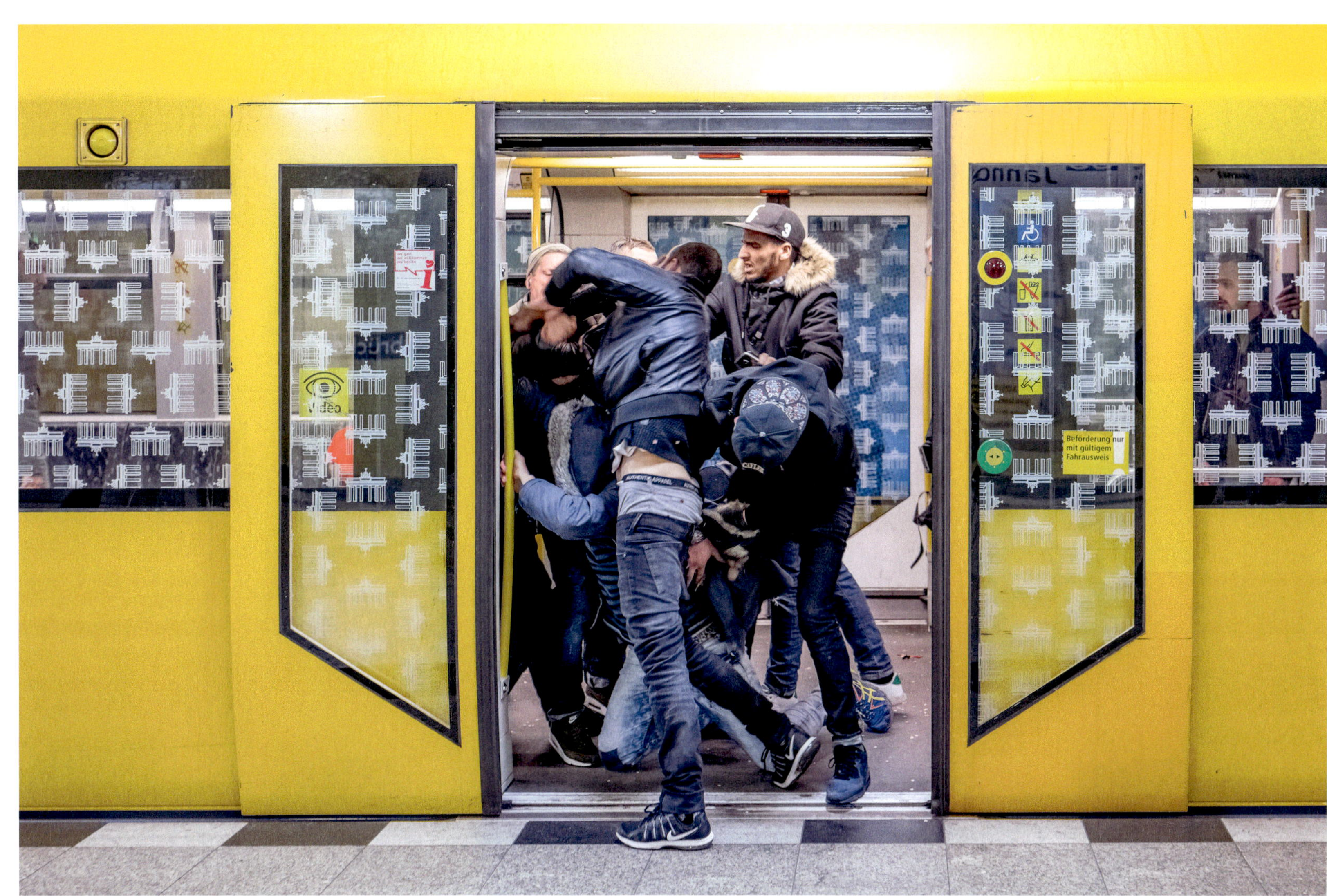
Video
Beförderung nur
mit gültigem
Fahrausweis

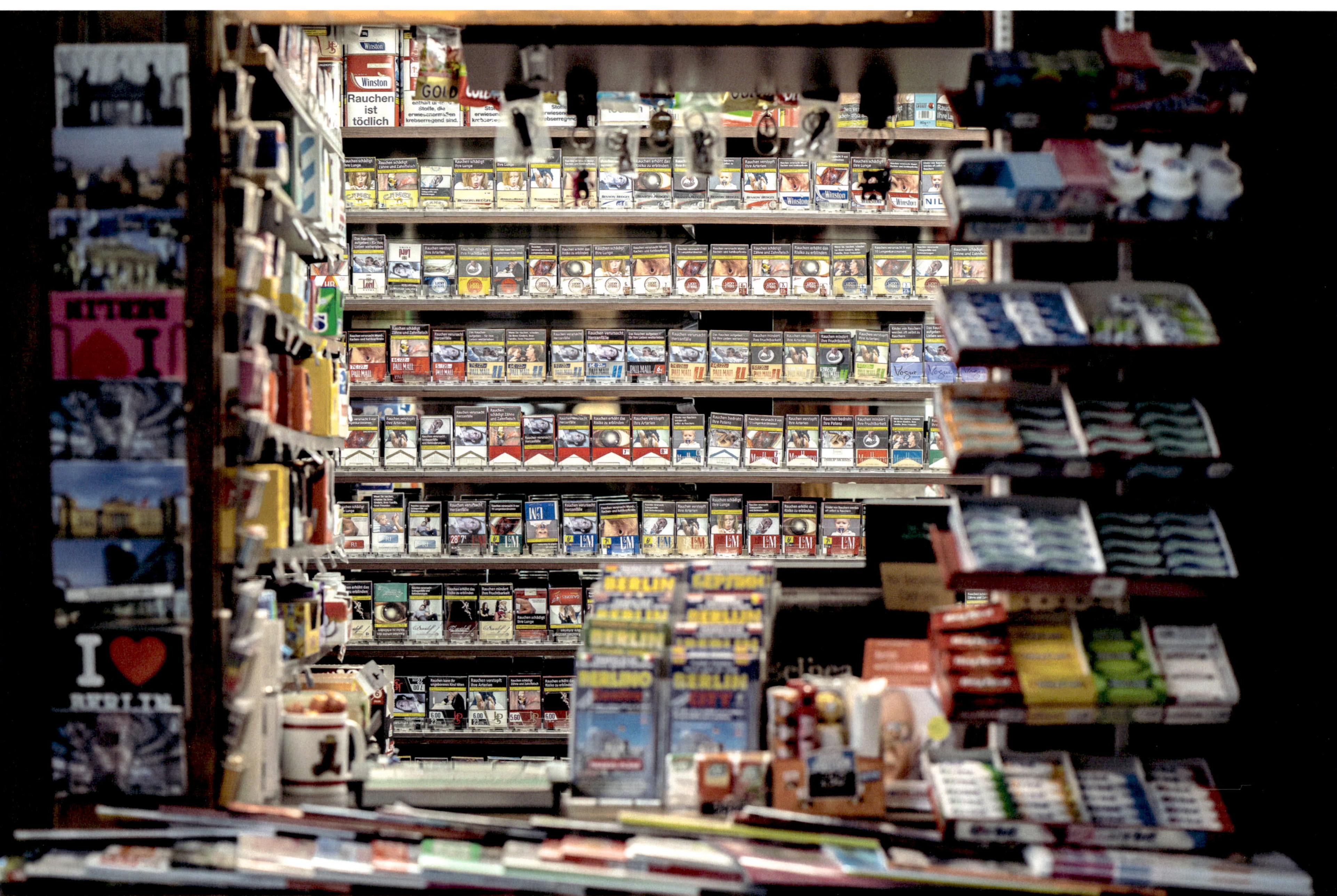

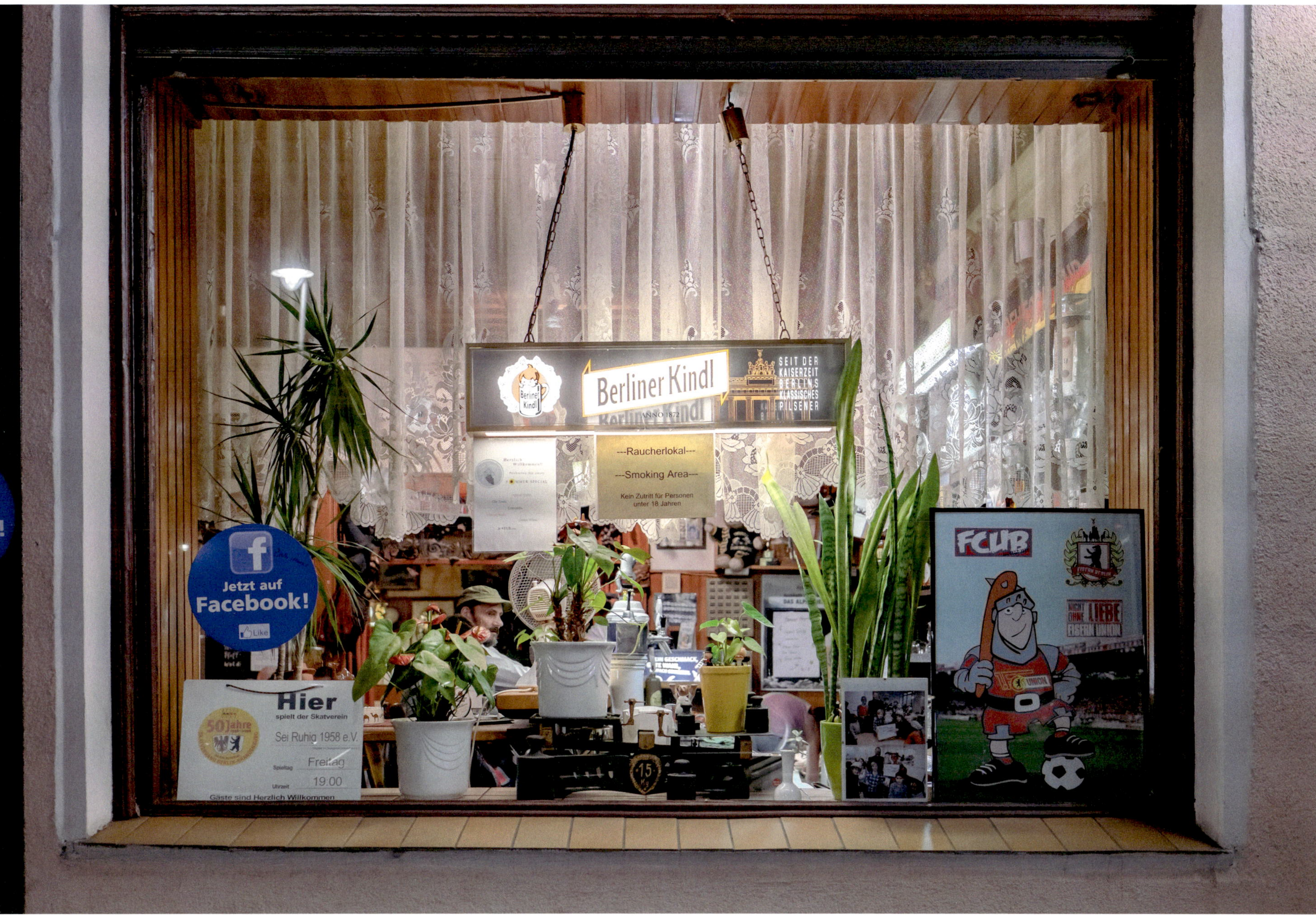
Berliner Kindl
---Raucherlokal---
---Smoking Area---
Kein Zutritt für Personen
unter 18 Jahren
Jetzt auf Facebook!
Hier
spielt der Skatverein
50 Jahre
Sei Ruhig 1958 e.V.
Spieltag   Freitag
Uhrzeit   19:00
Gäste sind Herzlich Willkommen
FCUB
NICHT OHNE LIEBE EISERN UNION

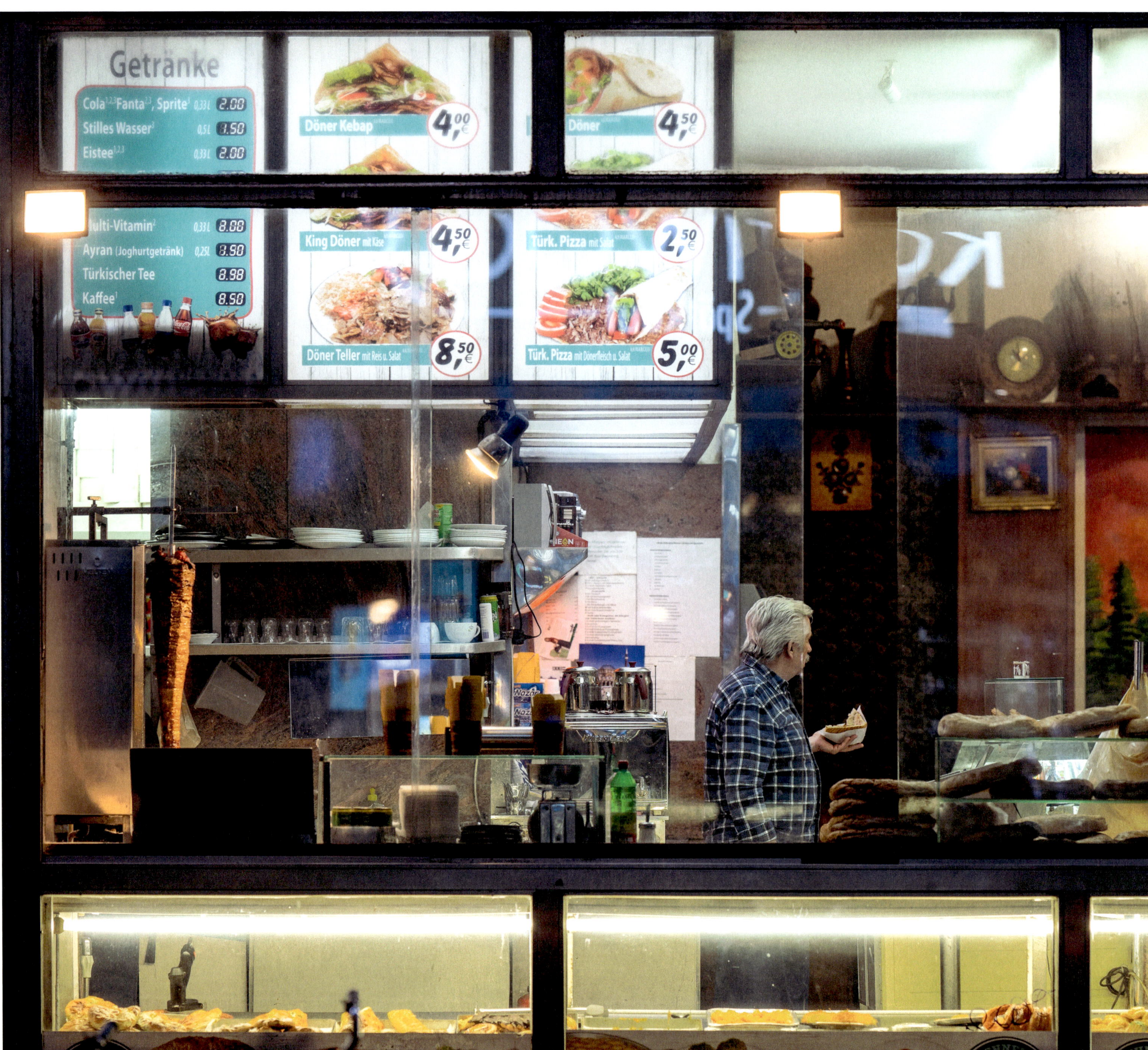
Getränke
Cola, Fanta, Sprite 0,33l 2.00
Stilles Wasser 0,5l 3.50
Eistee 0,33l 2.00
Multi-Vitamin 0,33l 8.88
Ayran (Joghurtgetränk) 0,25l 3.90
Türkischer Tee 3.98
Kaffee 3.50
Döner Kebap 4,00 €
Döner 4,50 €
King Döner mit Käse 4,50 €
Döner Teller mit Reis u. Salat 8,50 €
Türk. Pizza mit Salat 2,50 €
Türk. Pizza mit Dönerfleisch u. Salat 5,00 €

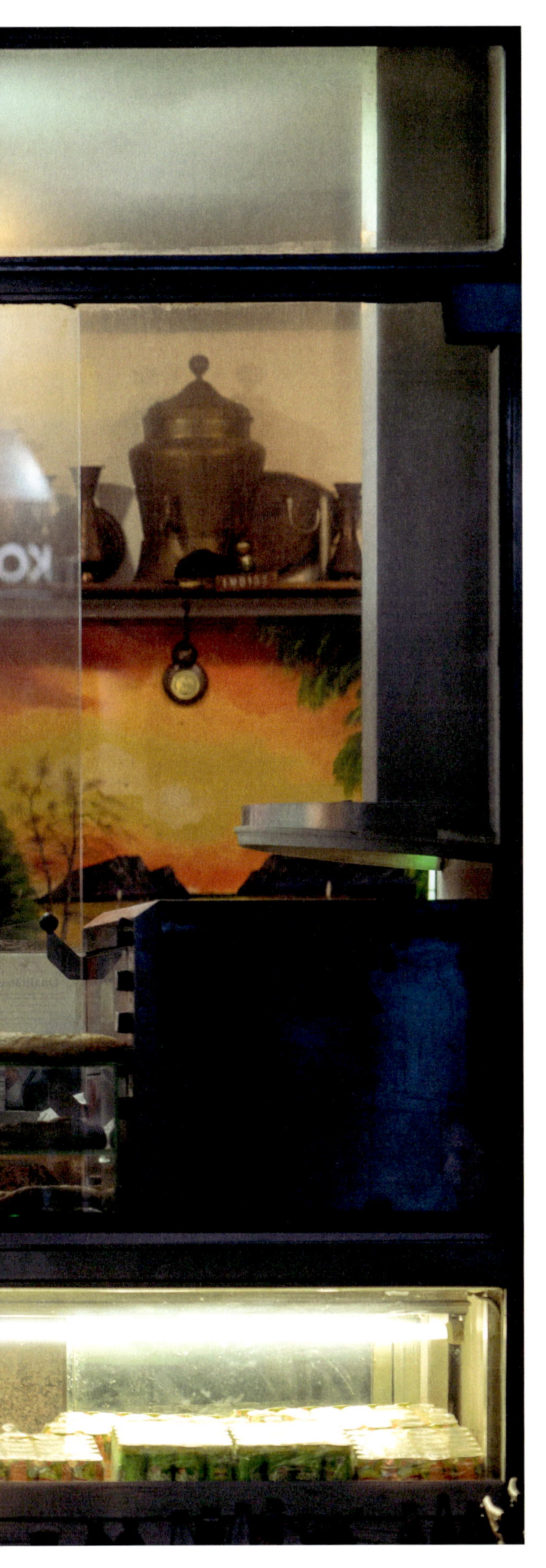

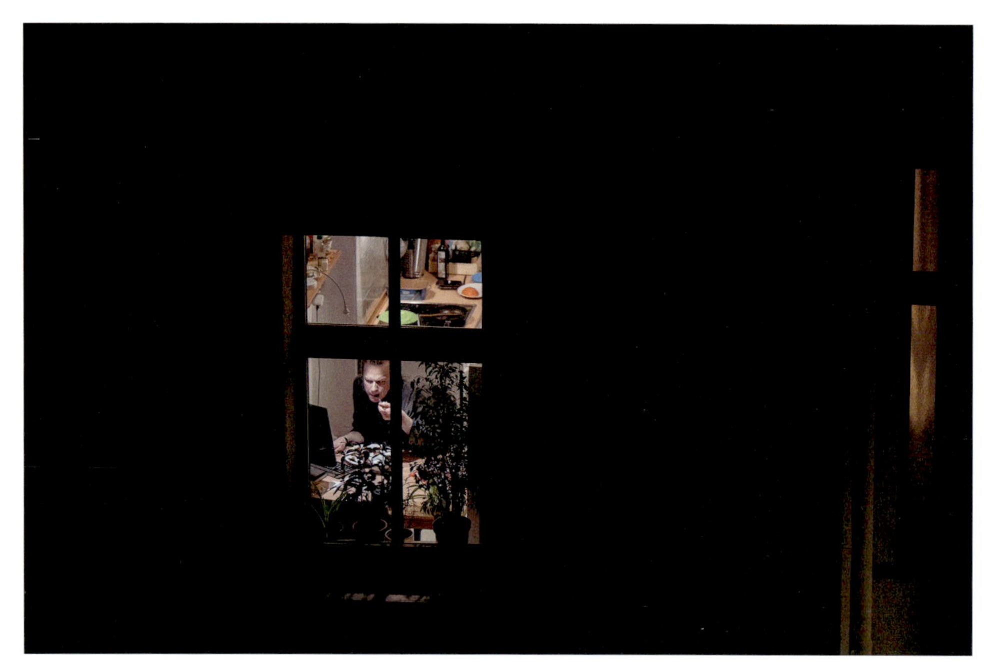

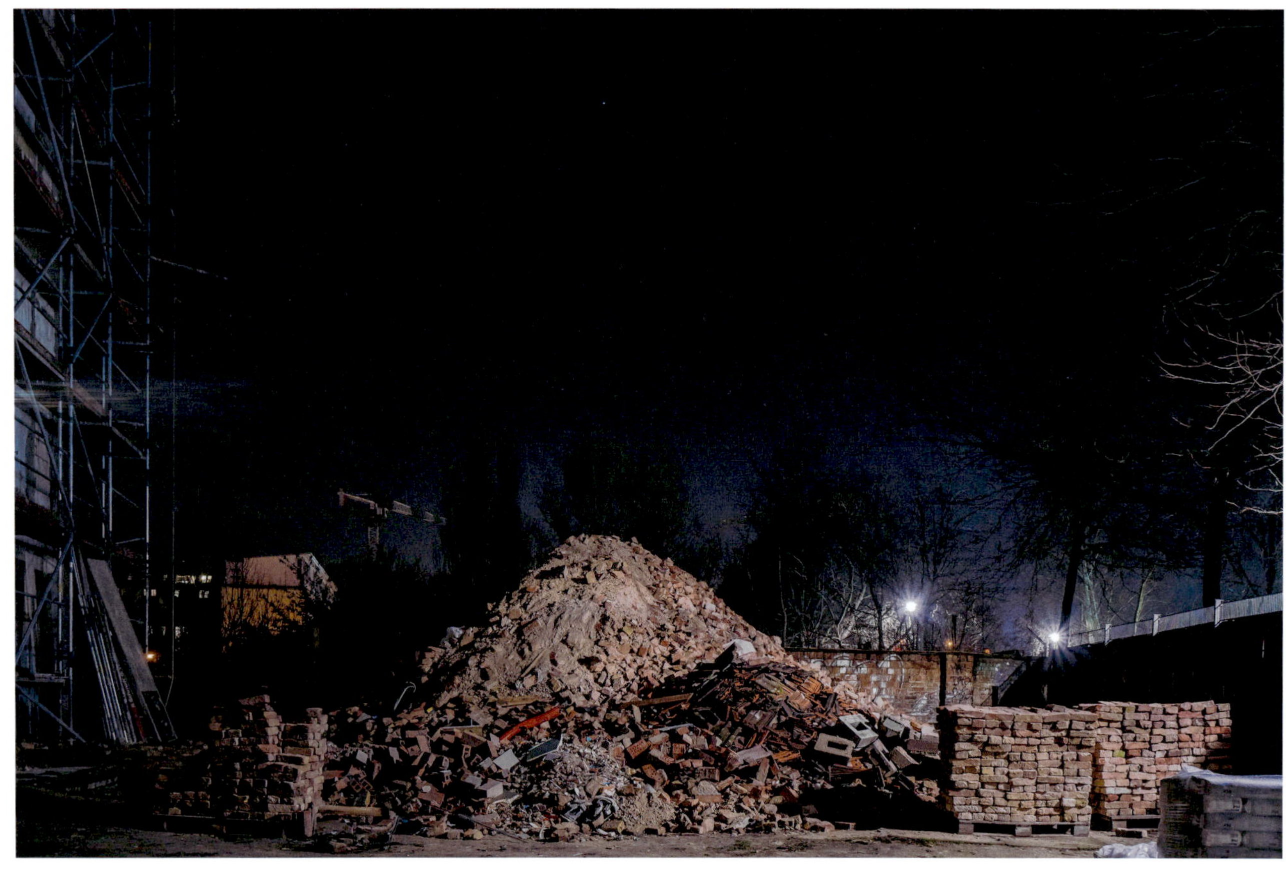

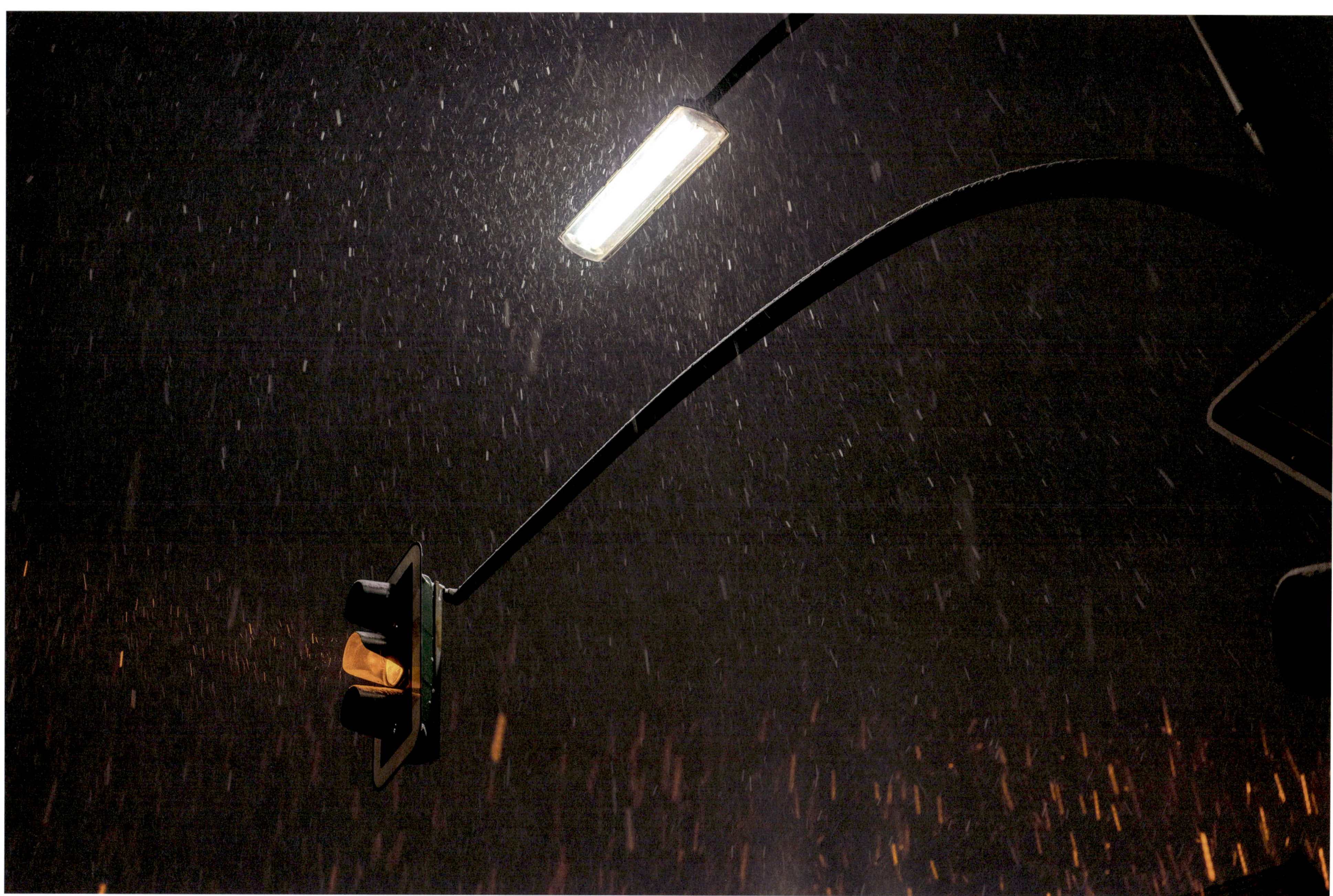

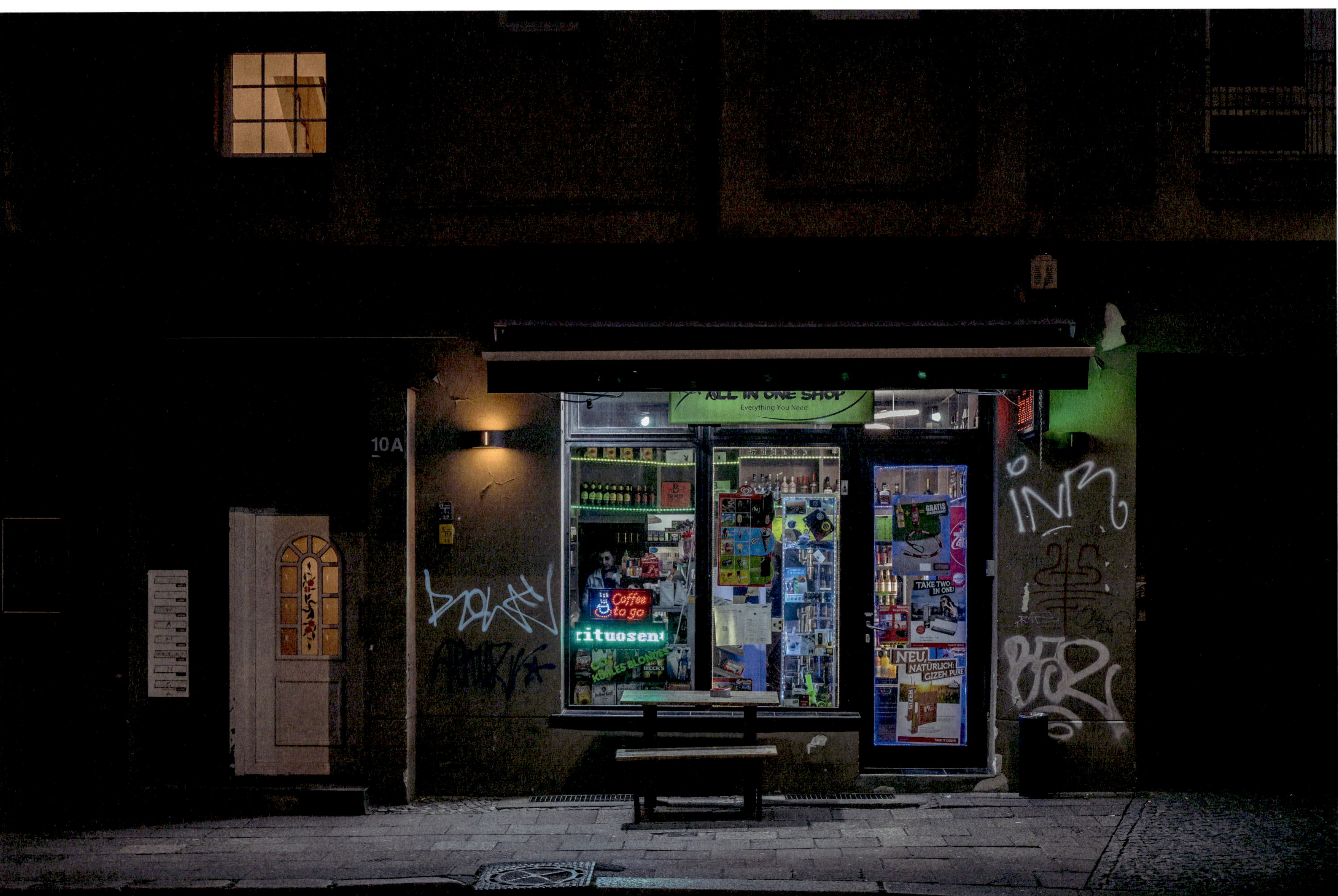
10 A
ALL IN ONE SHOP
Everything You Need
Coffee
to go
rituosen
KÜHLES BLONDES
BECK'S
TAKE TWO
IN ONE
NEU
NATÜRLICH
GIZEH PURE

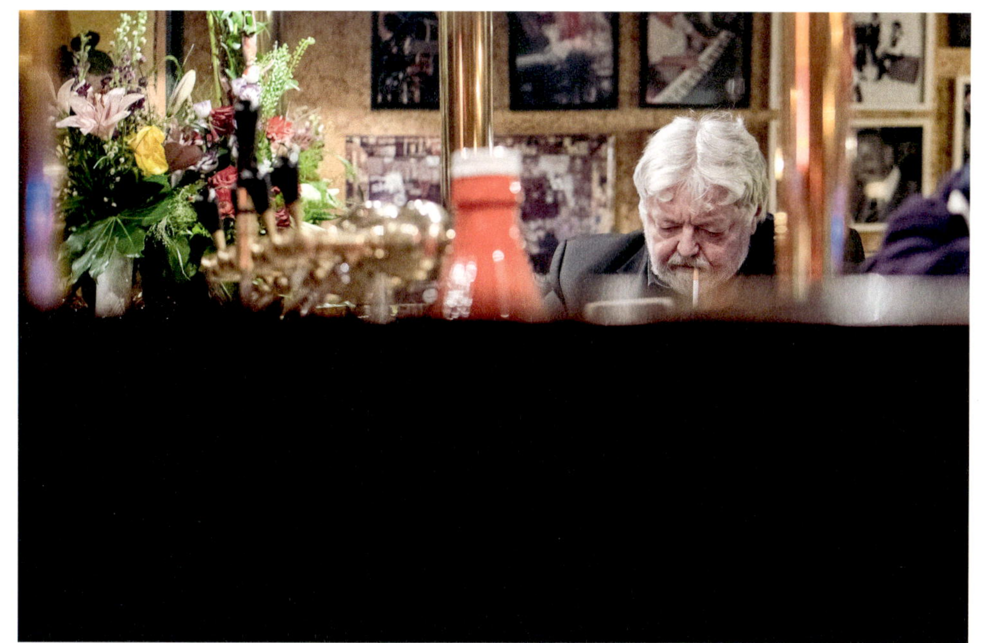

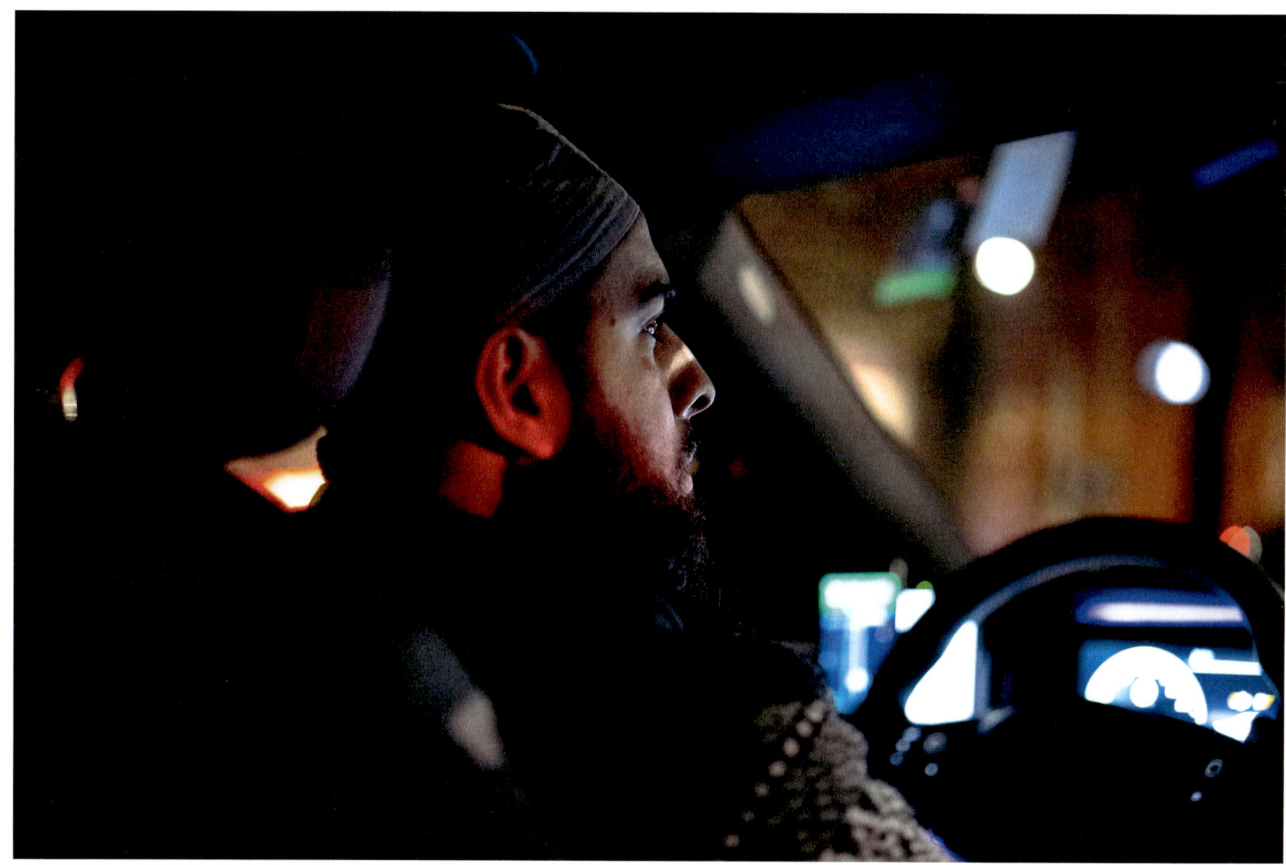

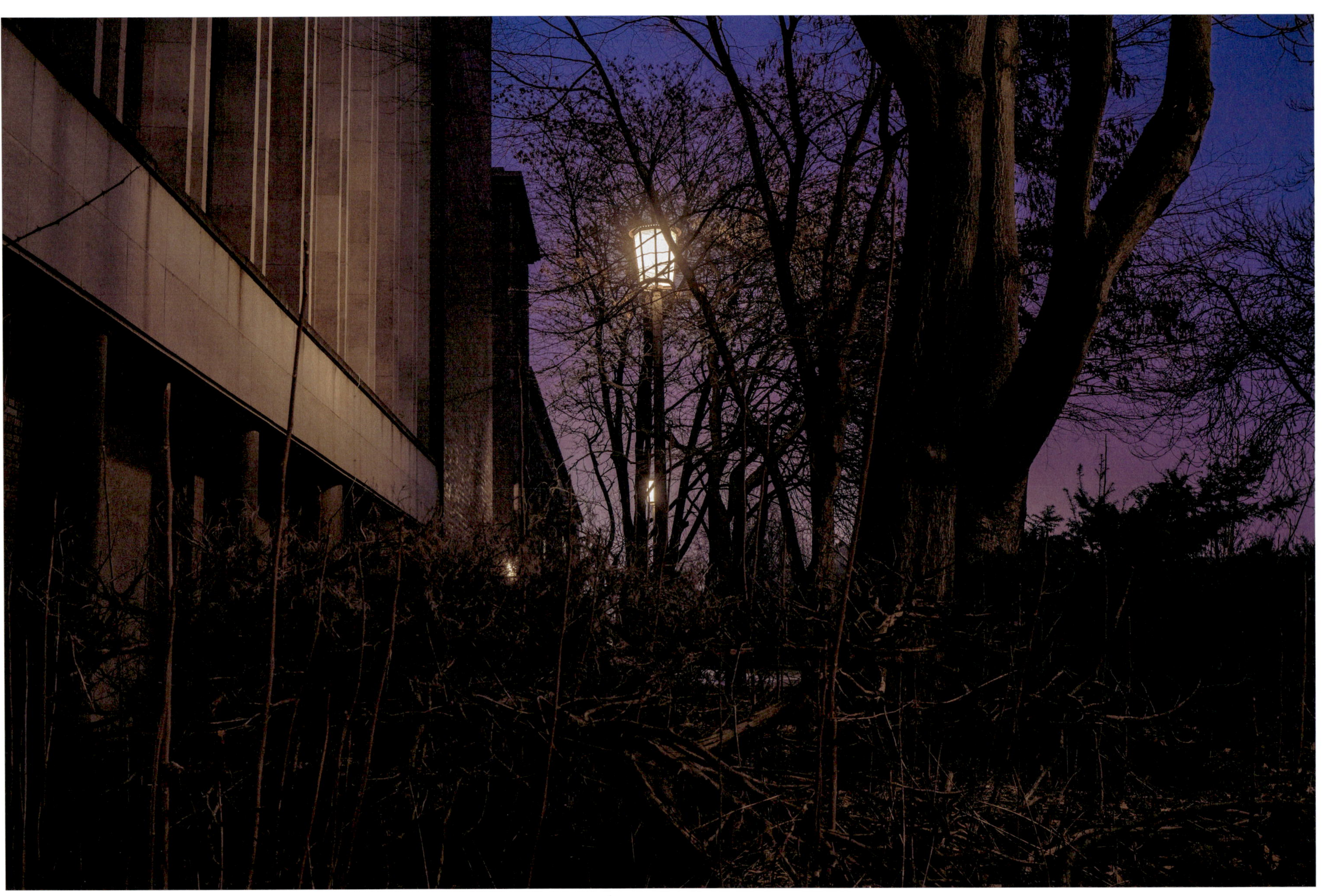

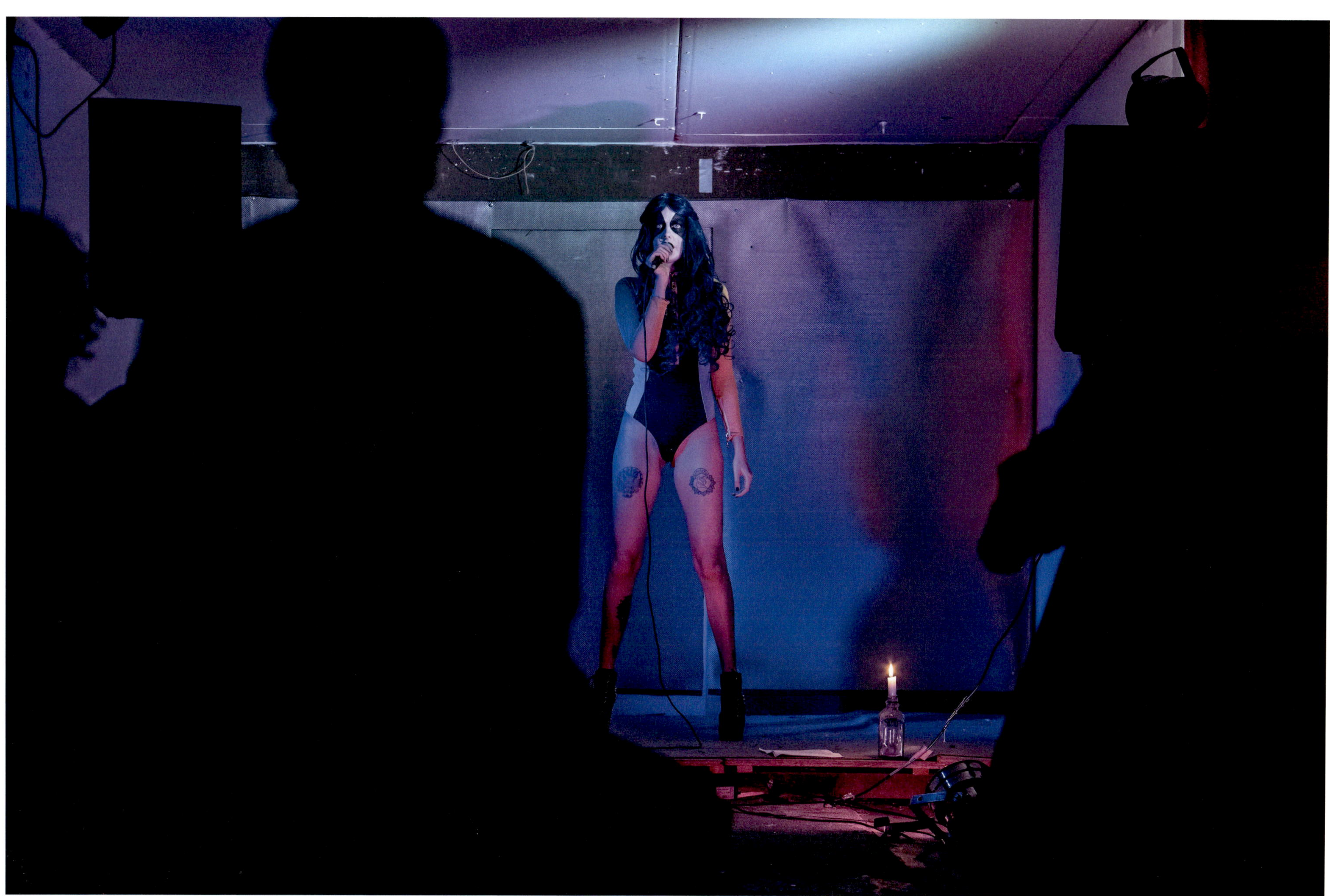

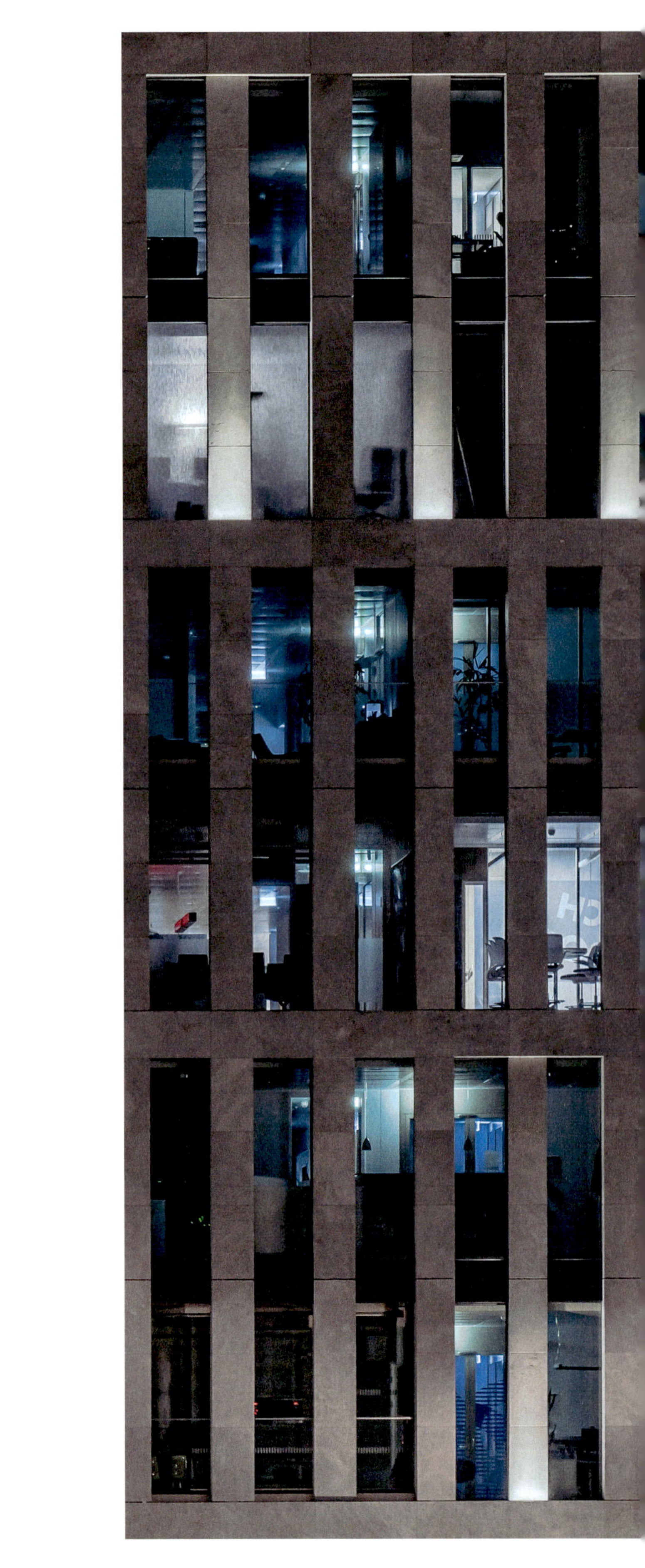

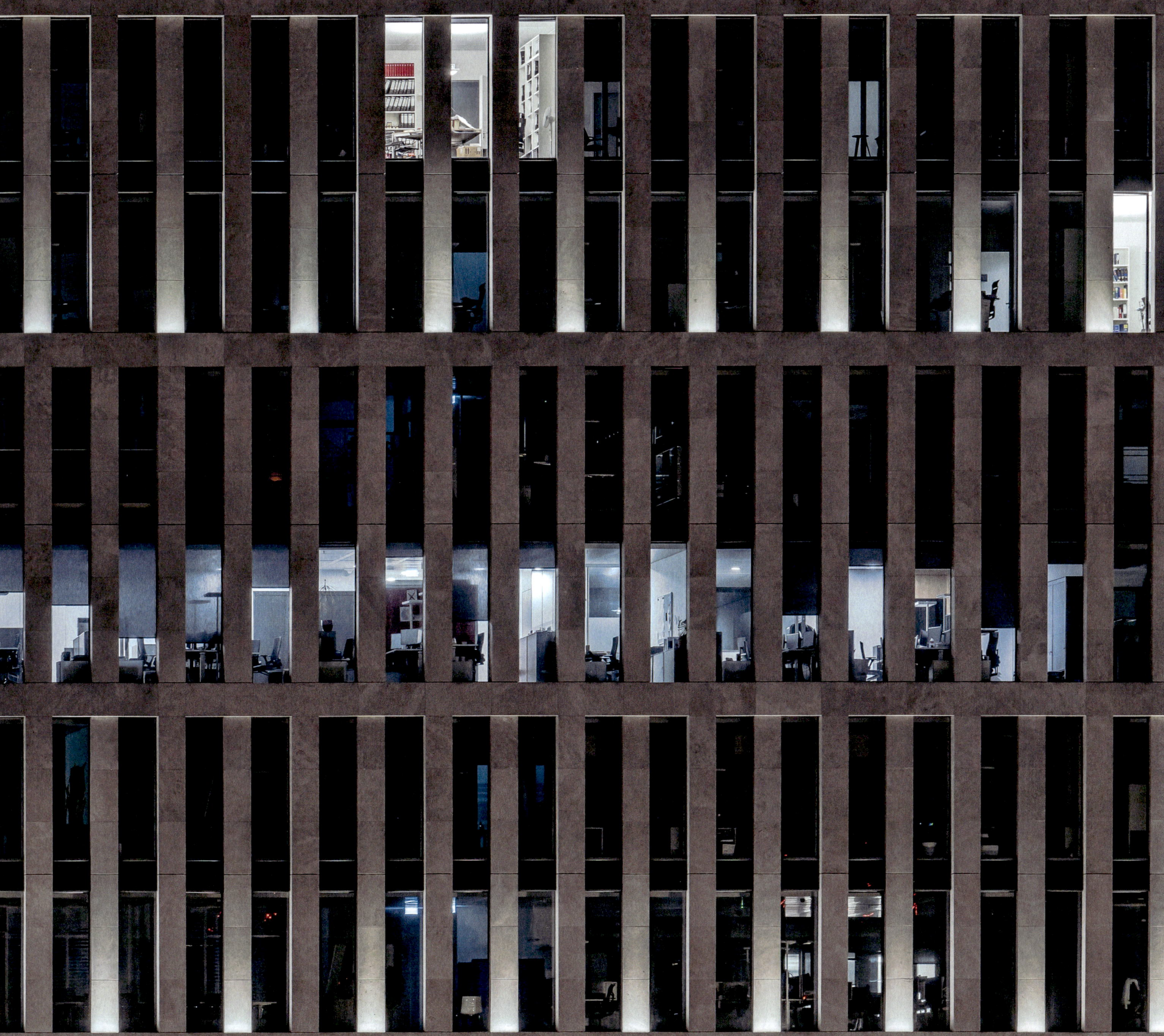

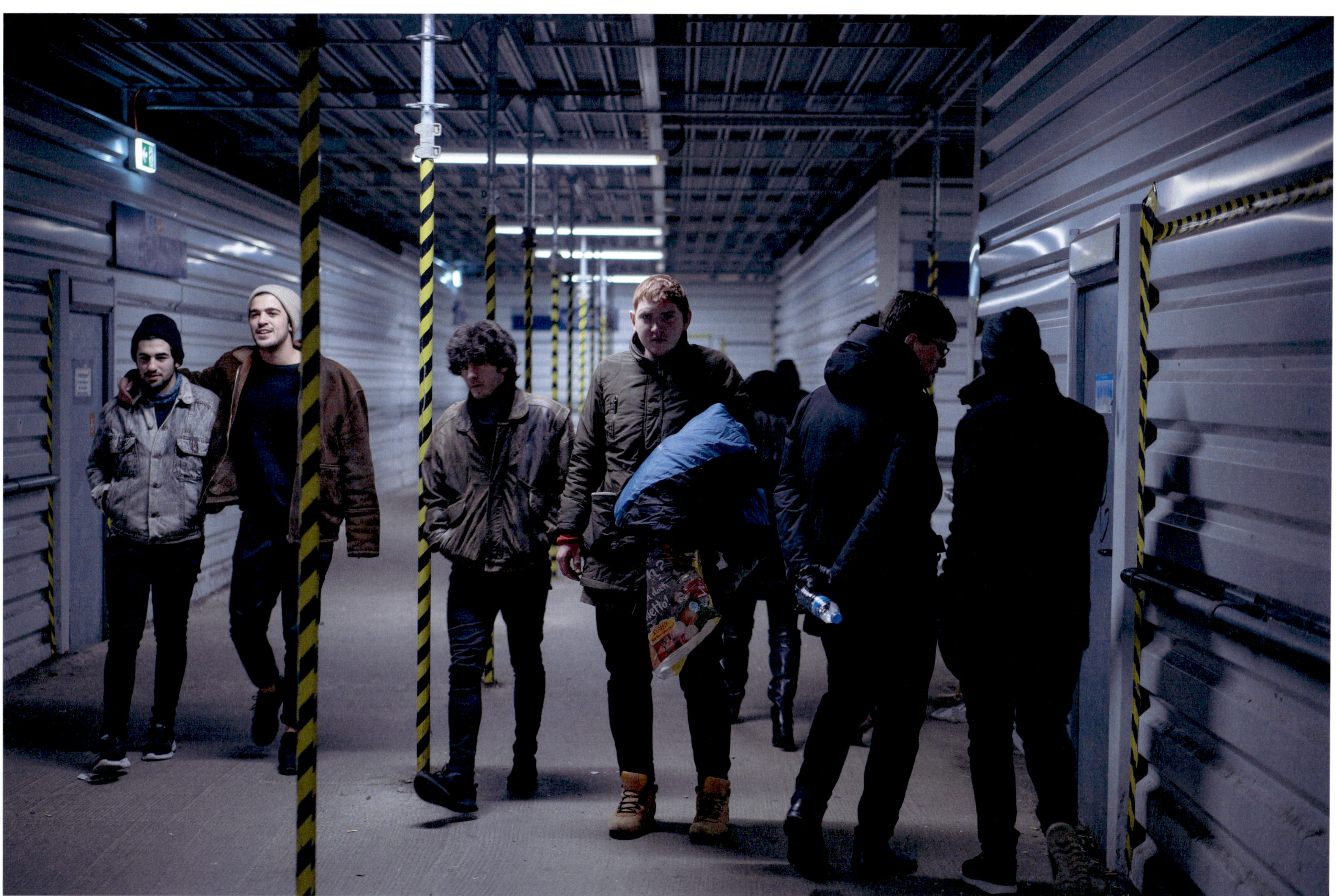

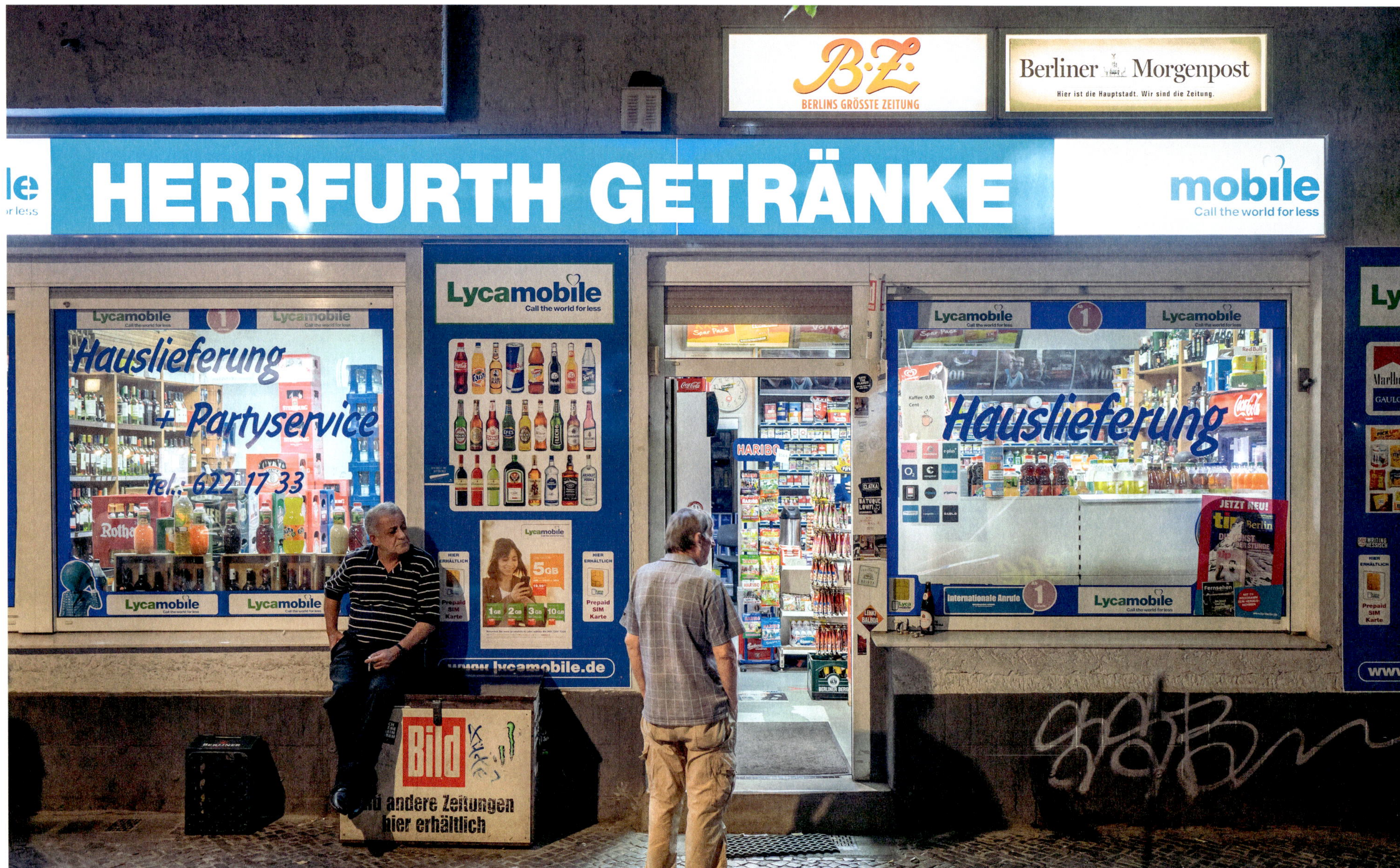

B·Z·
BERLINS GRÖSSTE ZEITUNG
Berliner Morgenpost
Hier ist die Hauptstadt. Wir sind die Zeitung.
HERRFURTH GETRÄNKE
mobile
Call the world for less
Lycamobile
Call the world for less
Hauslieferung
+ Partyservice
Tel.: 622 17 33
Lycamobile
Hauslieferung
Bild
und andere Zeitungen
hier erhältlich

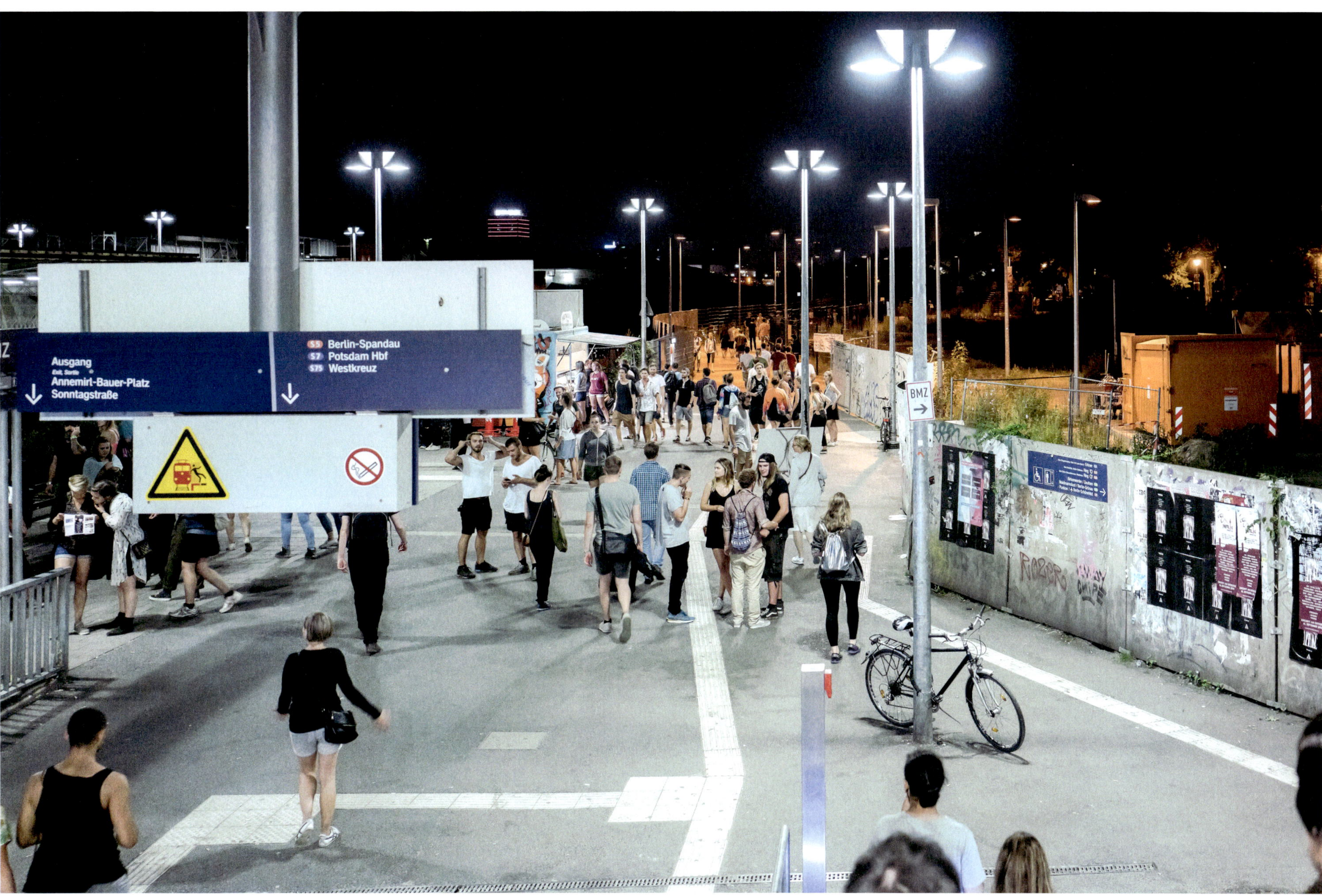

Ausgang
Exit, Sortie
Annemirl-Bauer-Platz
Sonntagstraße
S5 Berlin-Spandau
S7 Potsdam Hbf
S75 Westkreuz
BMZ

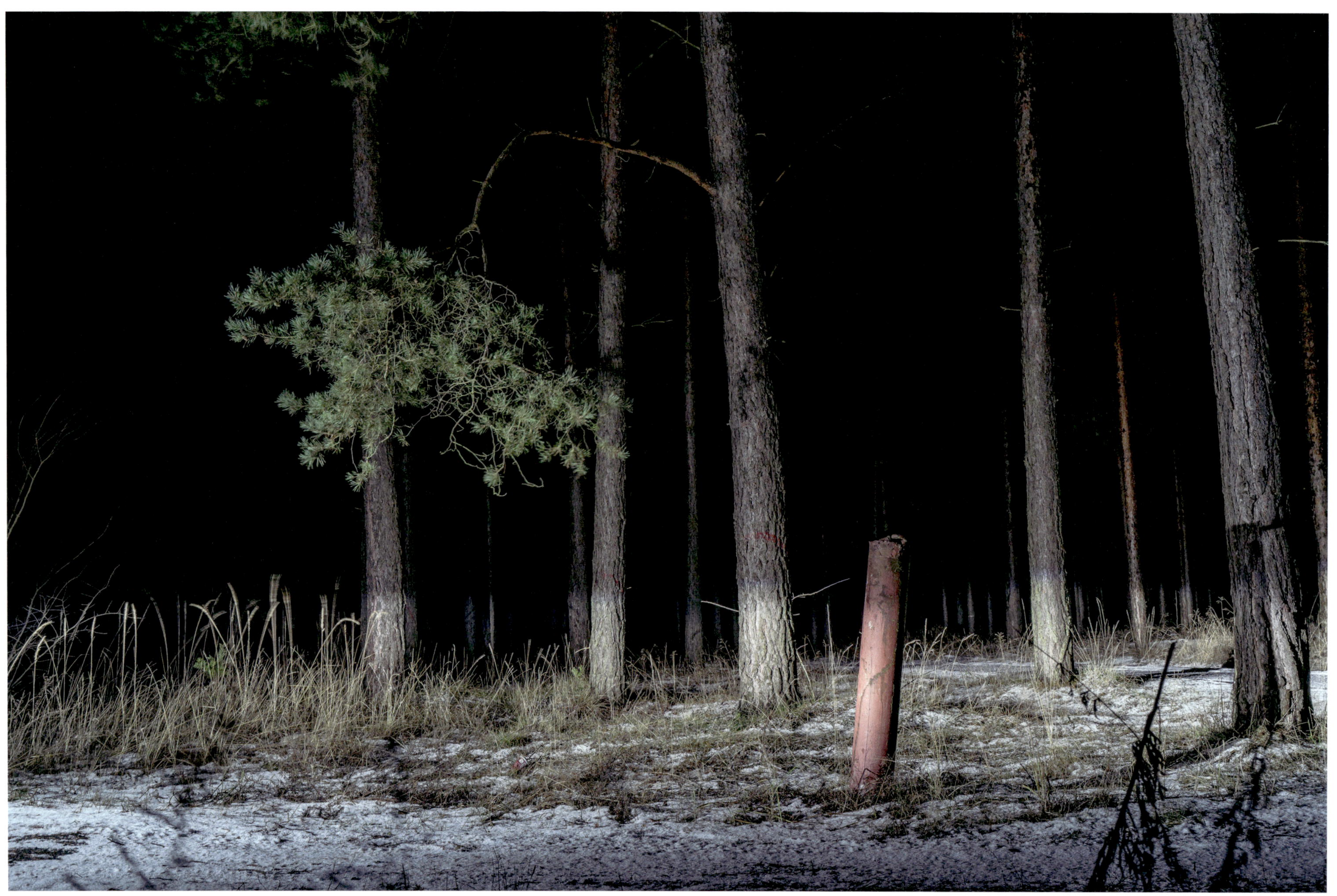

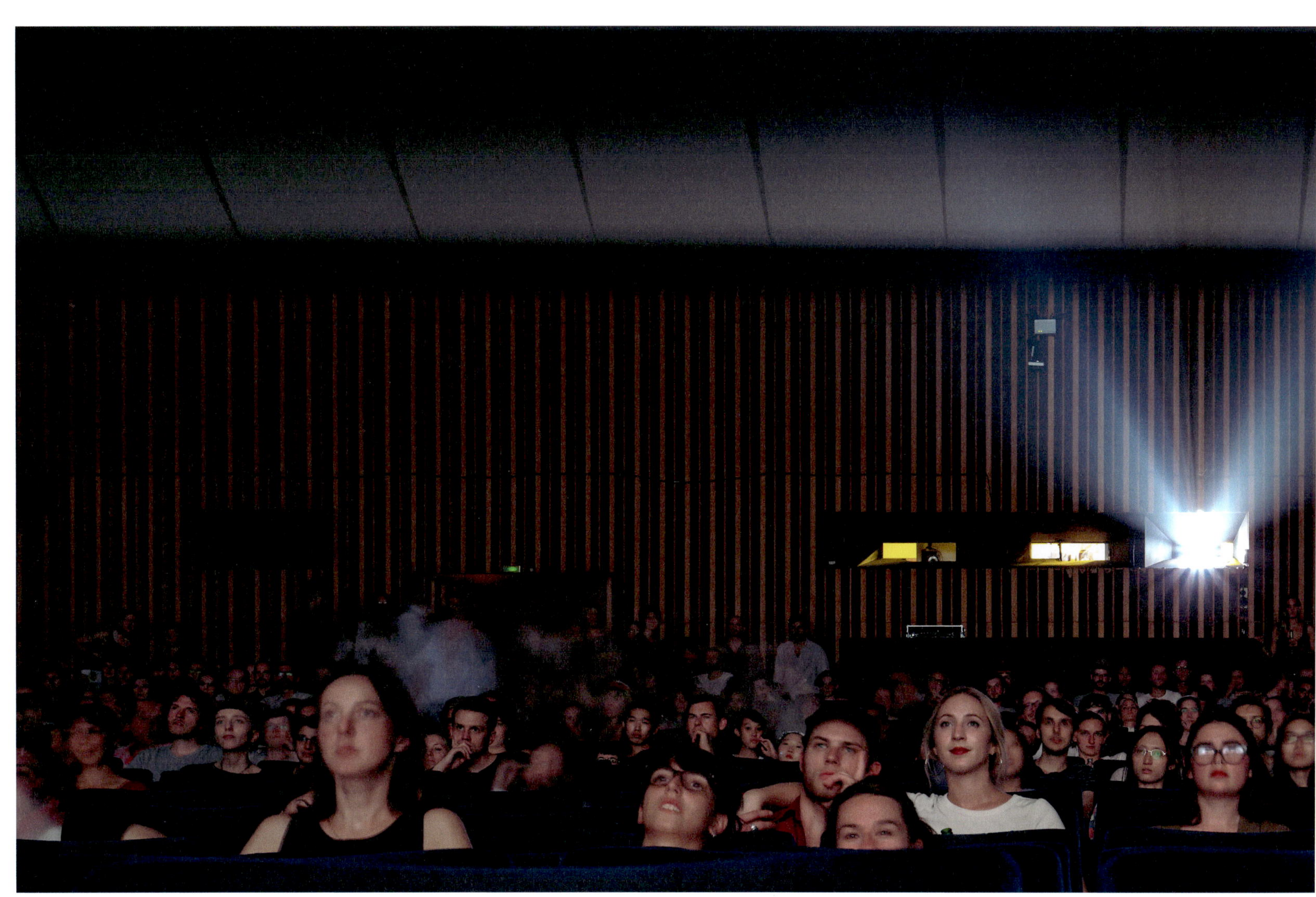

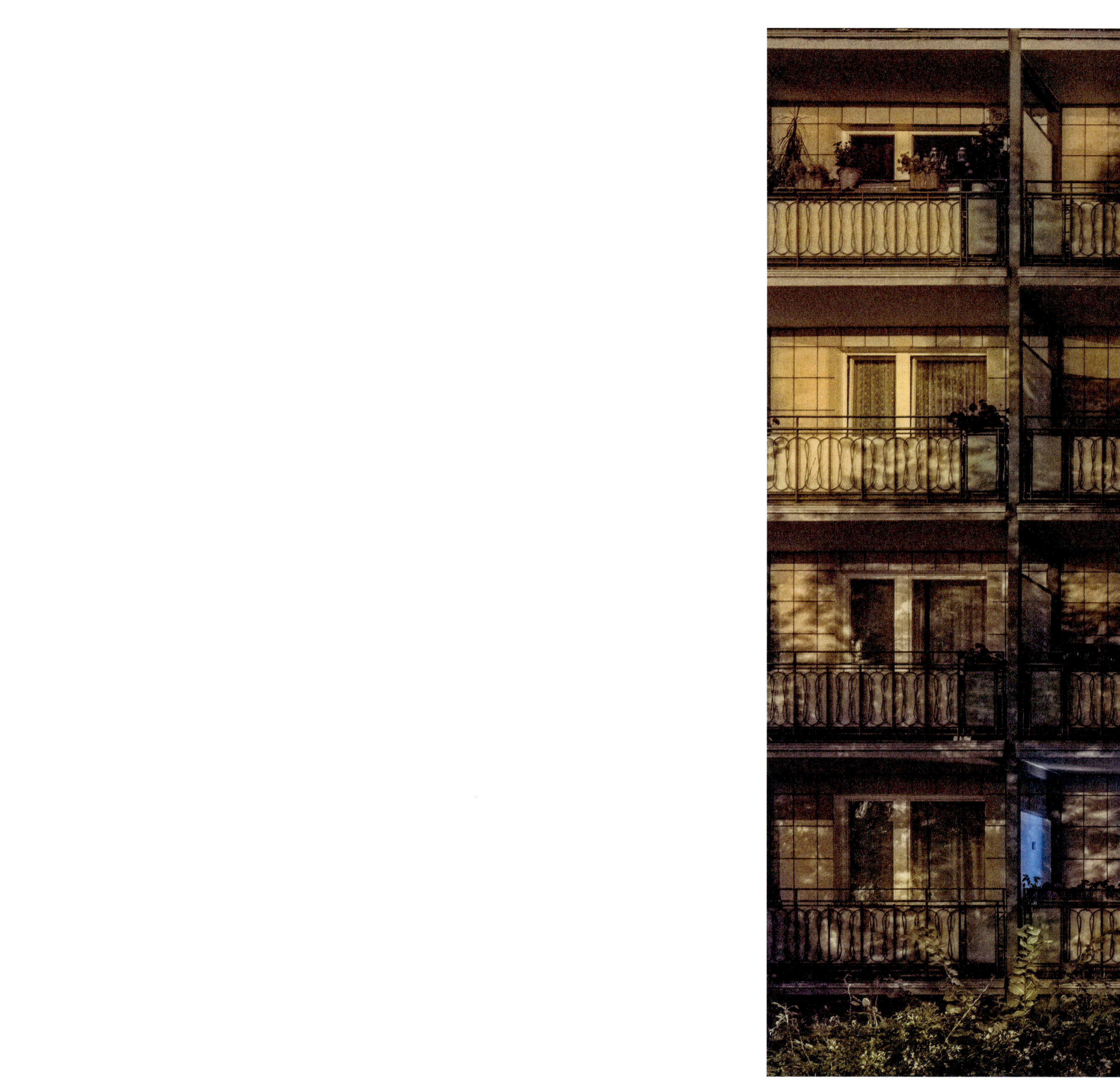

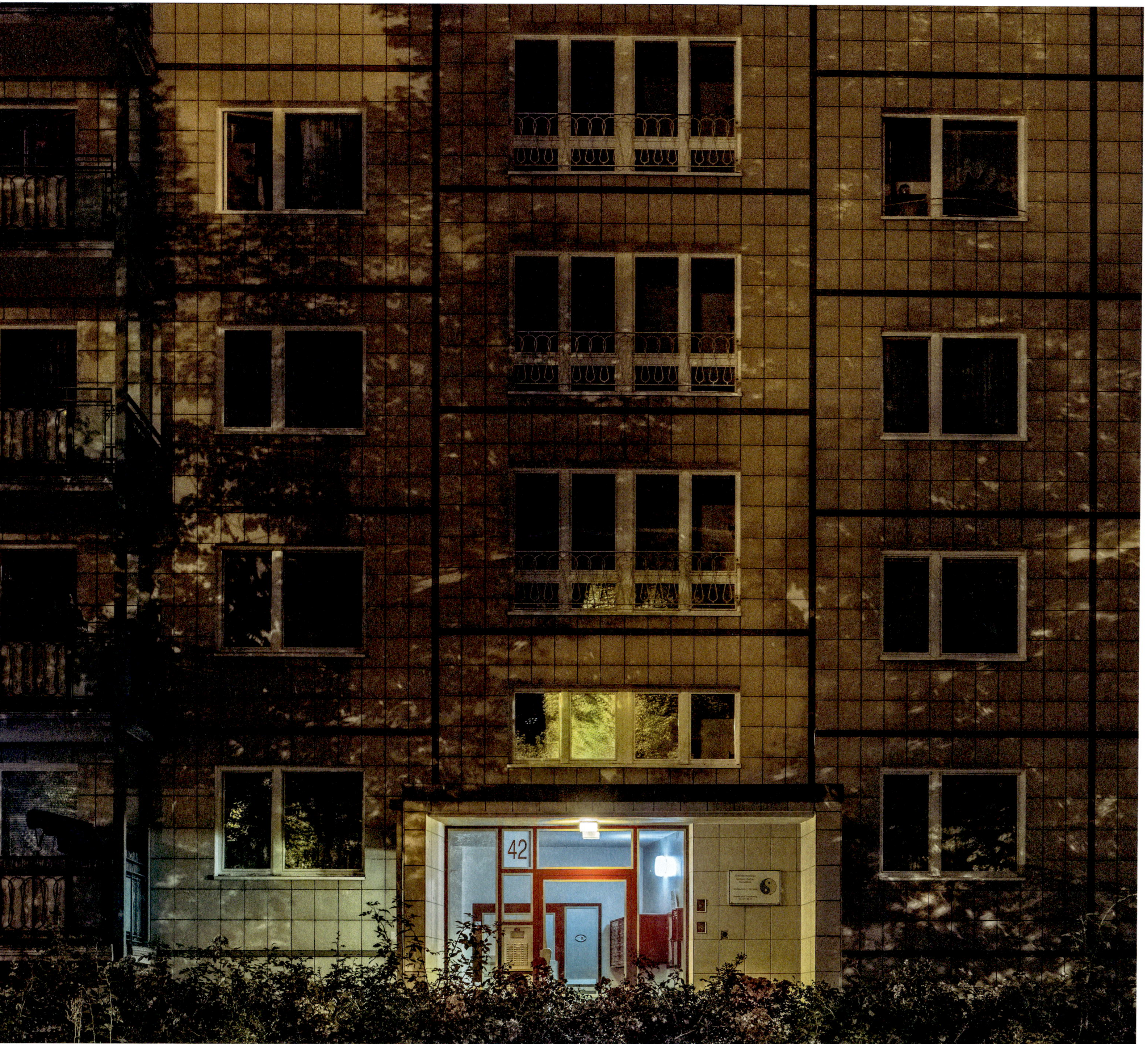

42

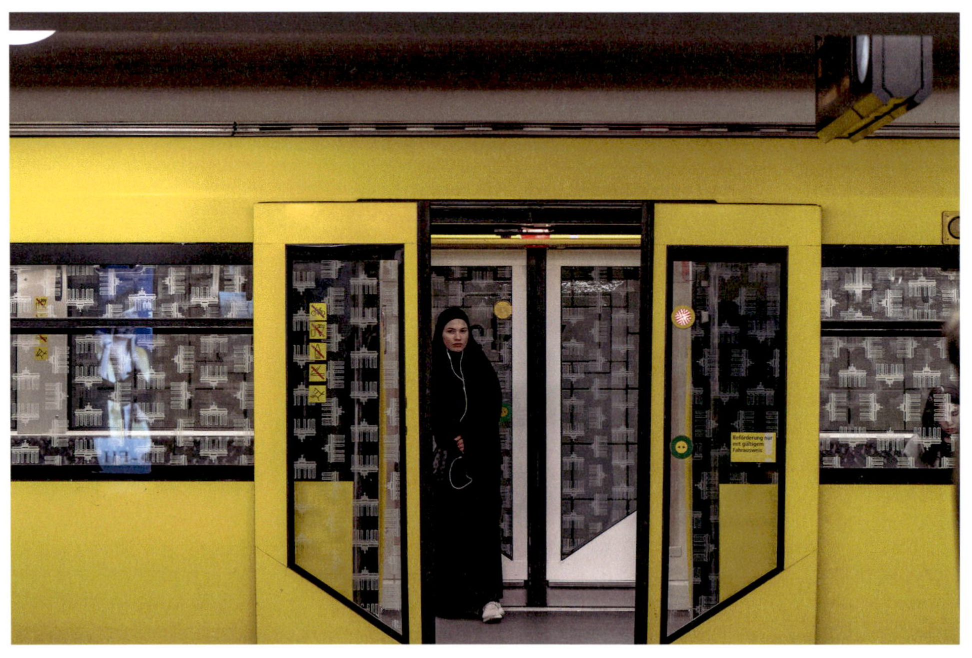

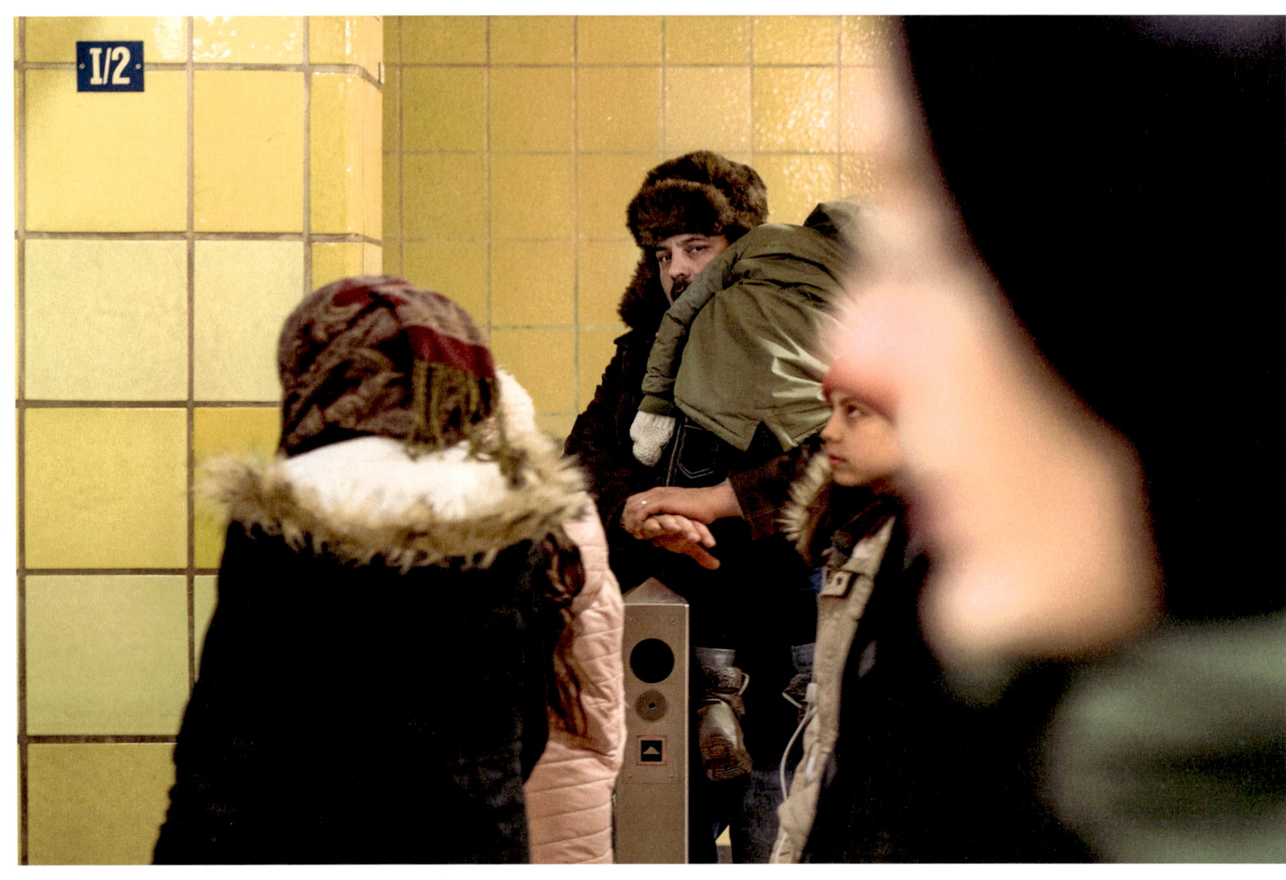

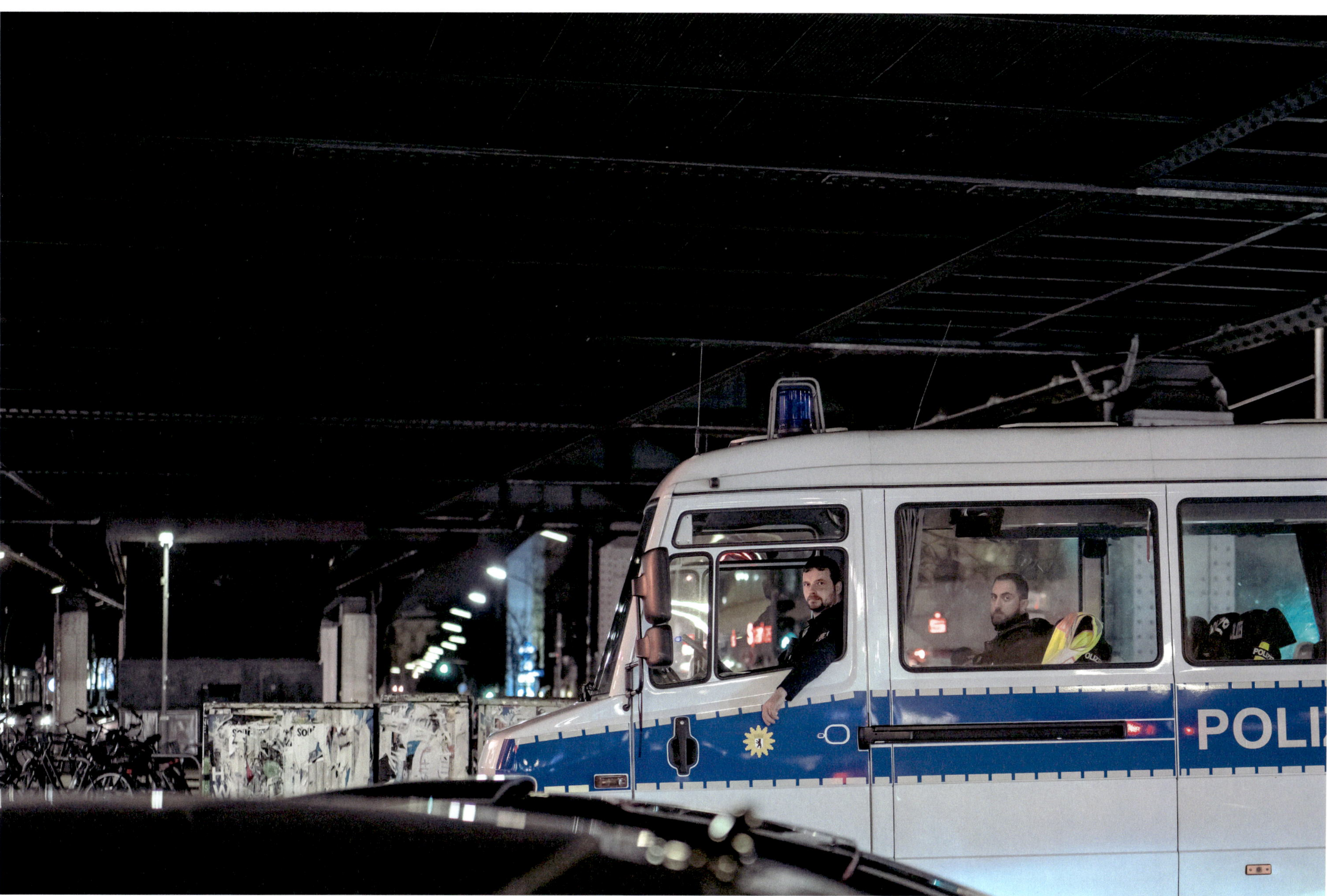

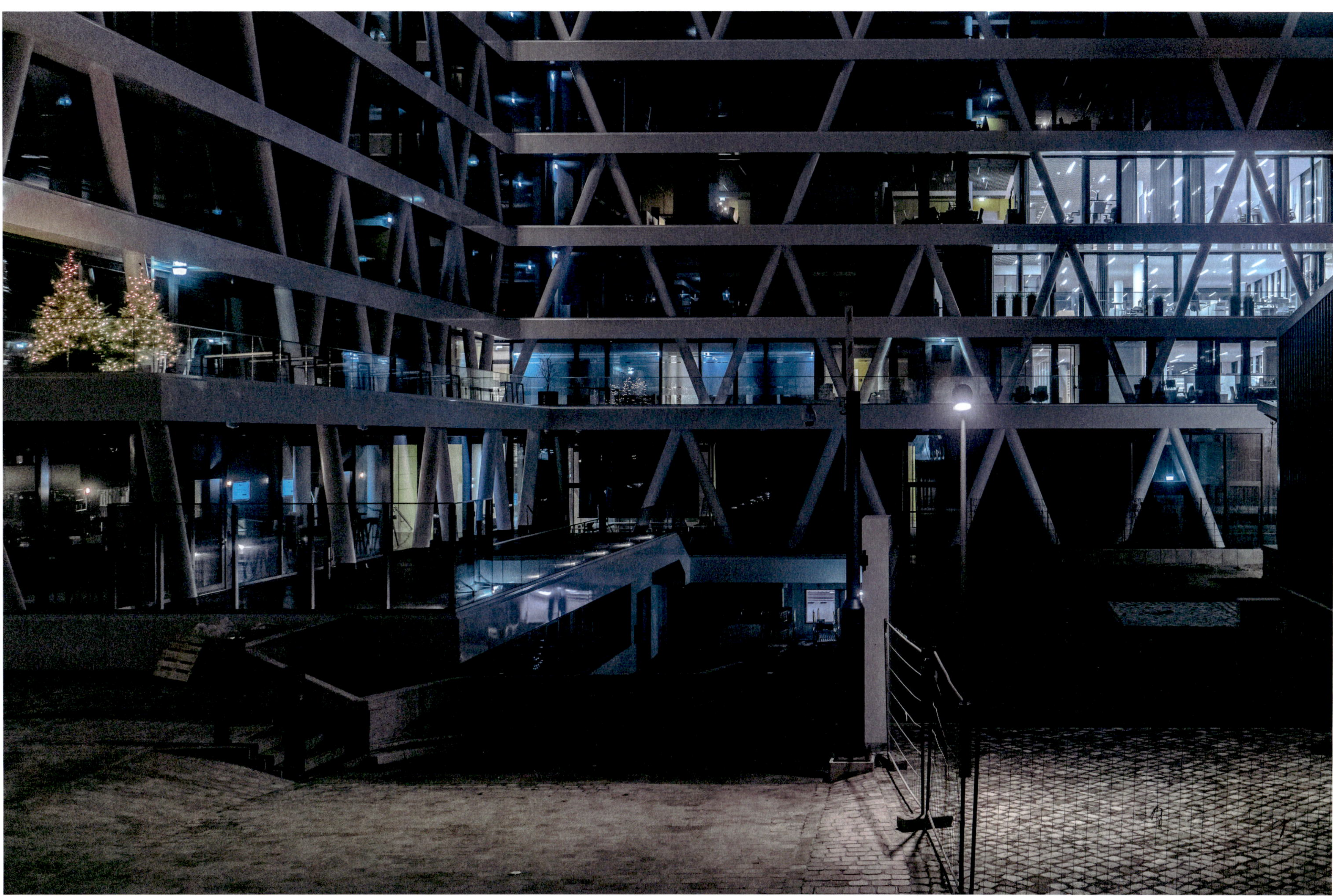

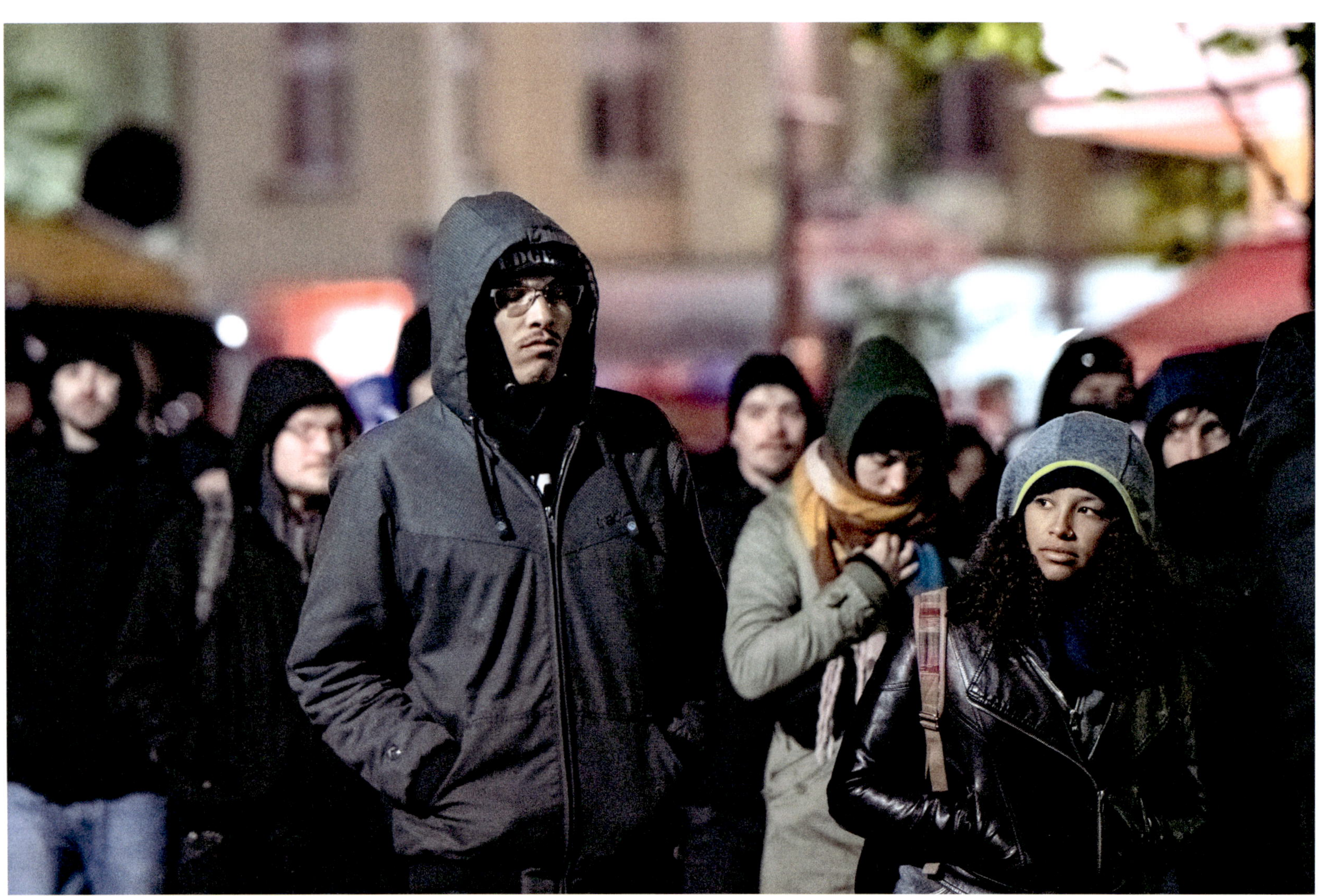

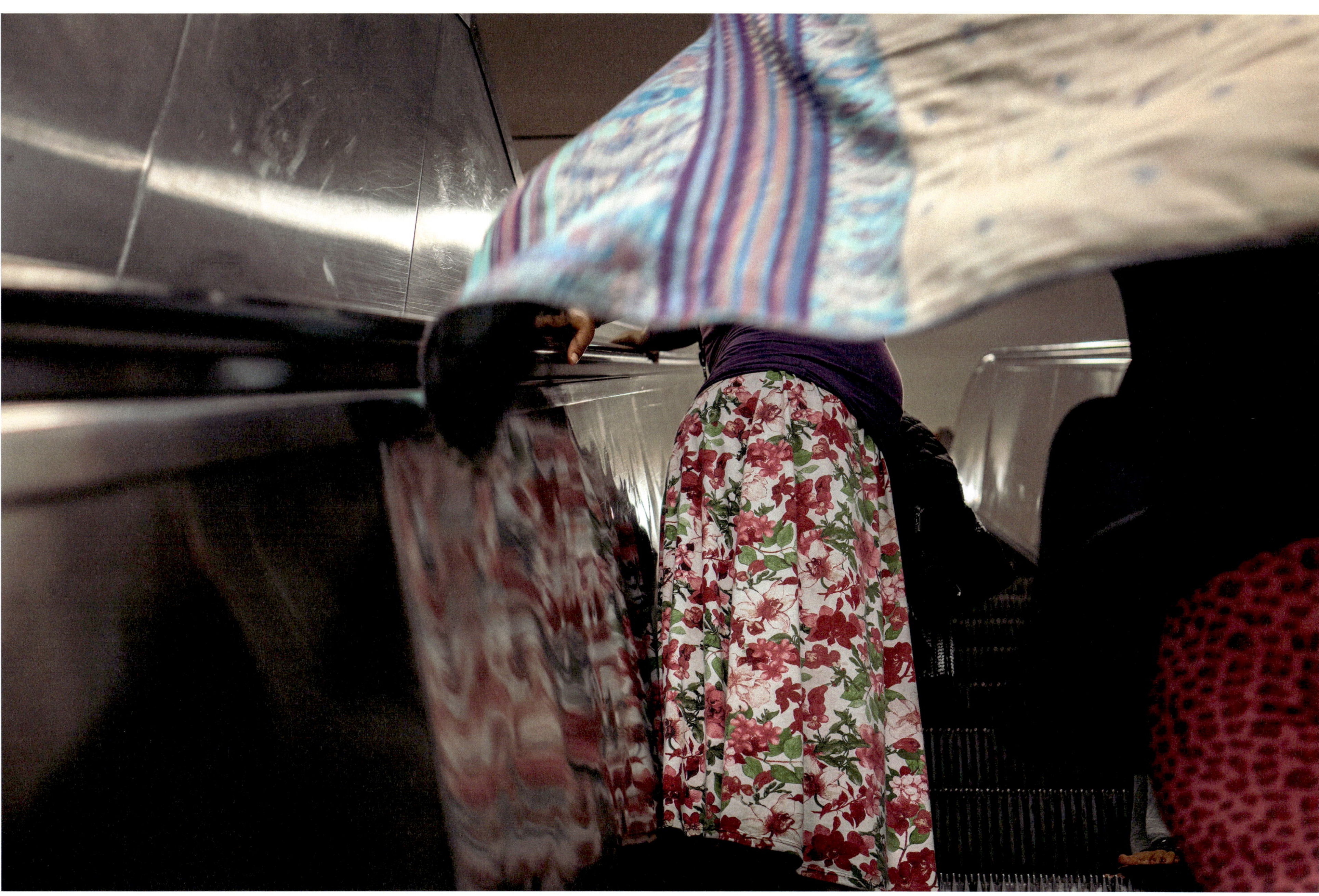

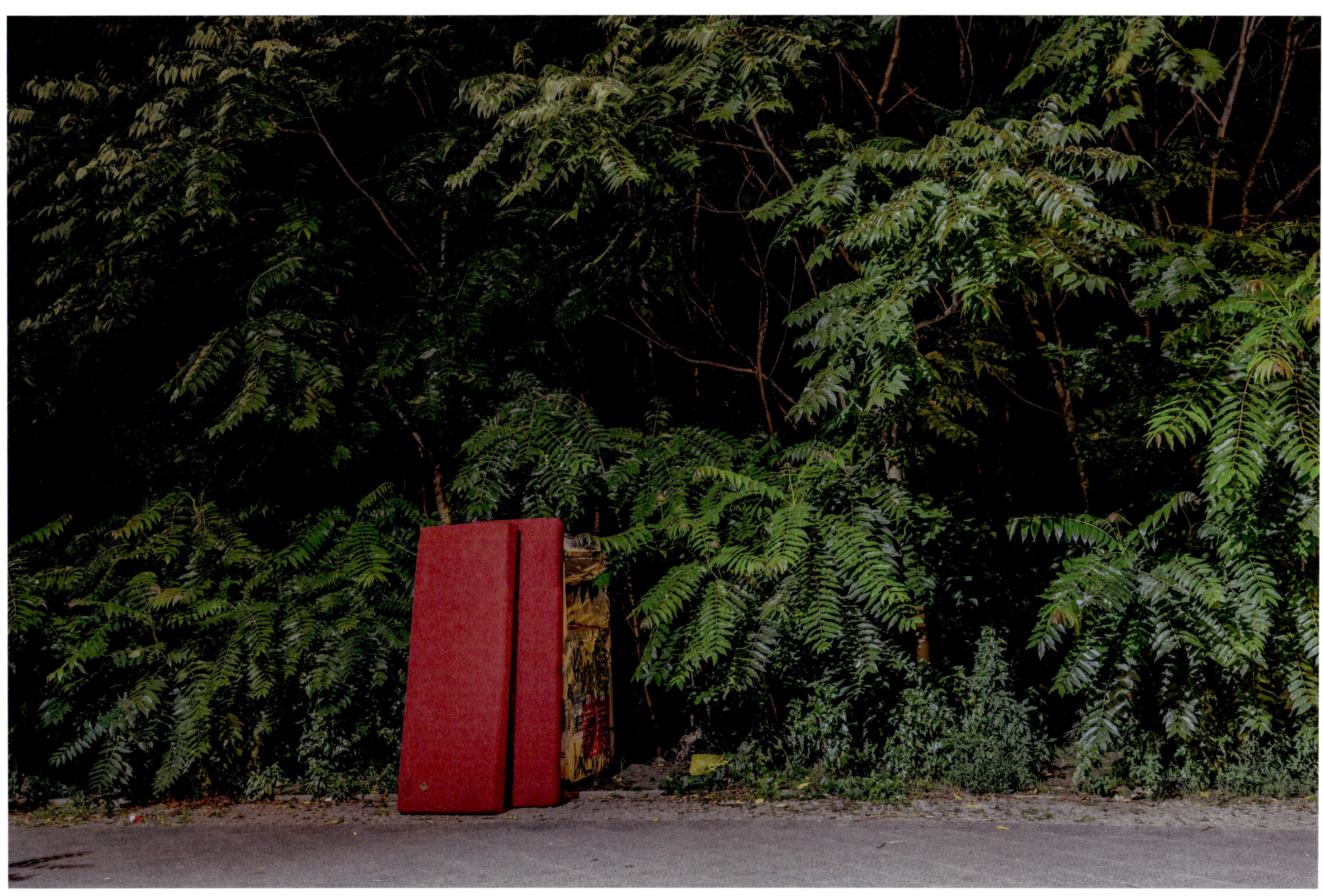

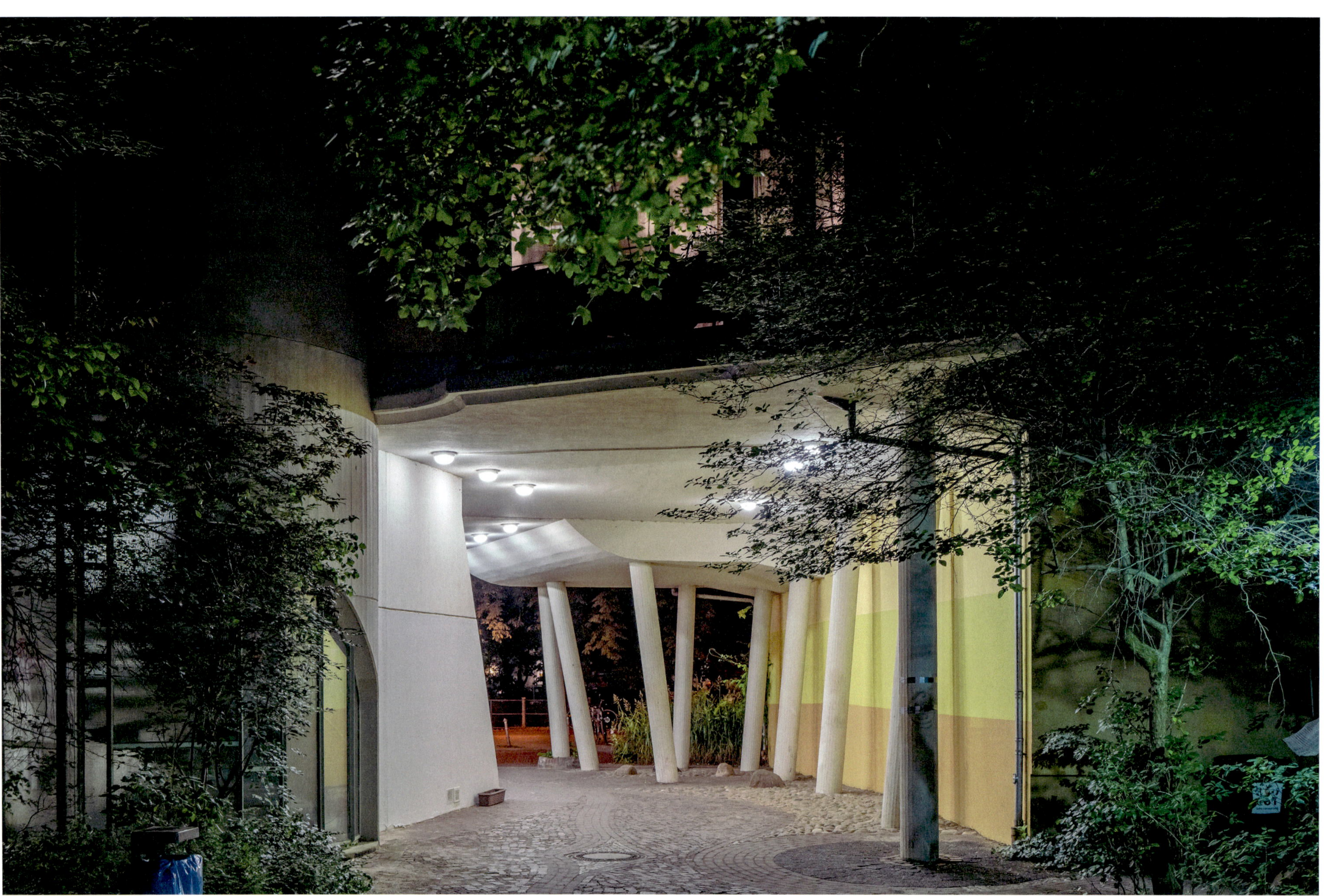

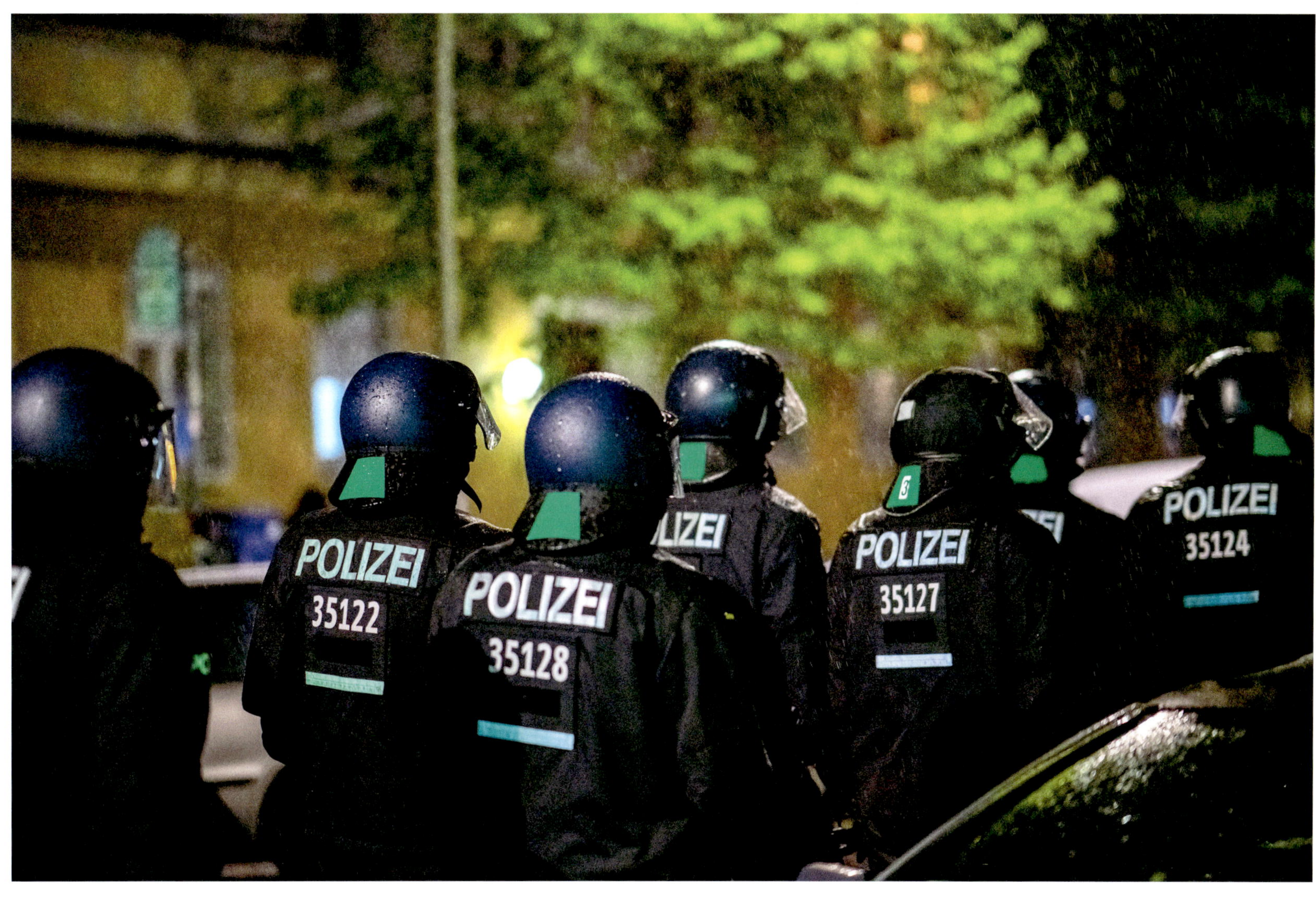

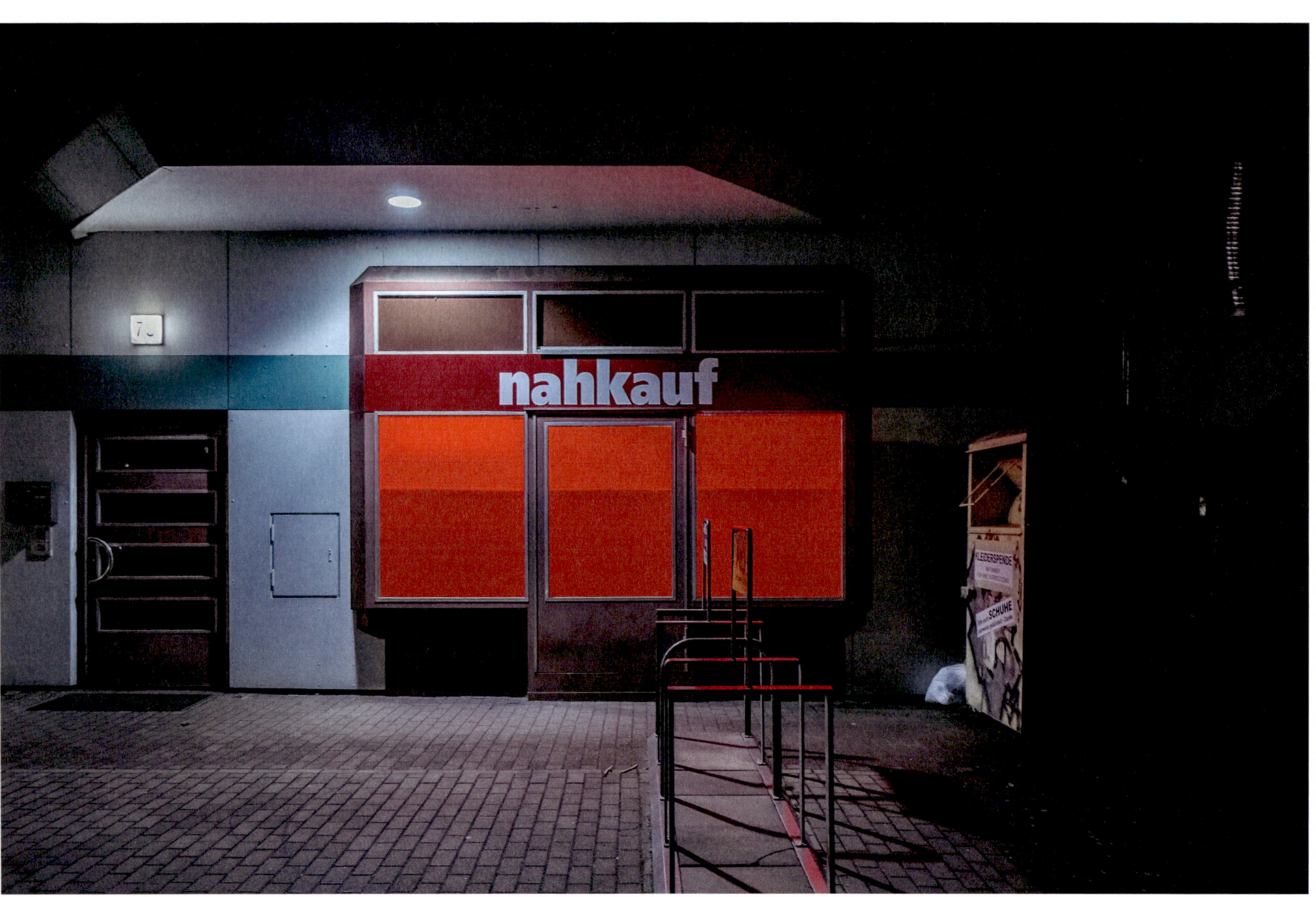

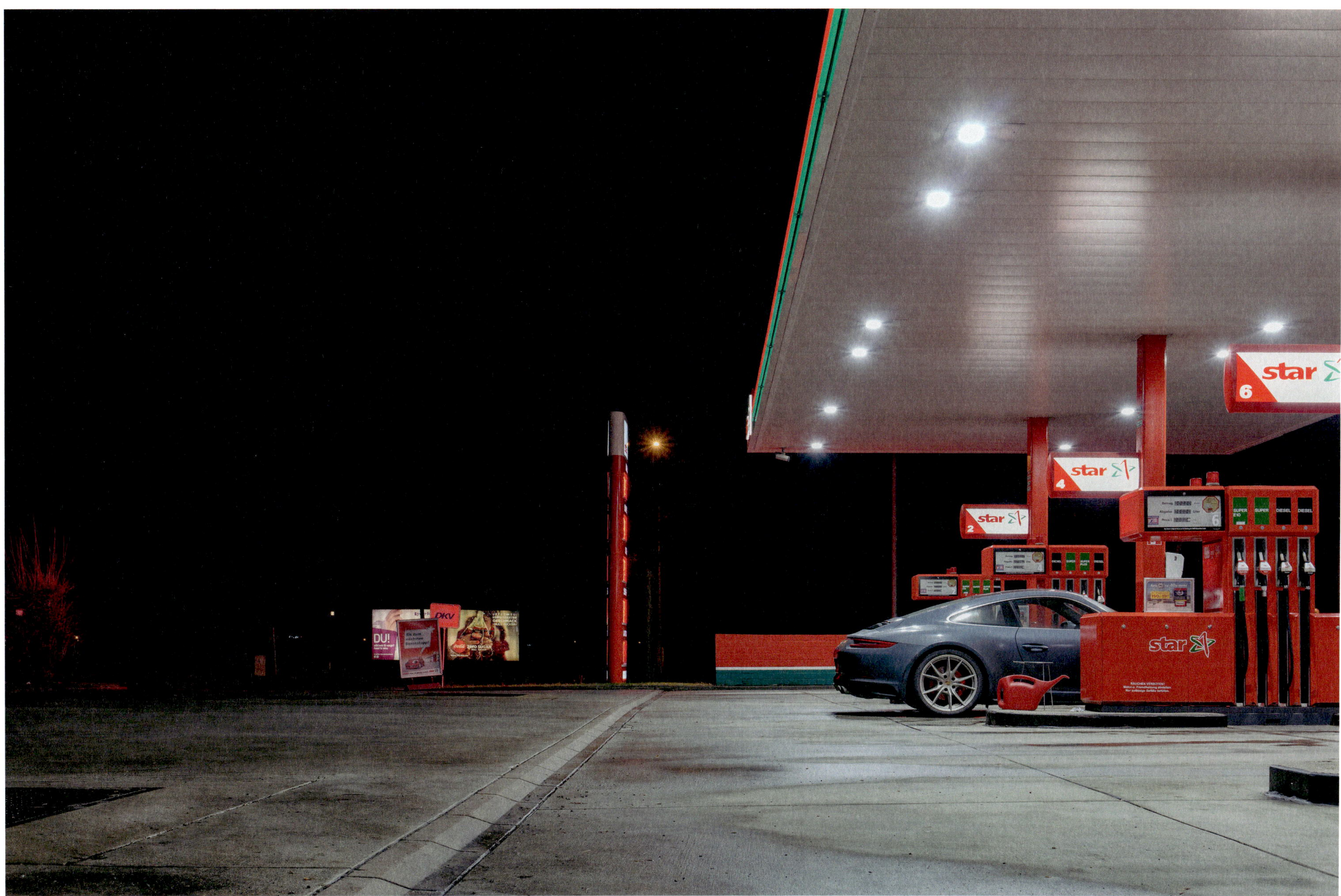

star
6
star
4
star
2
star
DKV
DU!

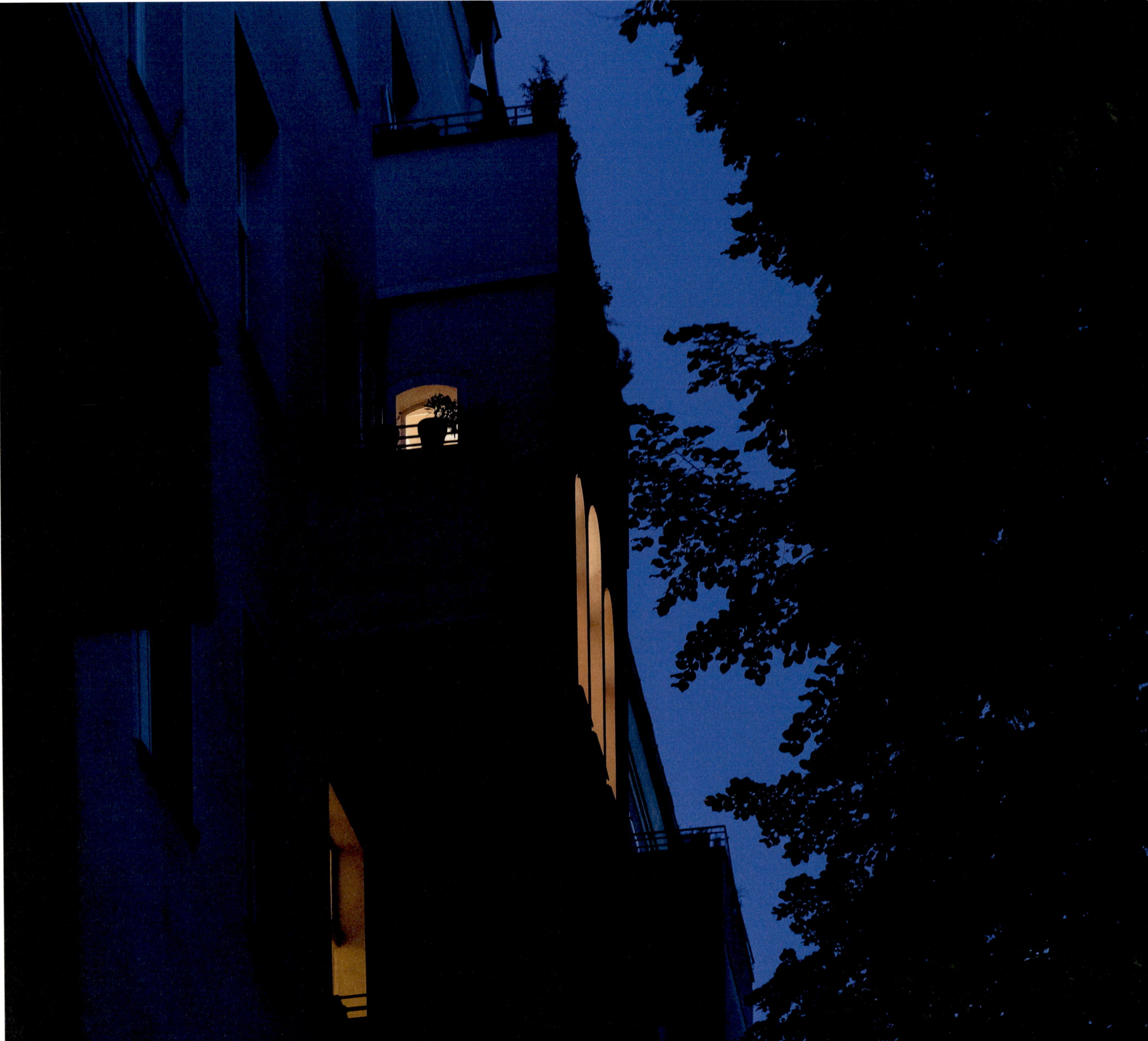

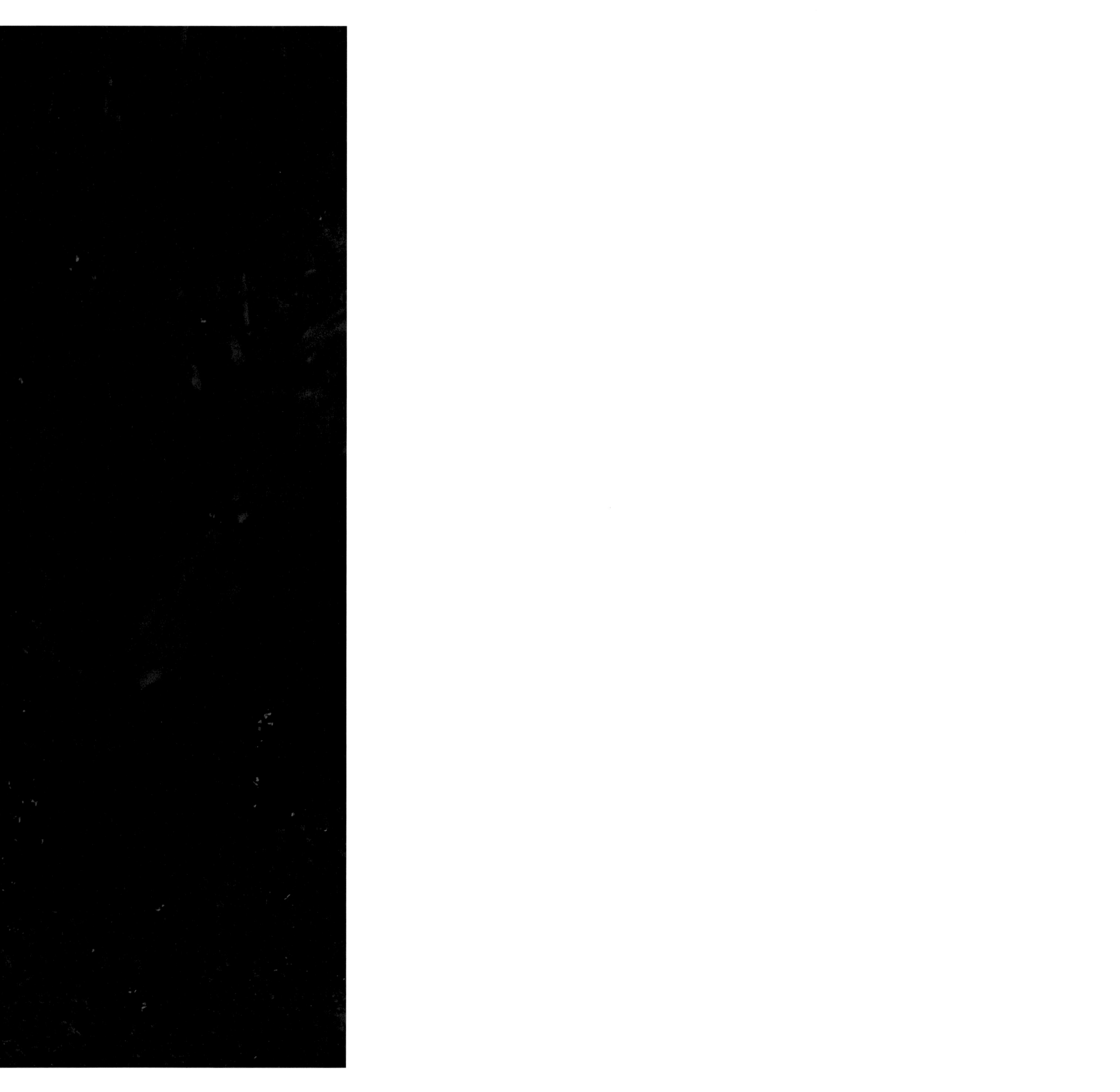

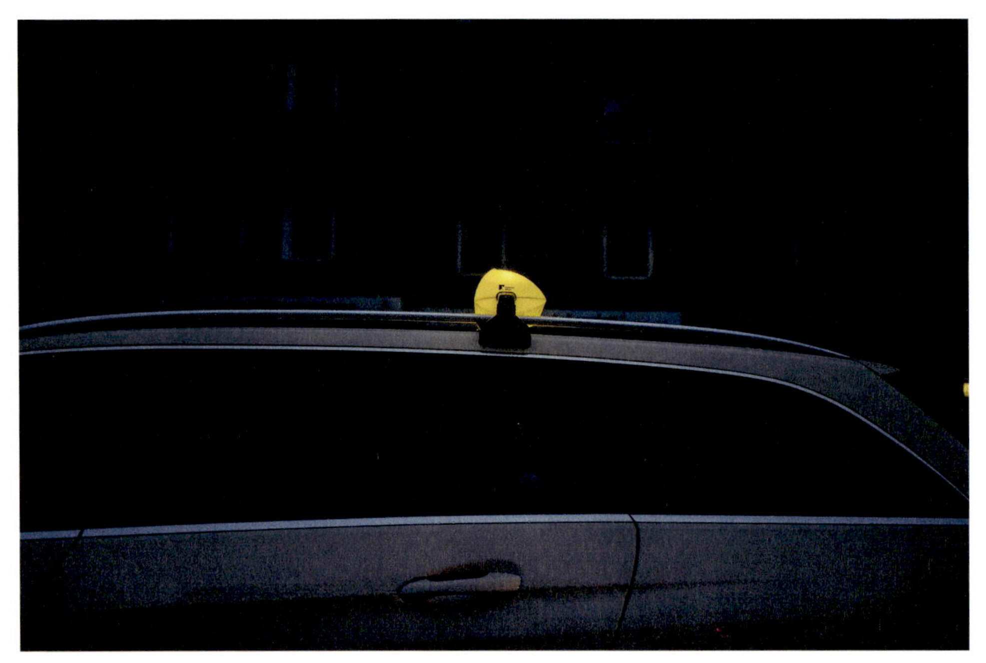

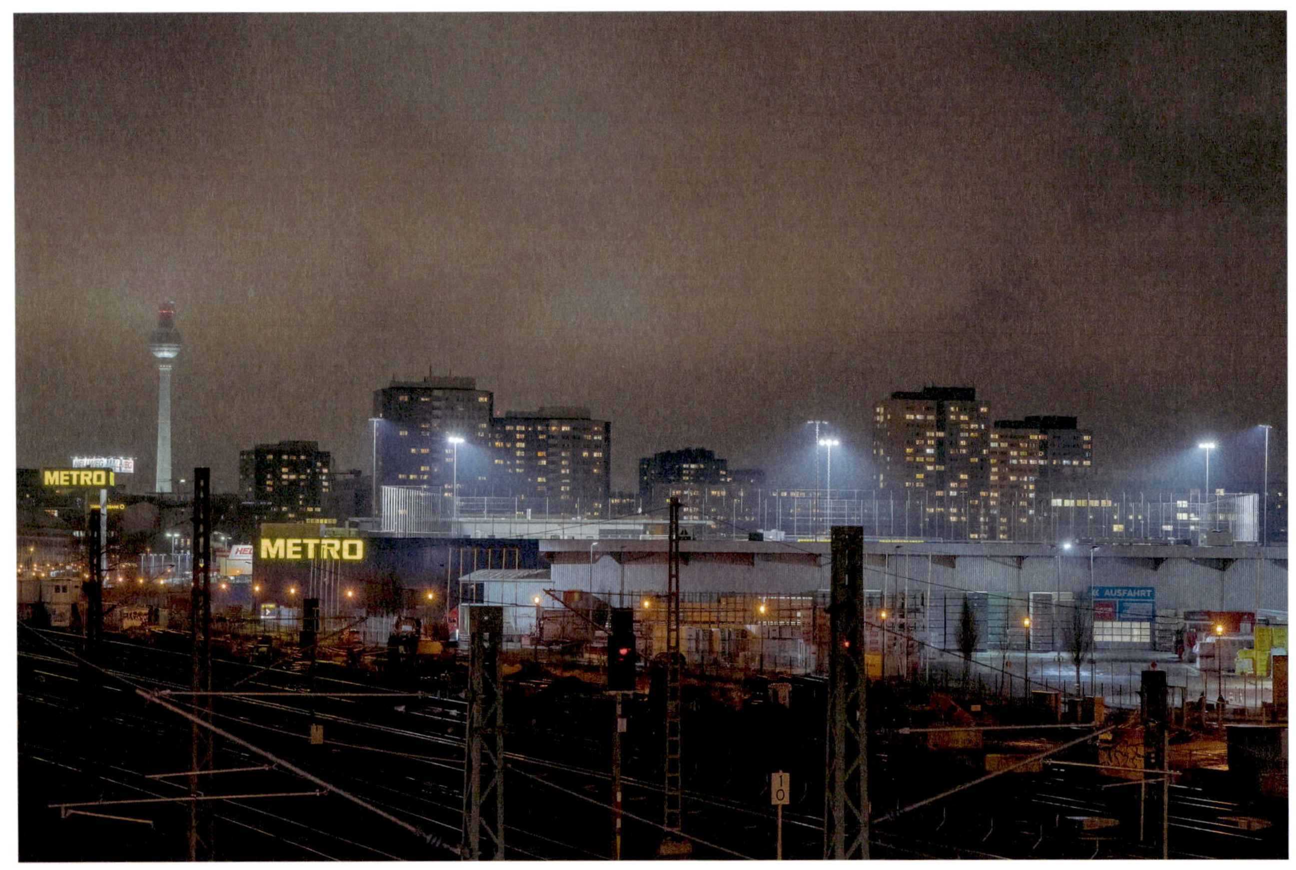
METRO
METRO
AUSFAHRT

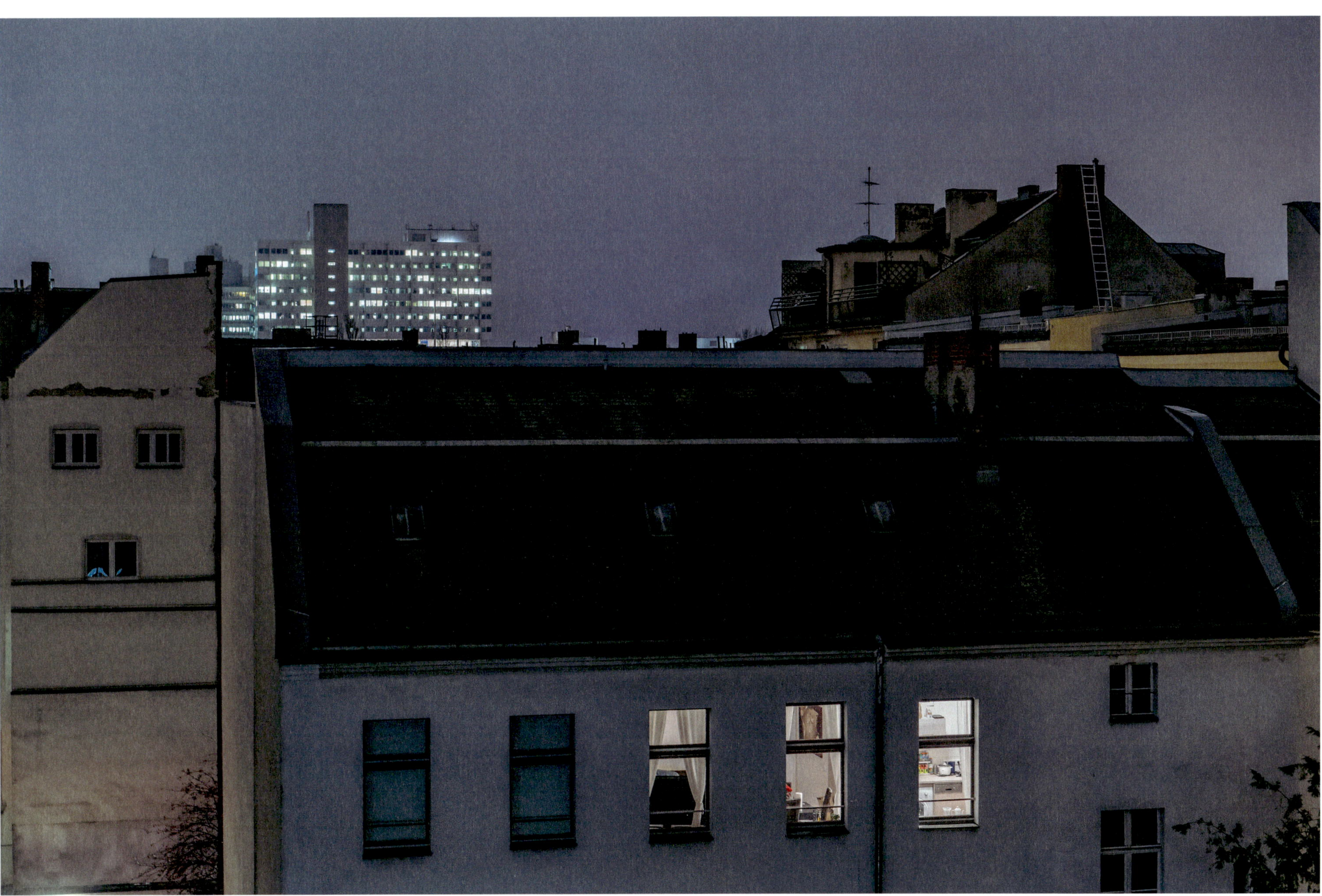

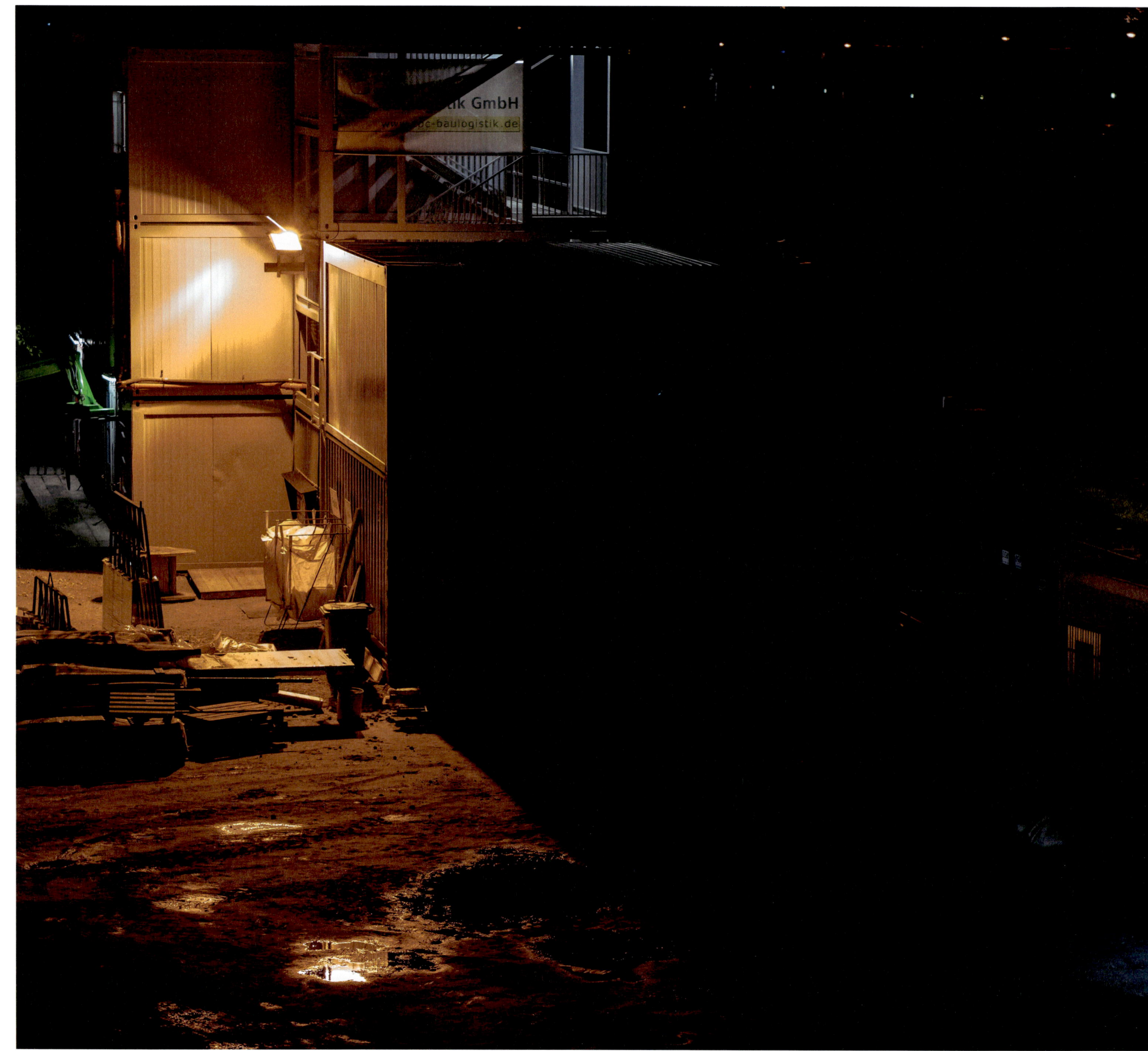
tik GmbH
www. c-baulogistik.de

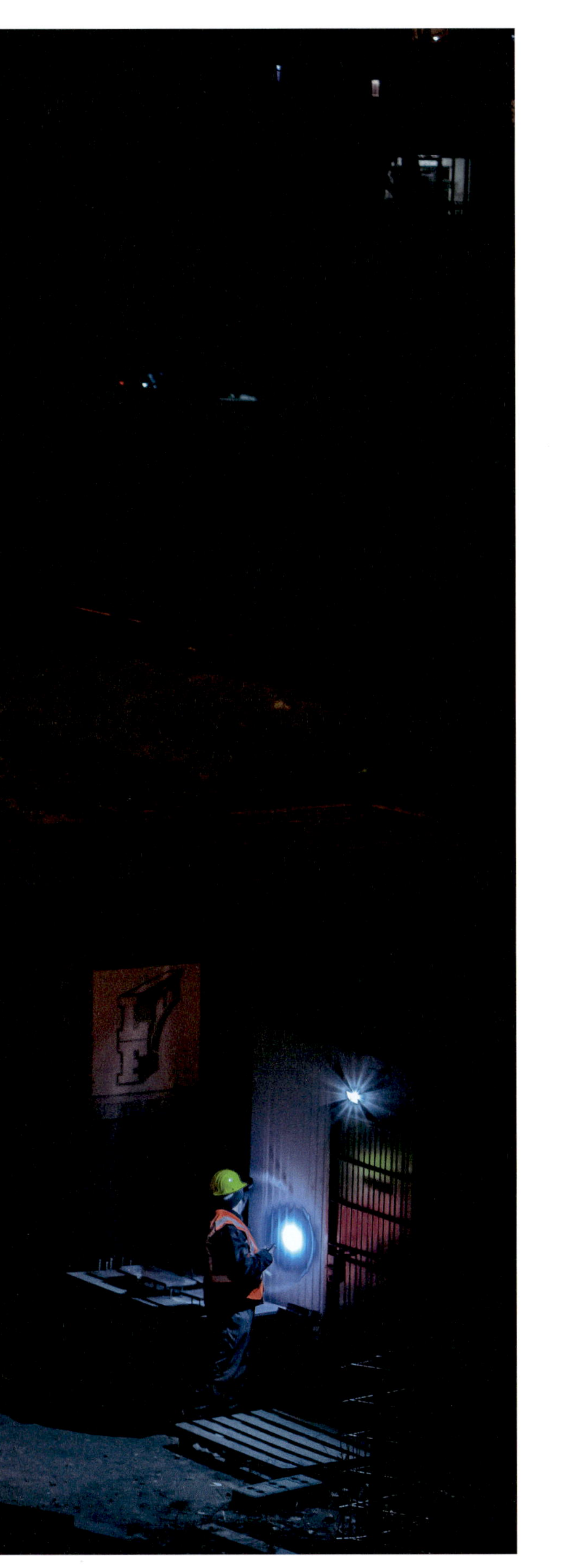

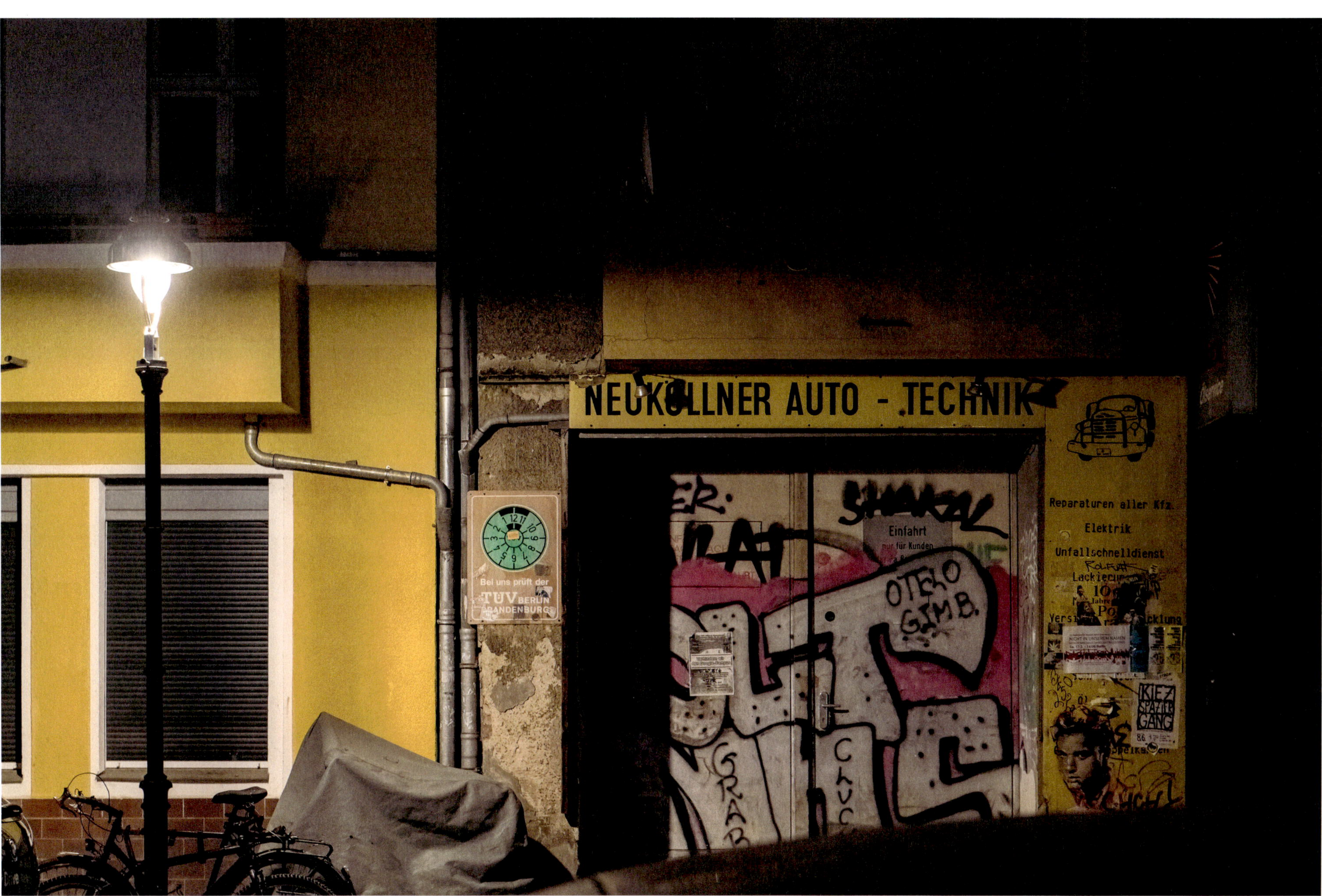
NEUKÖLLNER AUTO - TECHNIK
Reparaturen aller Kfz.
Elektrik
Unfallschnelldienst
Lackierung
Einfahrt
nur für Kunden
SHAKAL
OTELO
G.M.B.
KIEZ
SPAZIER
GANG
Bei uns prüft der
TÜV BERLIN
BRANDENBURG

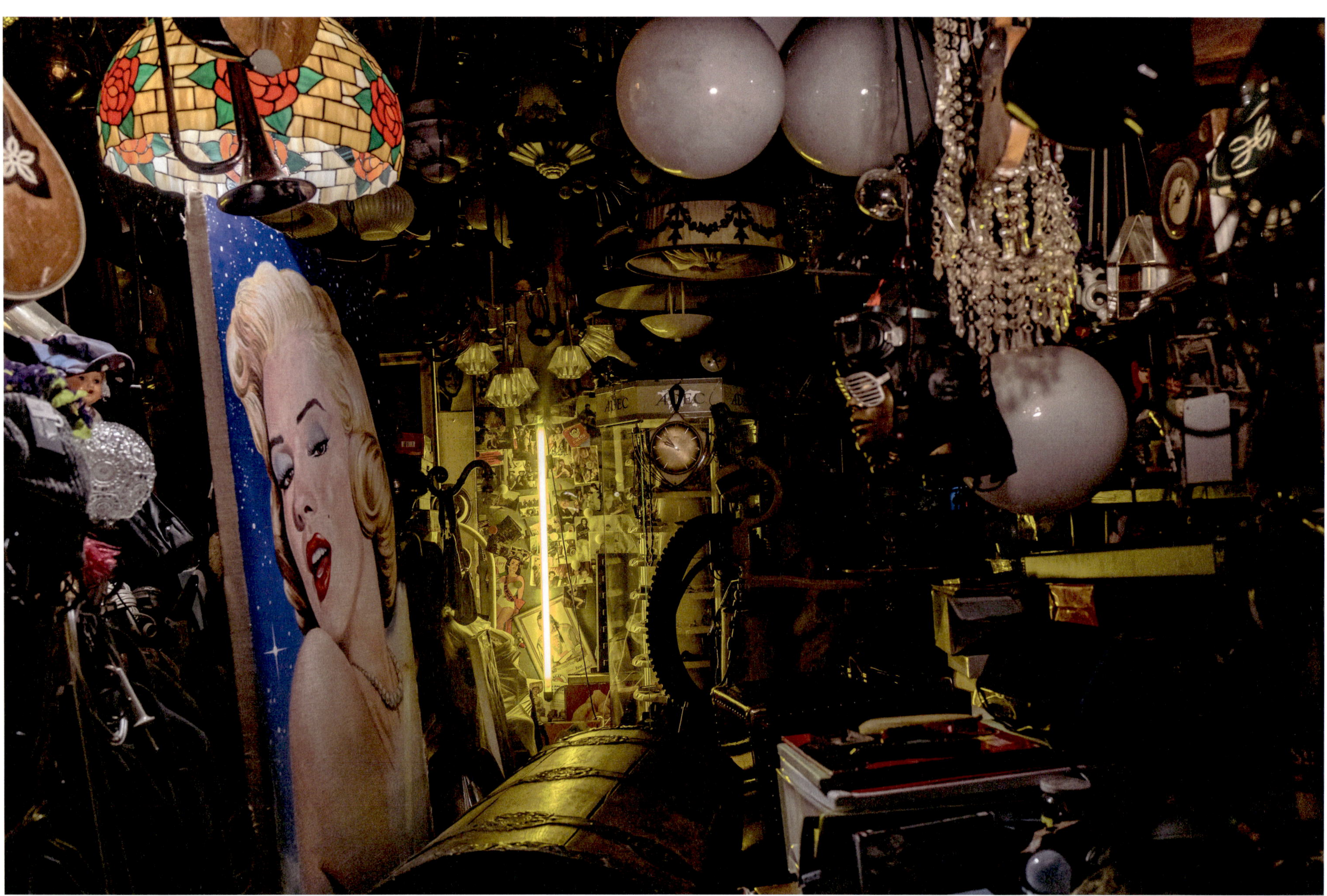

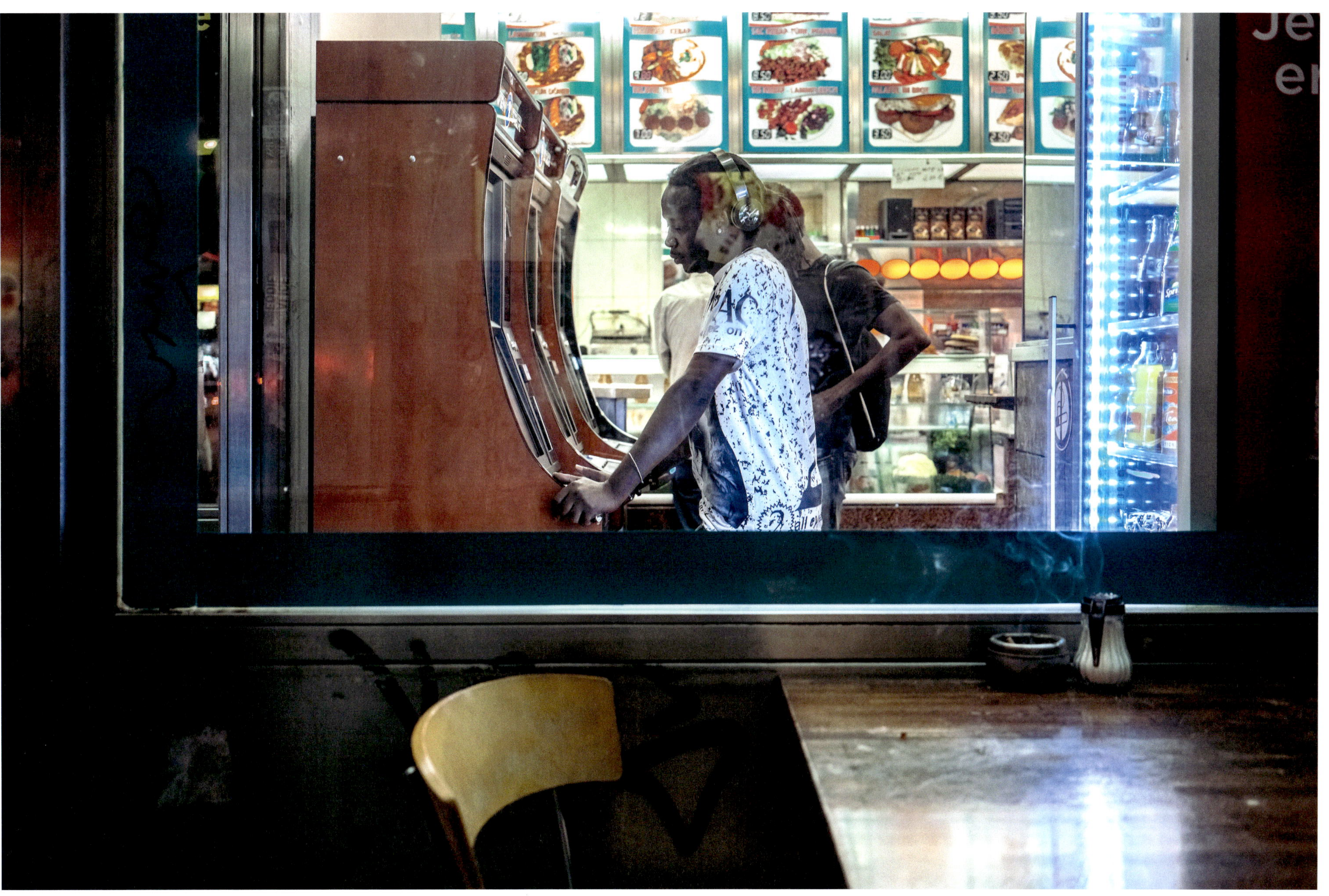

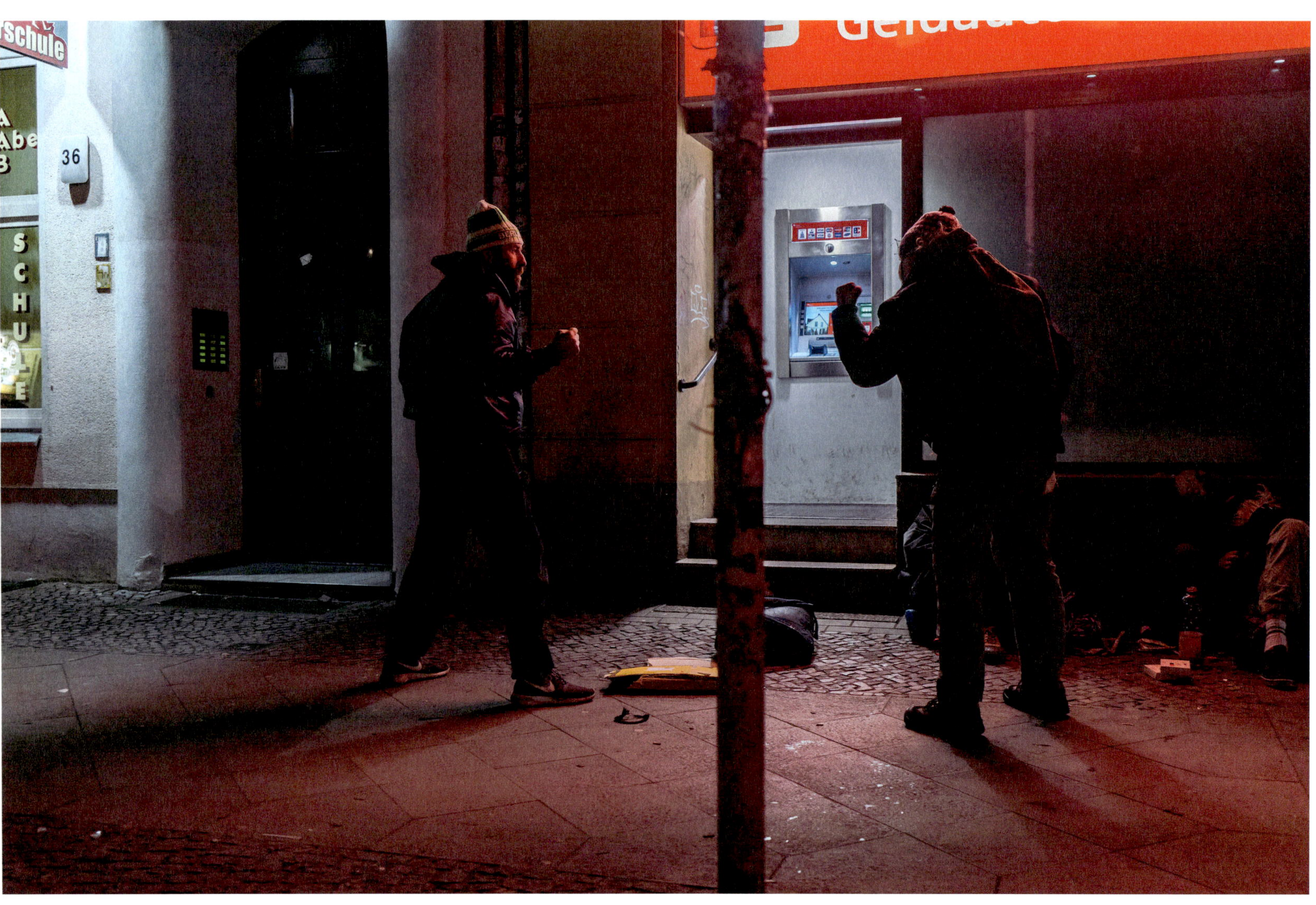

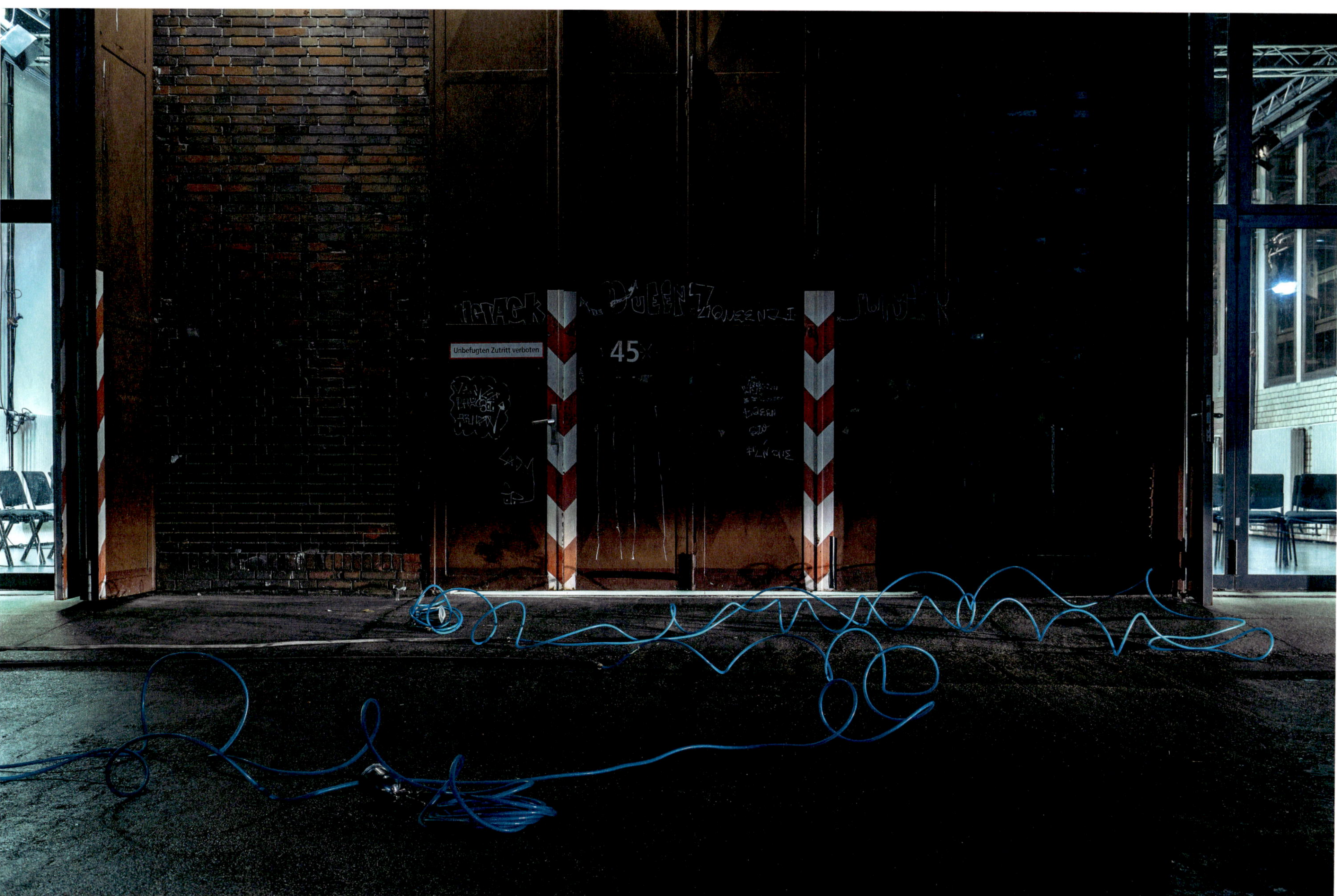

Unbefugten Zutritt verboten
45

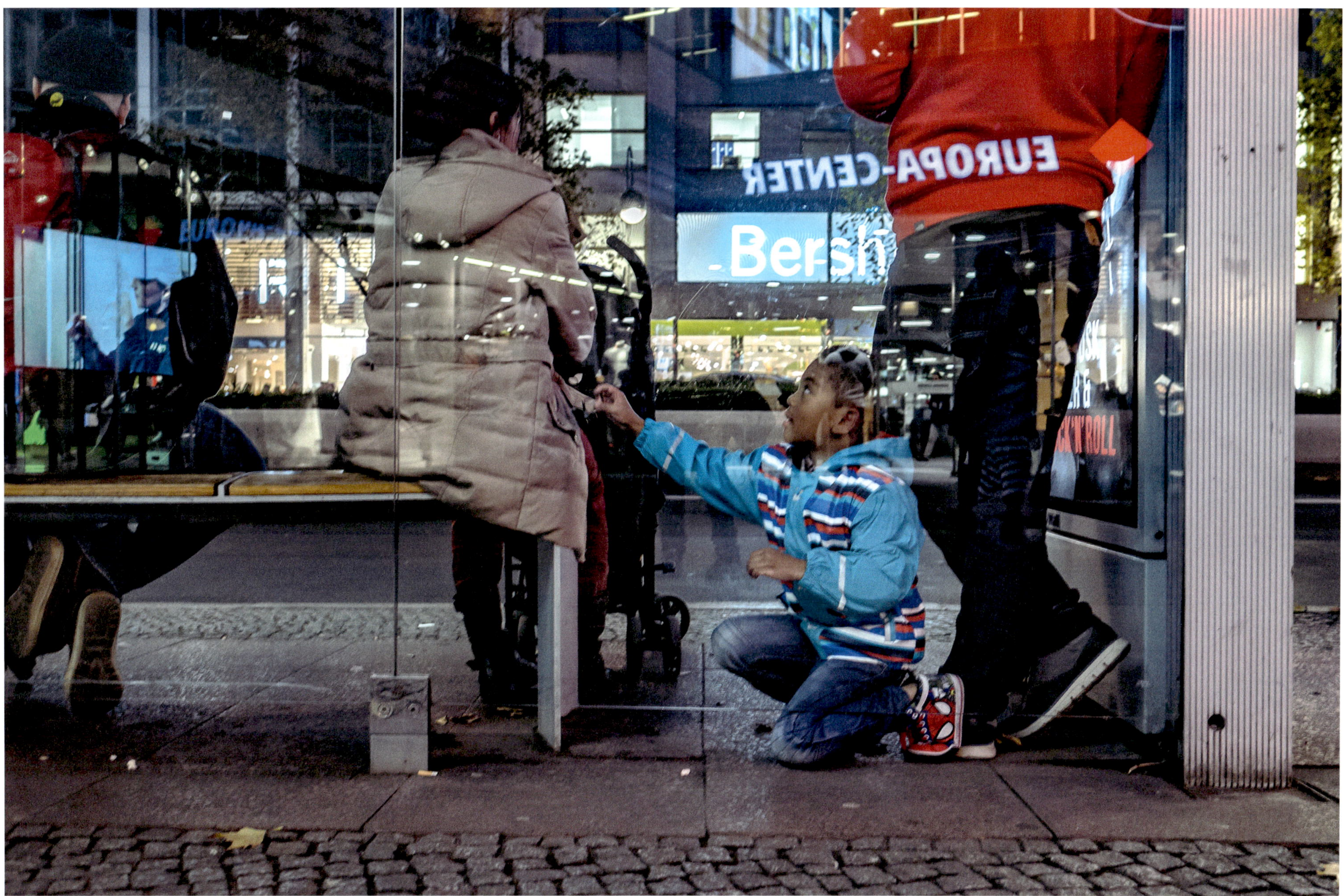

EUROPA-CENTER
Bersh

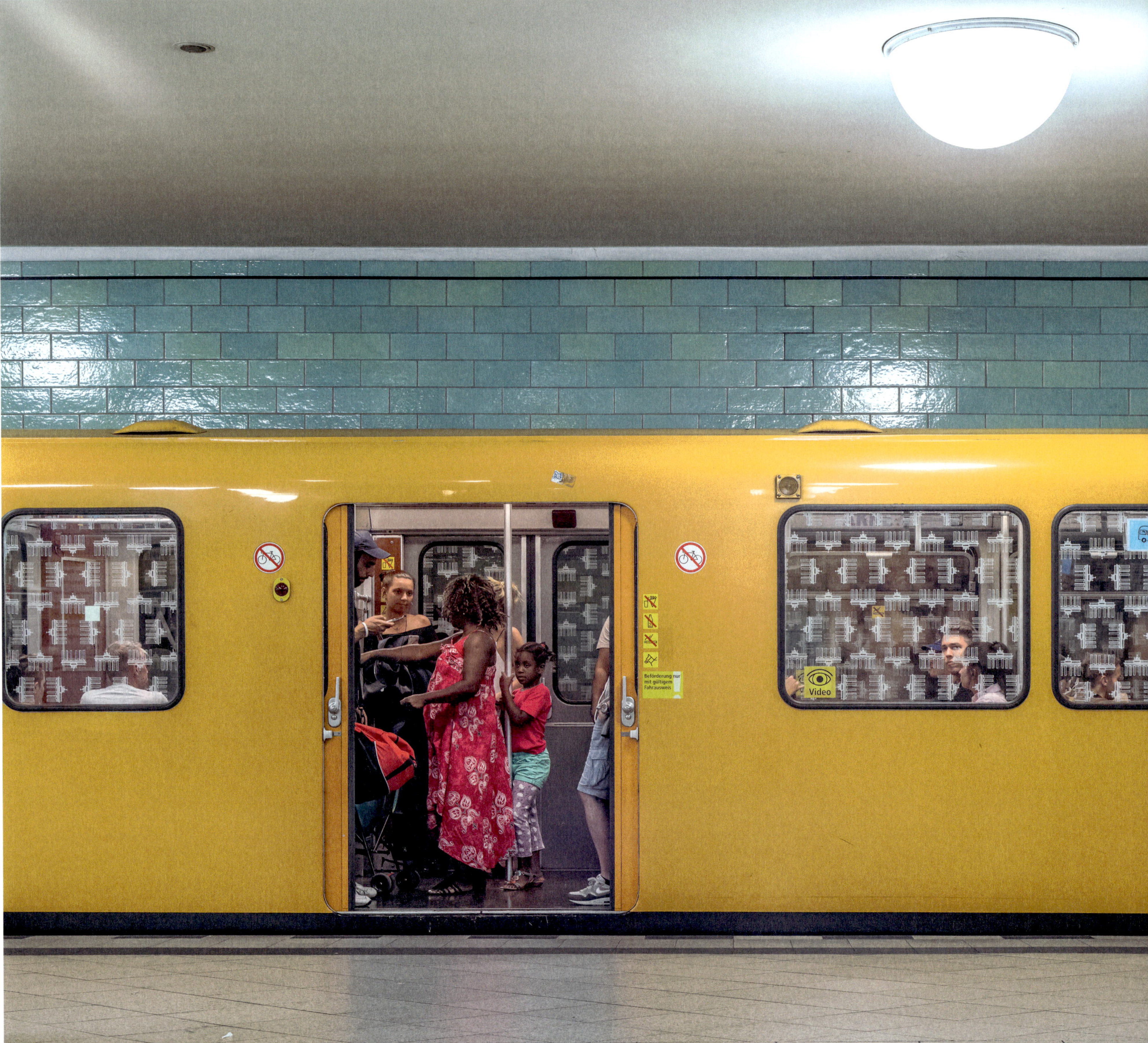

Beförderung nur
mit gültigem
Fahrausweis
Video

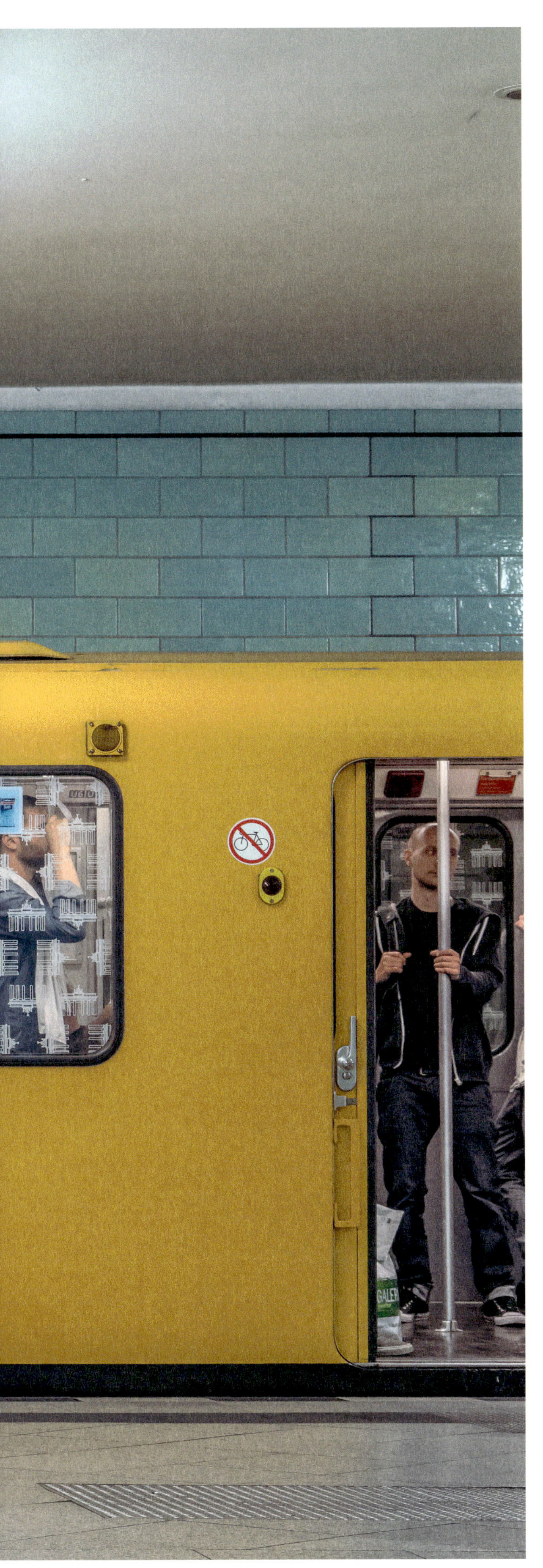

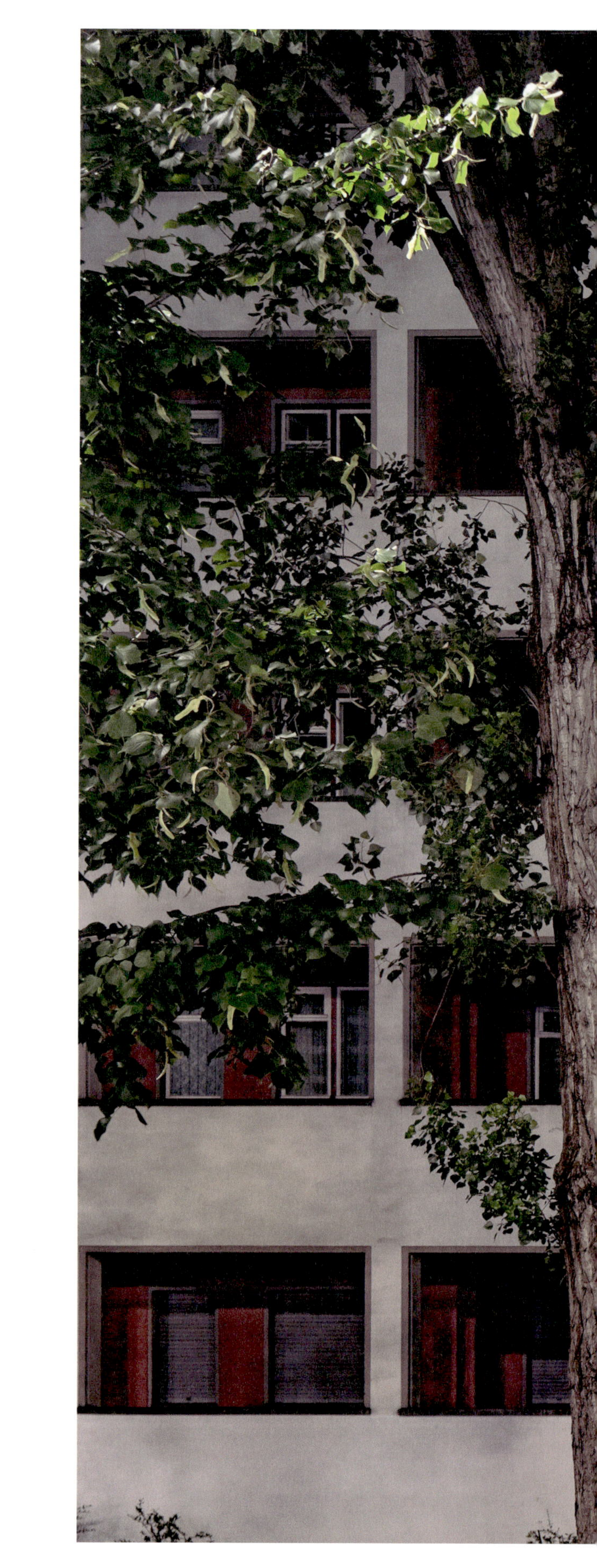

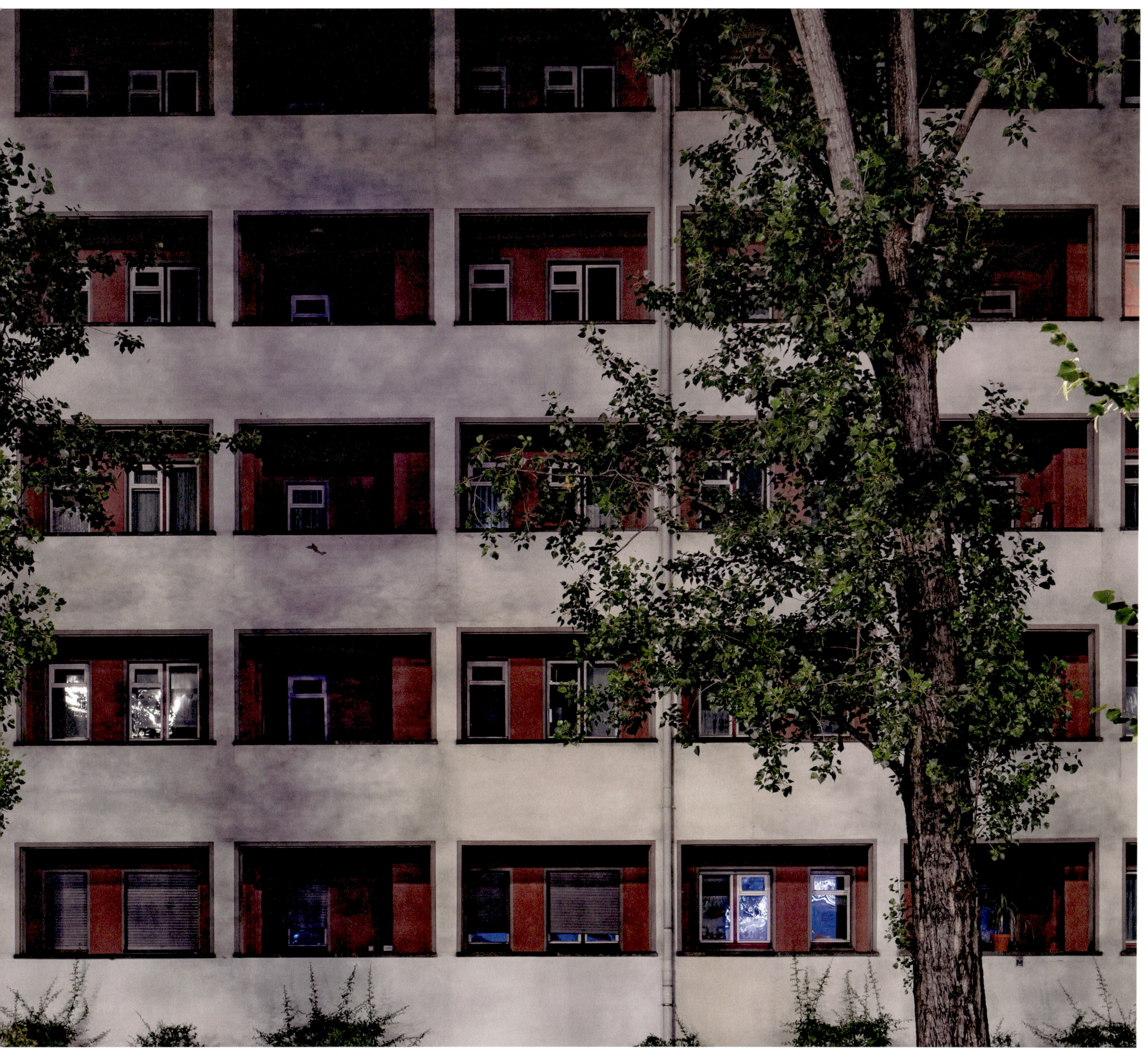

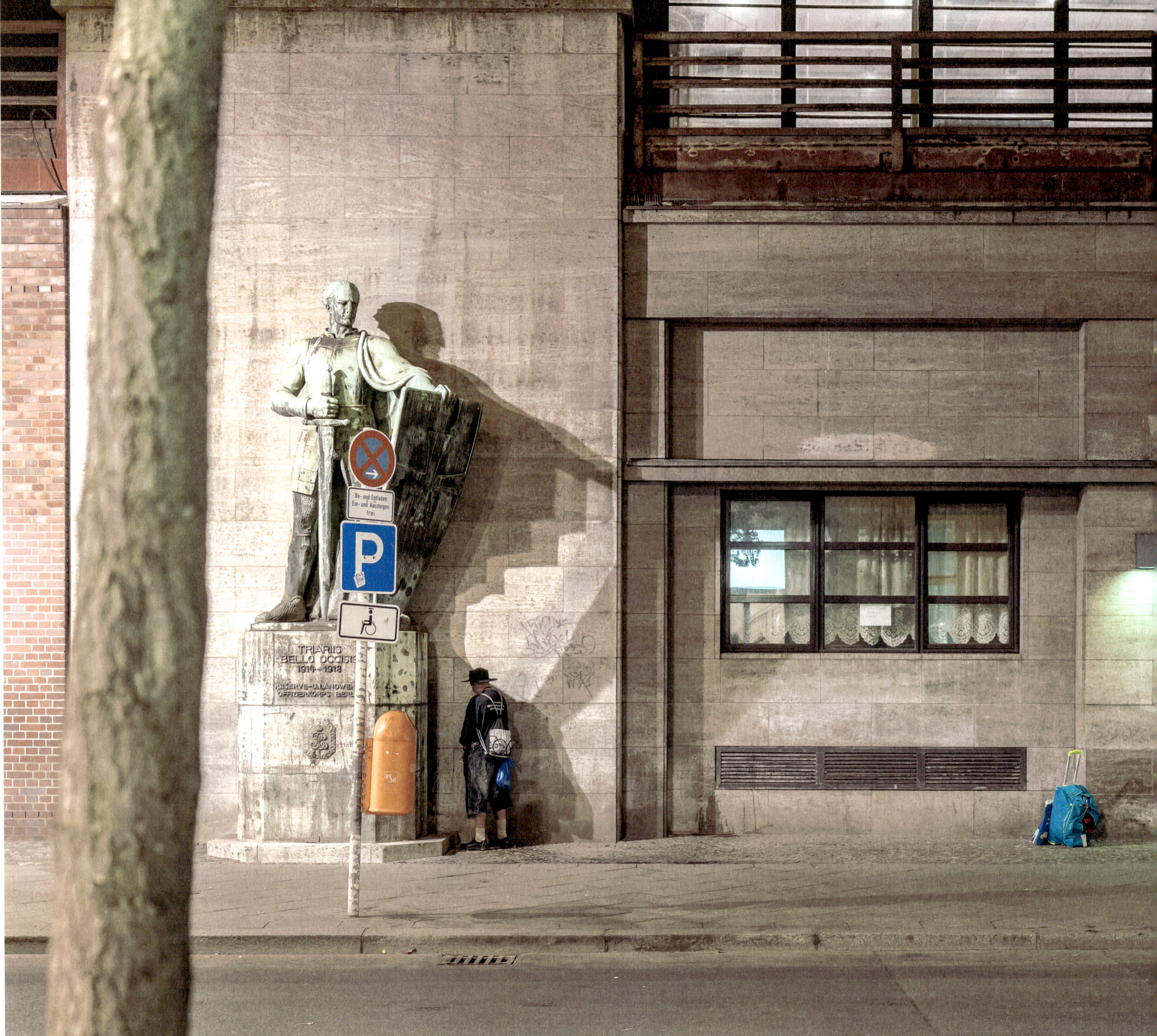

Be- und Entladen
Ein- und Aussteigen
frei
P
TRIARIIS
BELLO OCCISIS
1914—1918
RESERVE-U. LANDWEHR
OFFIZIERKORPS BERL
BSR

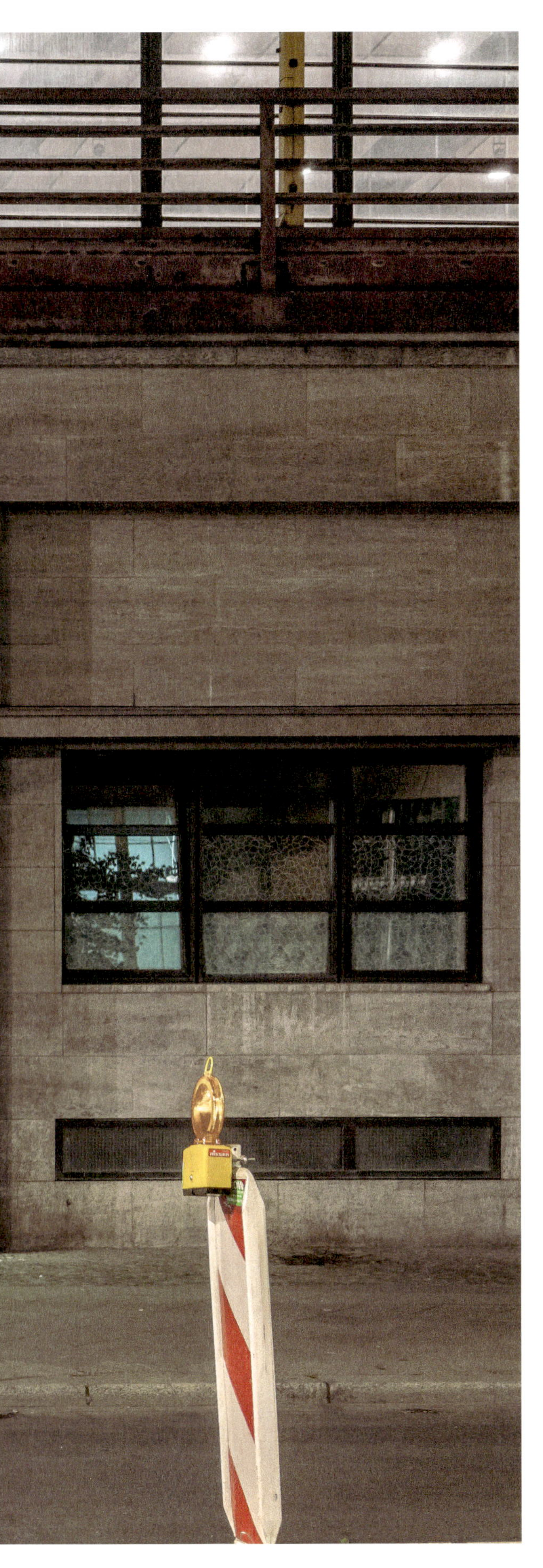

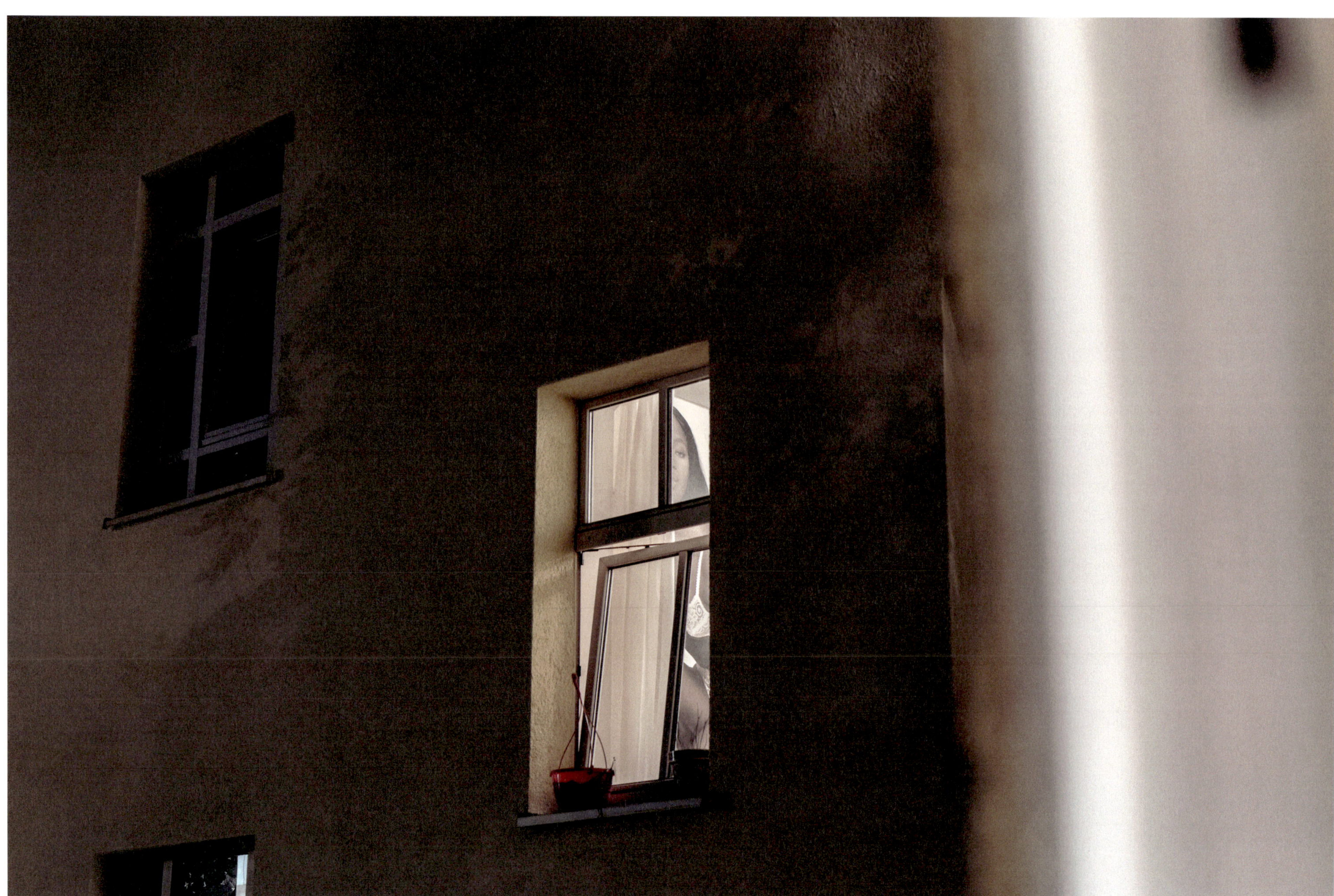

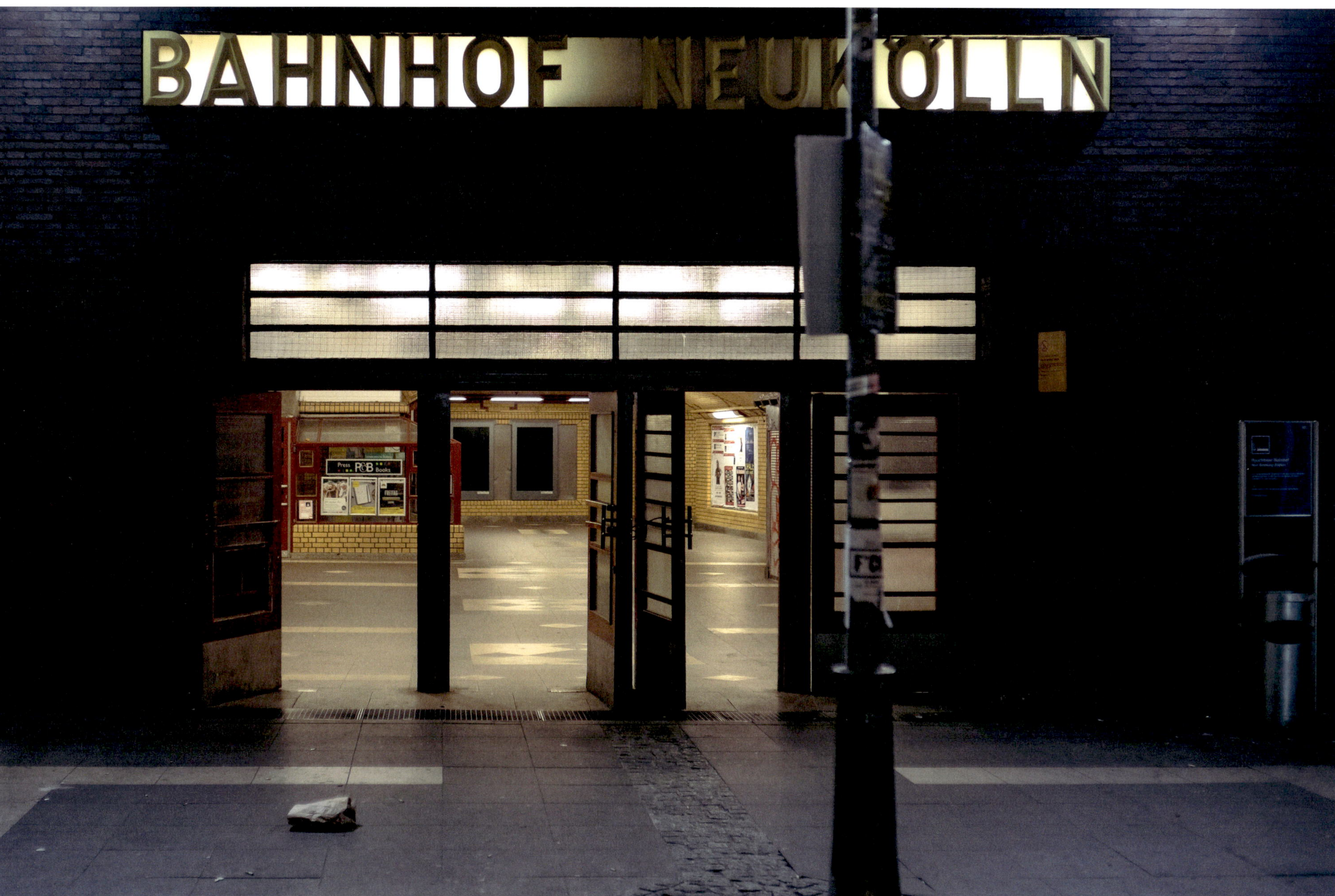

BAHNHOF NEUKÖLLN

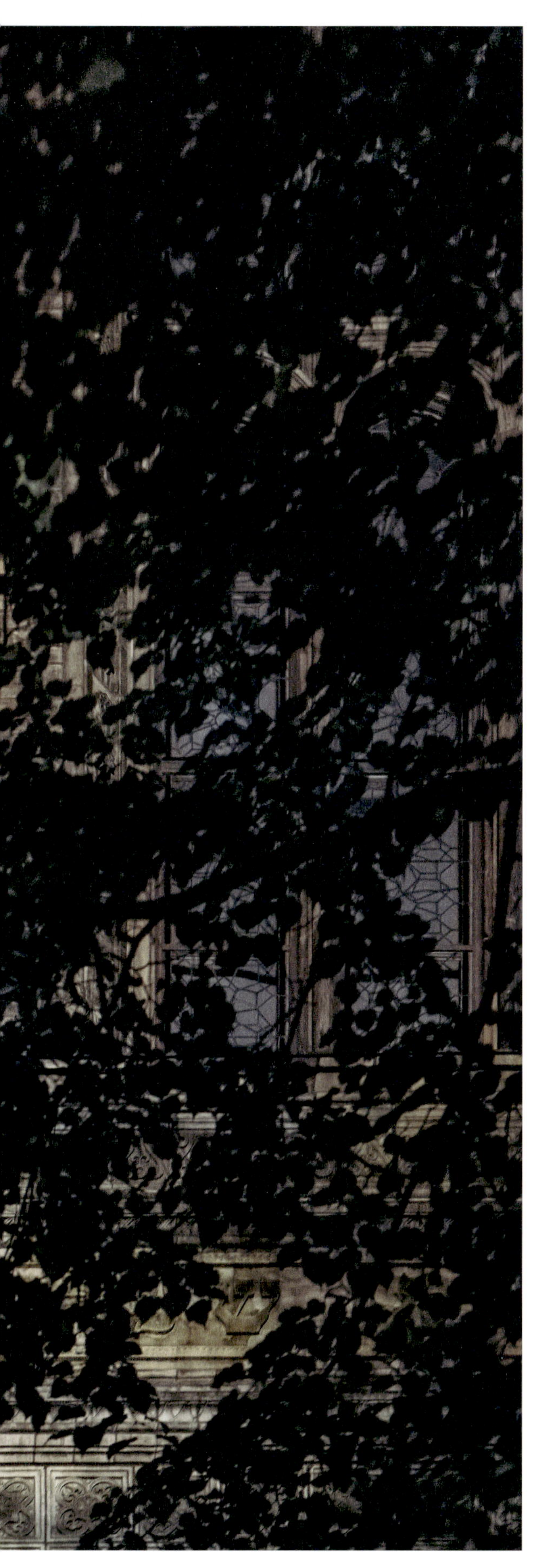

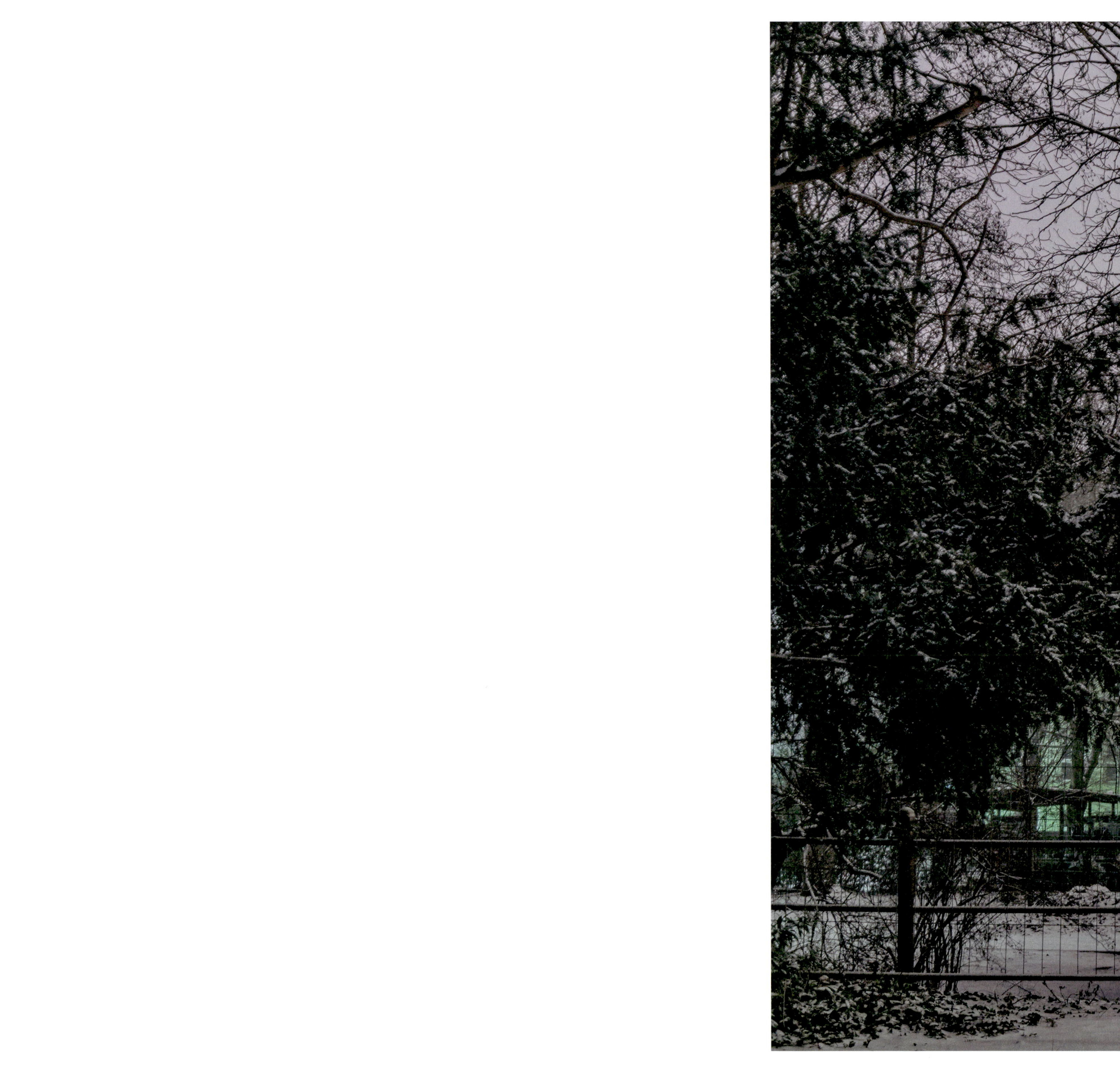

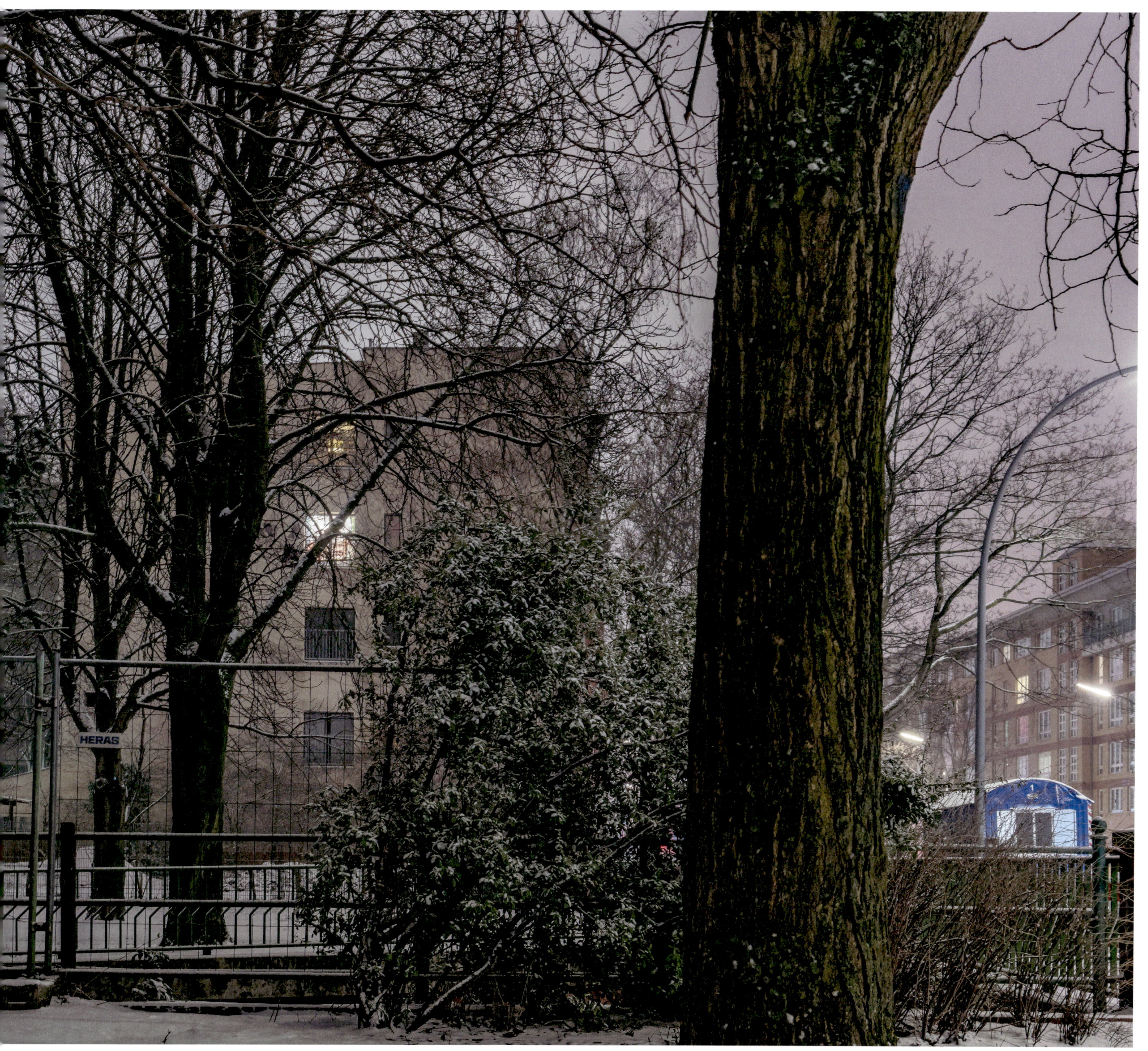
HERAS

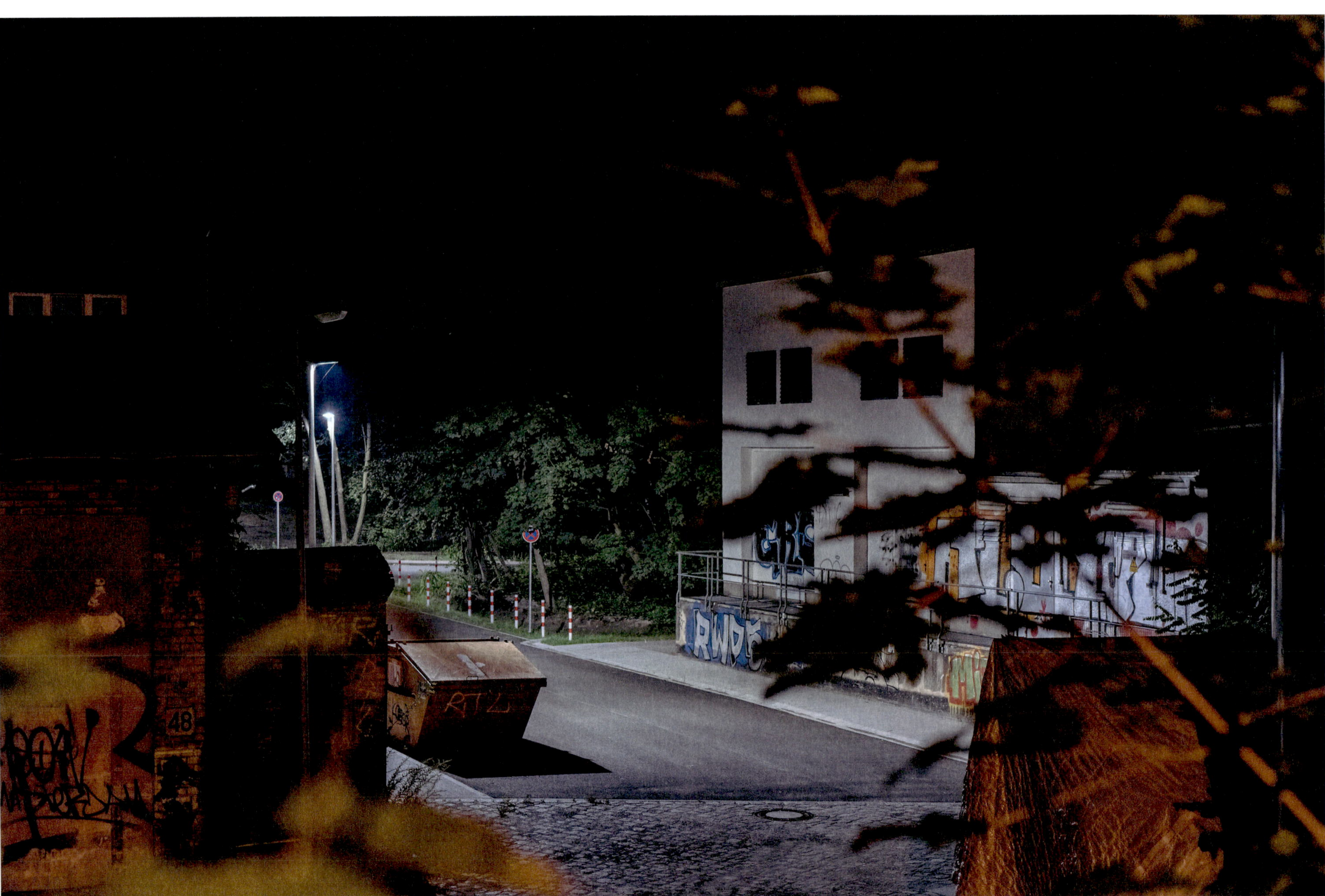

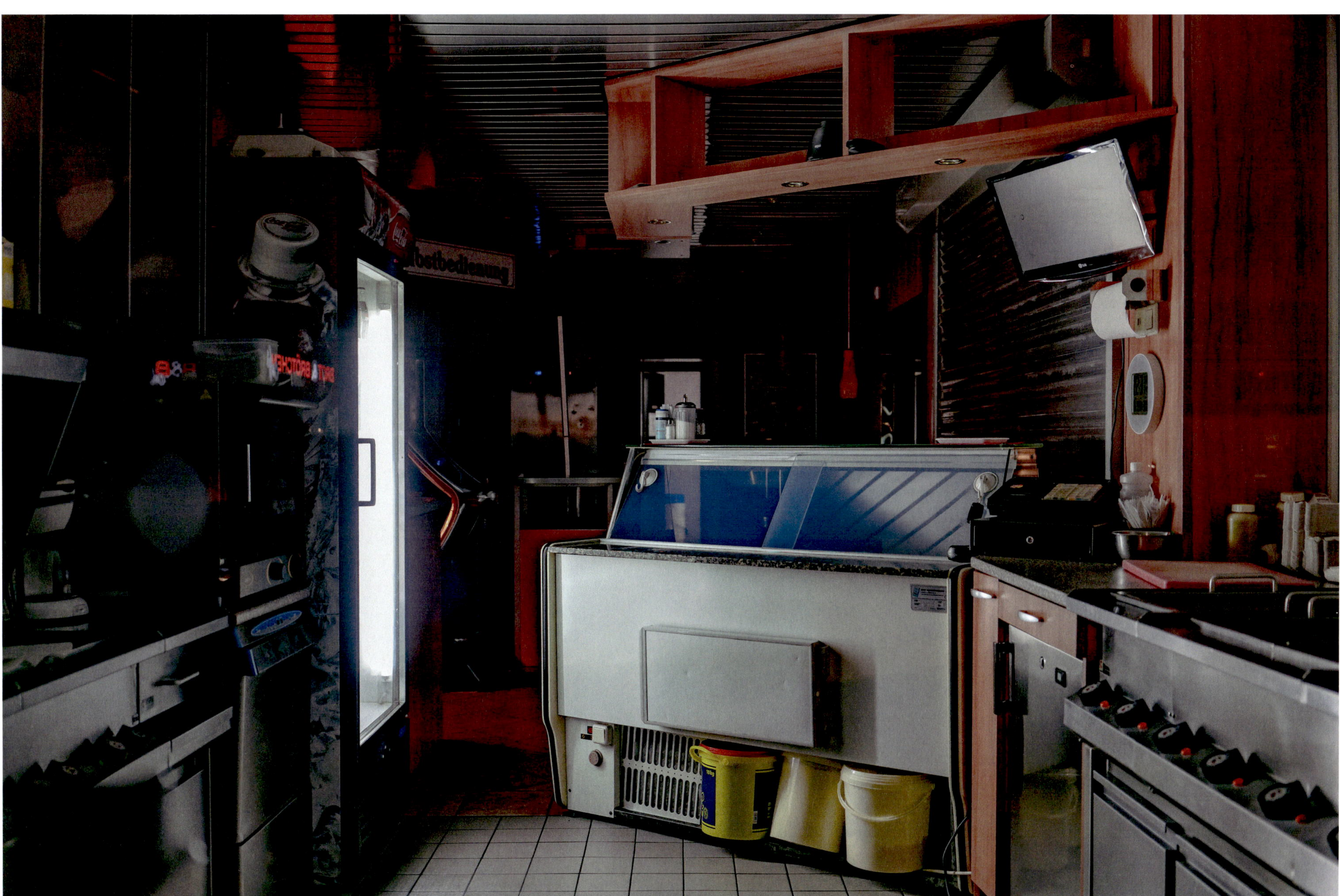

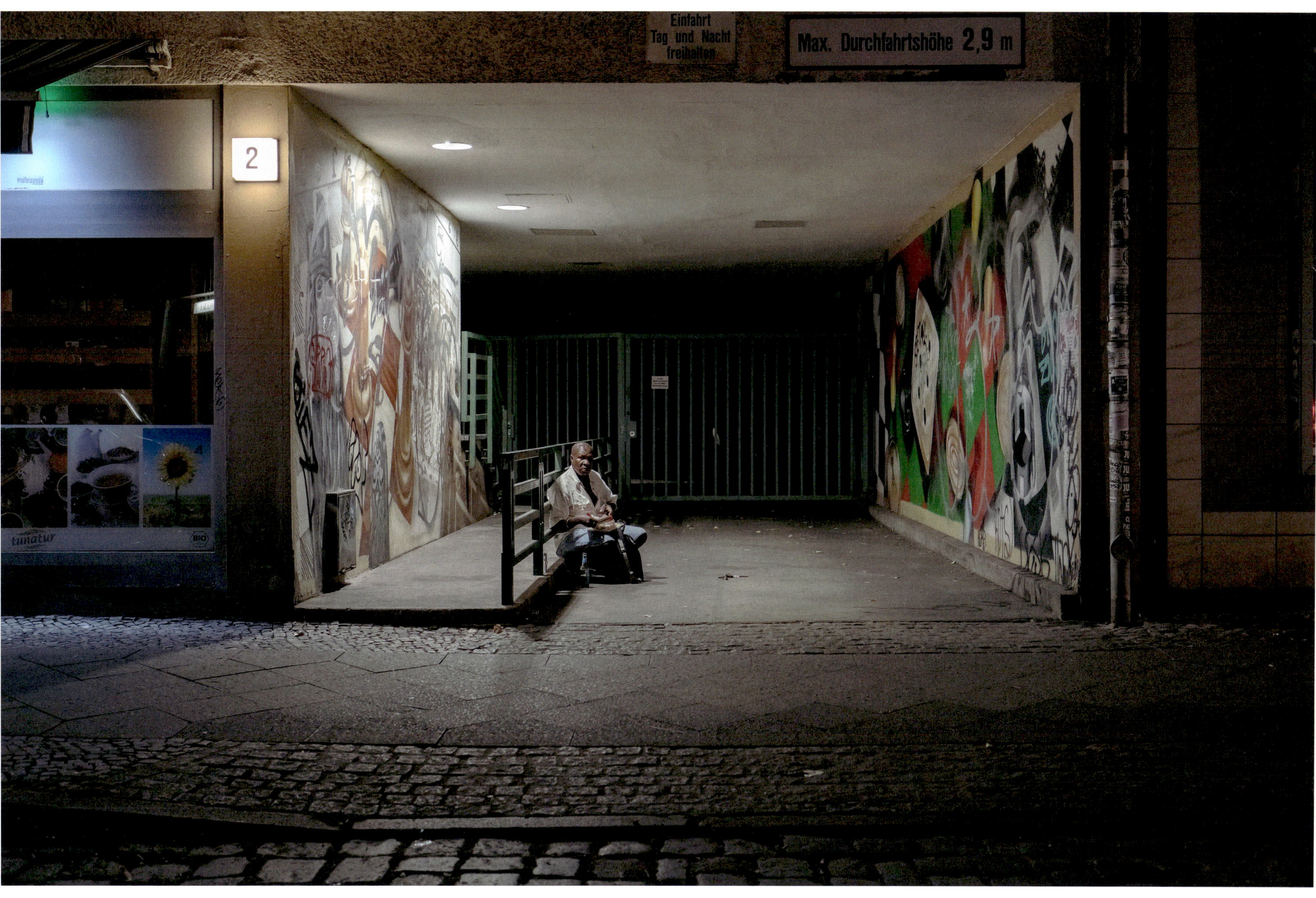
Einfahrt
Tag und Nacht
freihalten
Max. Durchfahrtshöhe 2,9 m
2

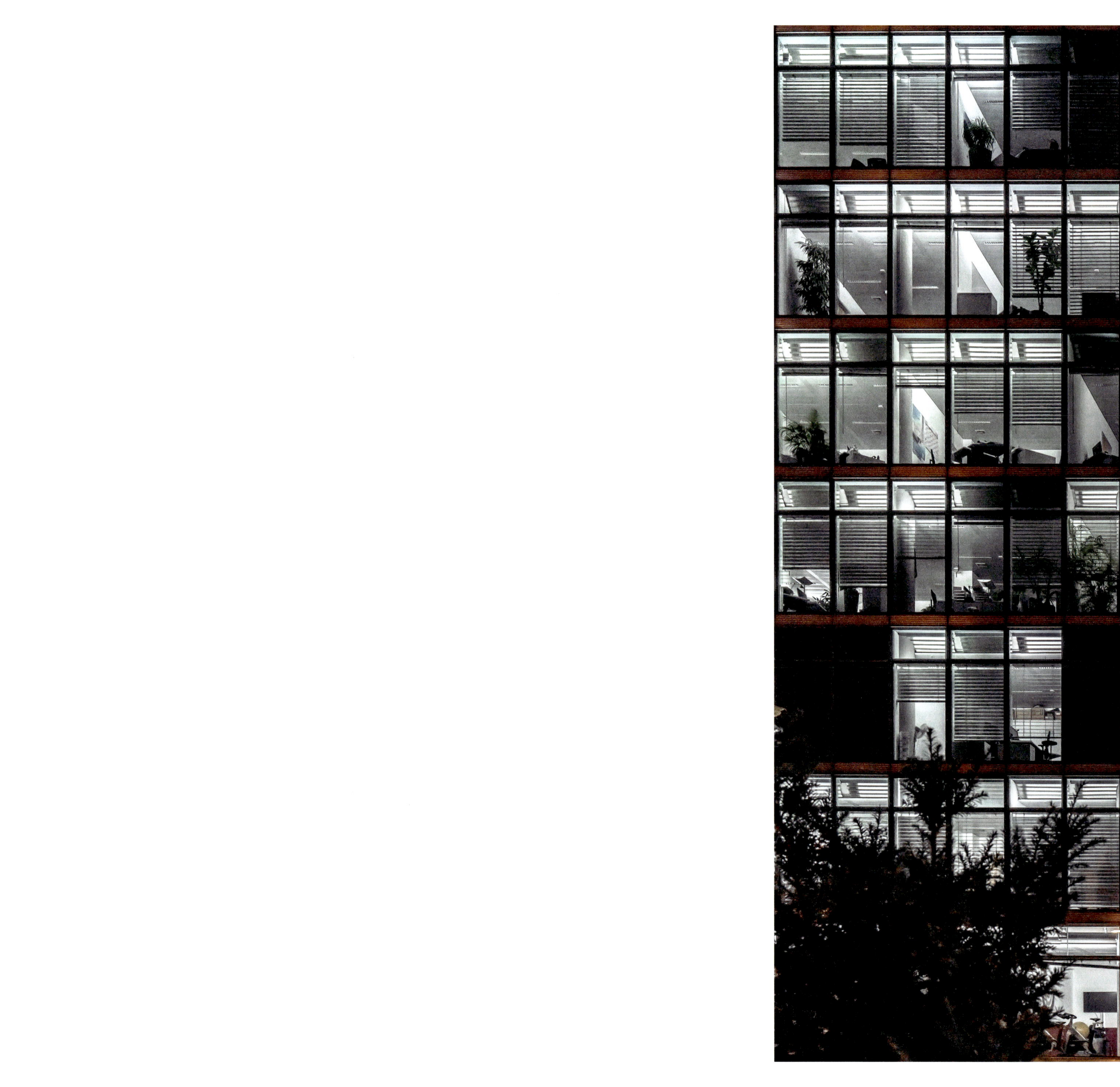

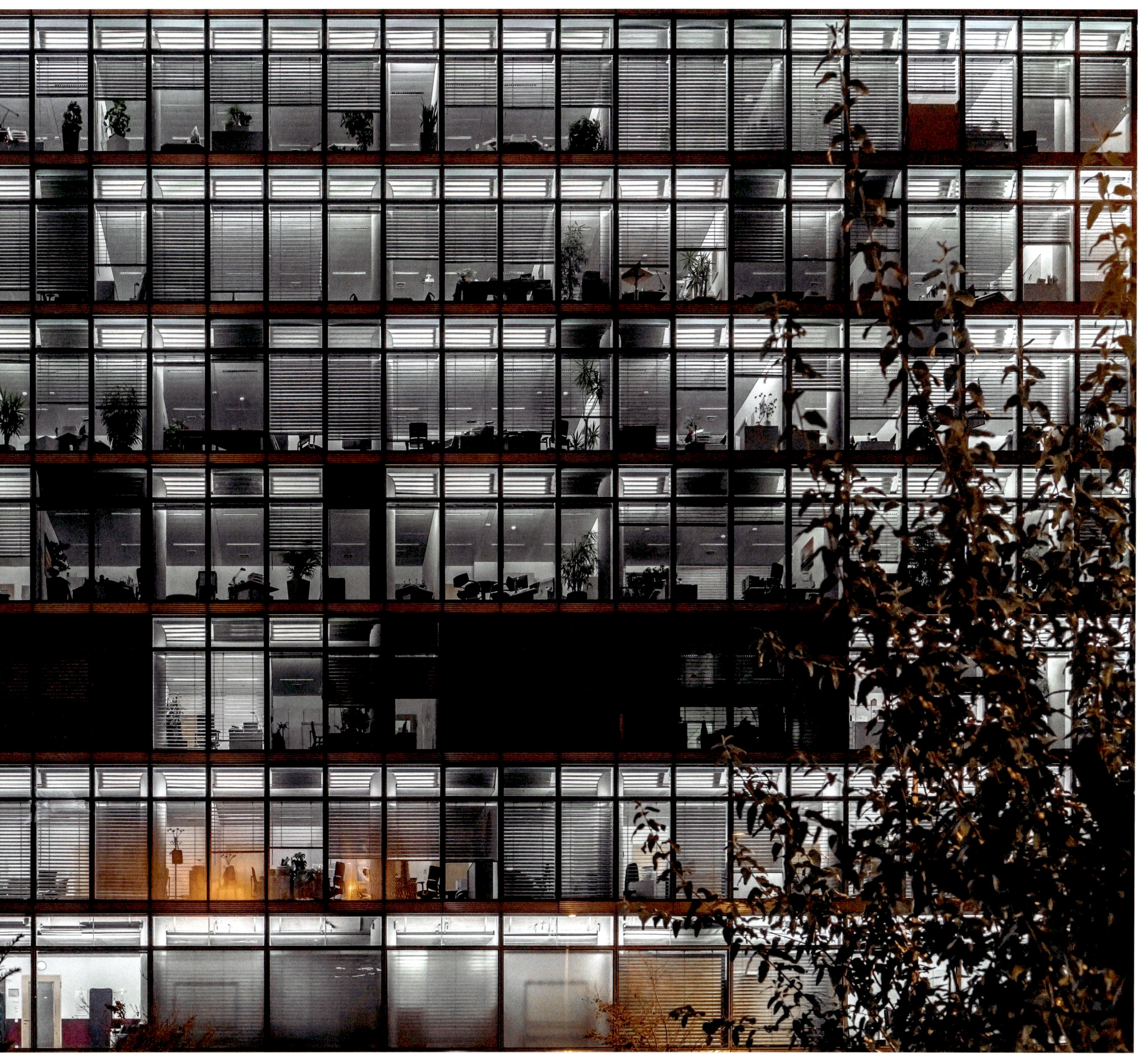

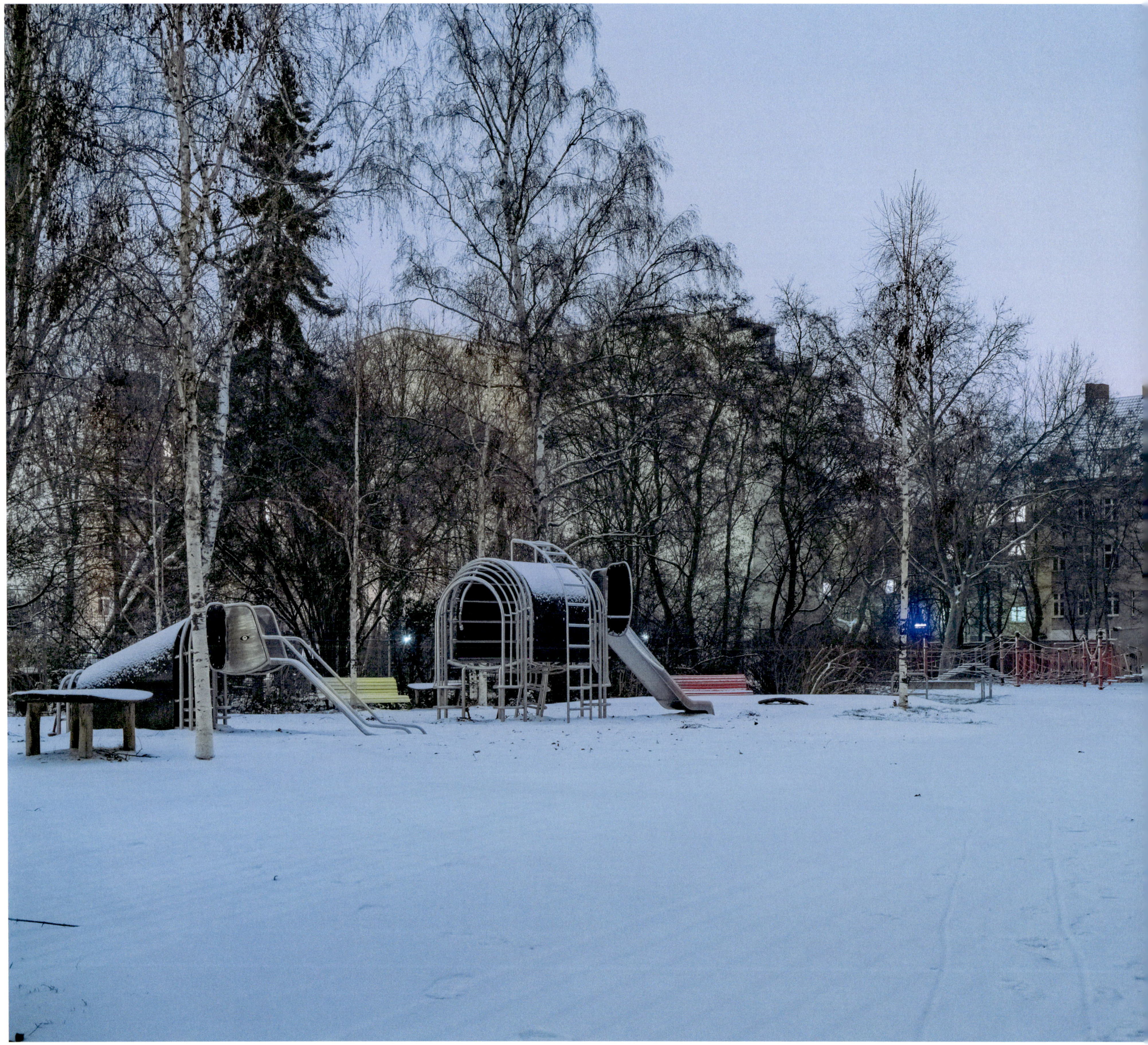

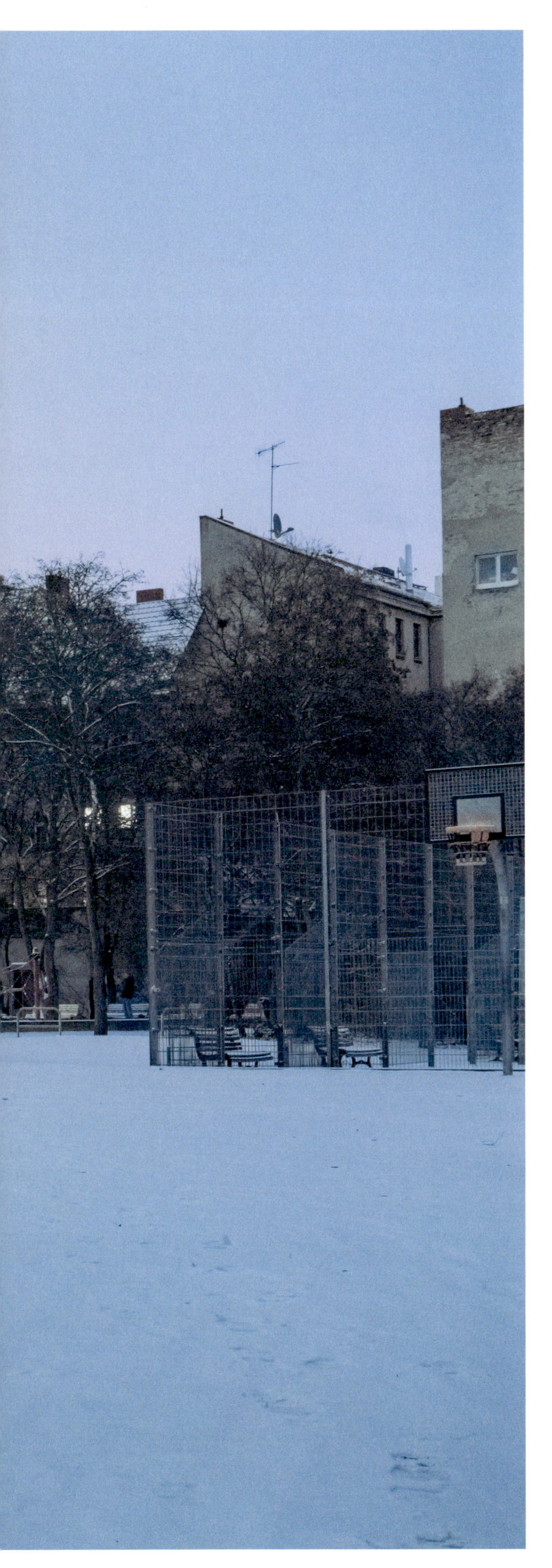

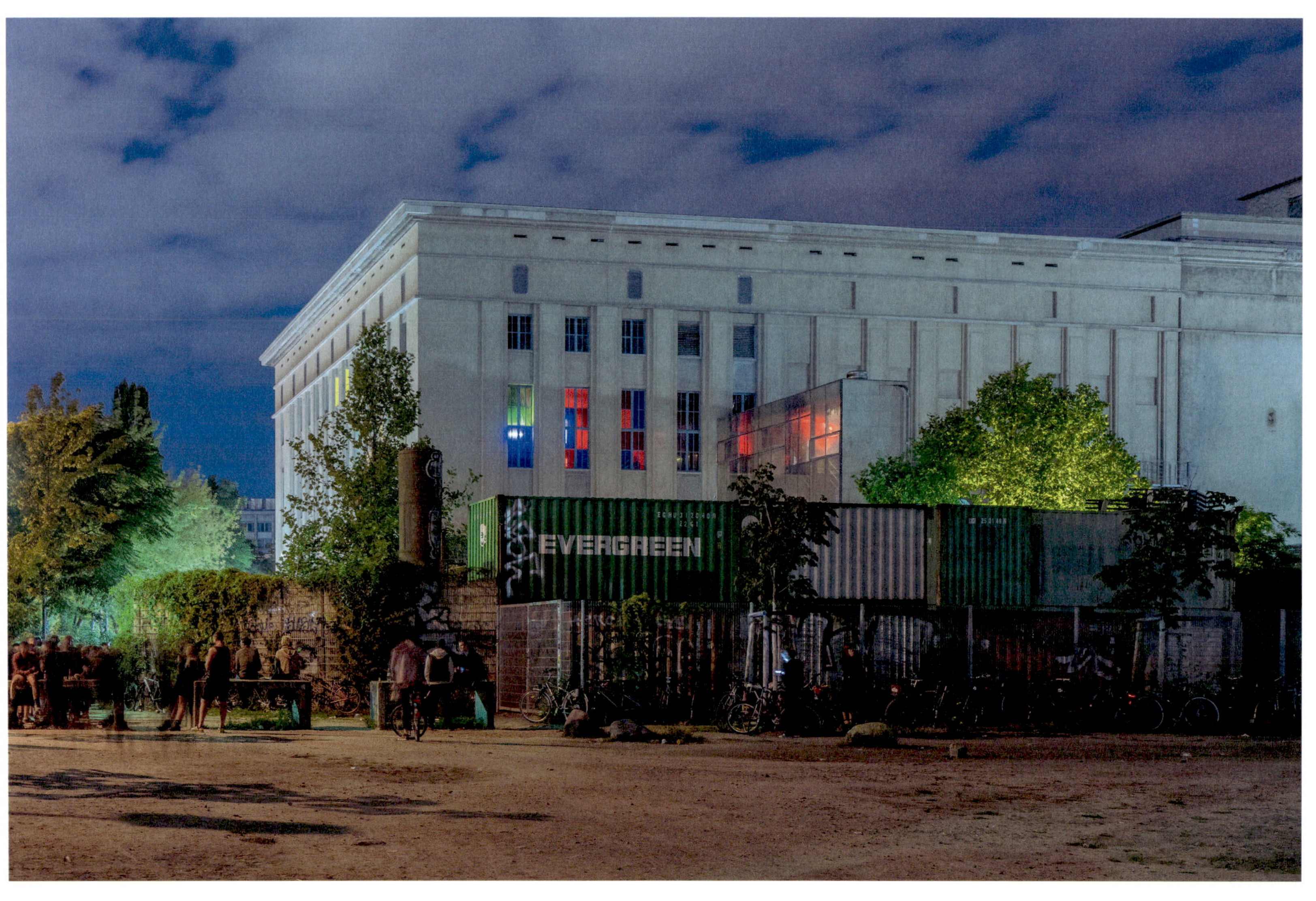

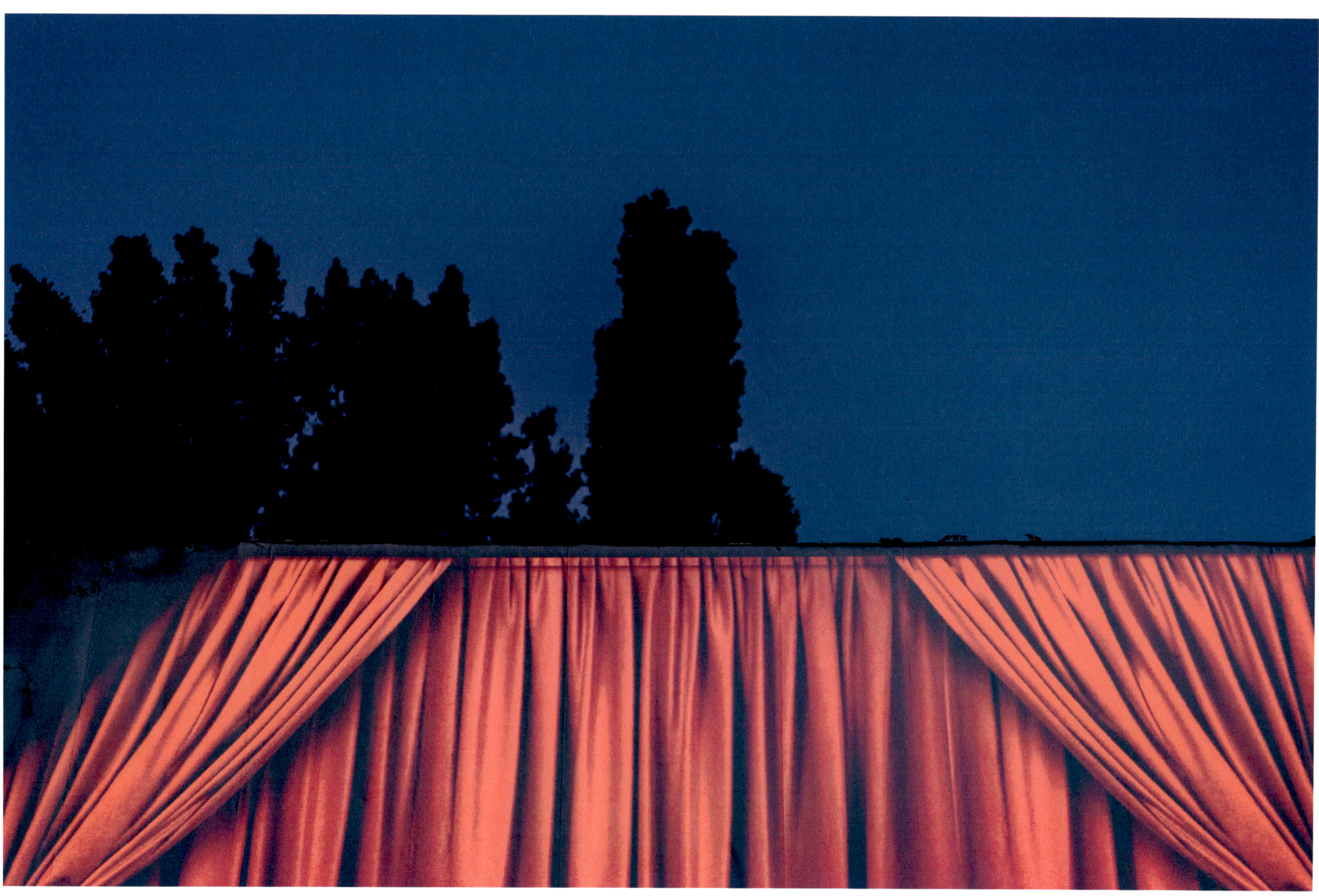

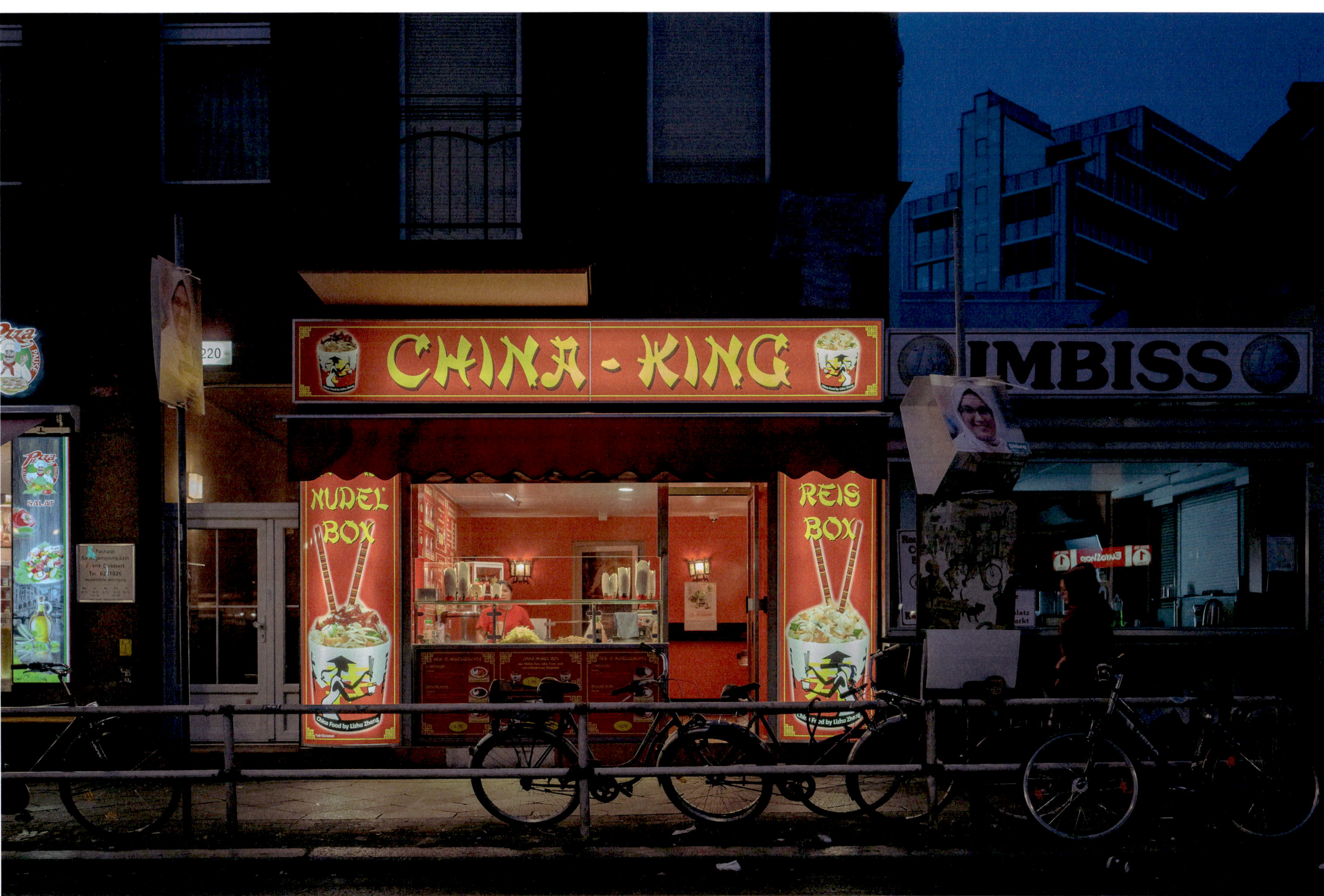
CHINA - KING
IMBISS
NUDEL BOX
REIS BOX
SALAT

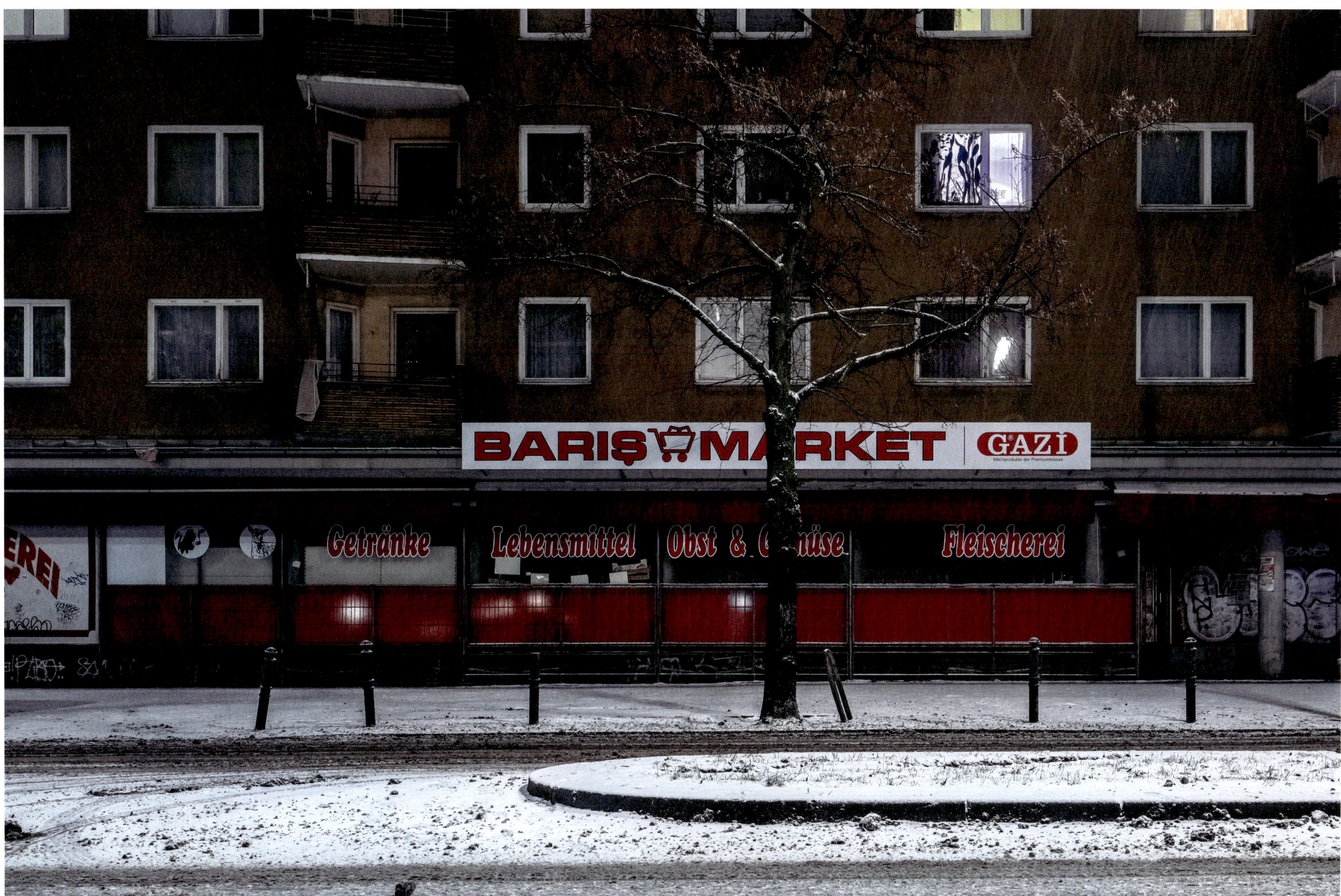

BARIŞ MARKET
GAZİ
Milchprodukte der Premiumklasse
Getränke
Lebensmittel
Obst & Gemüse
Fleischerei

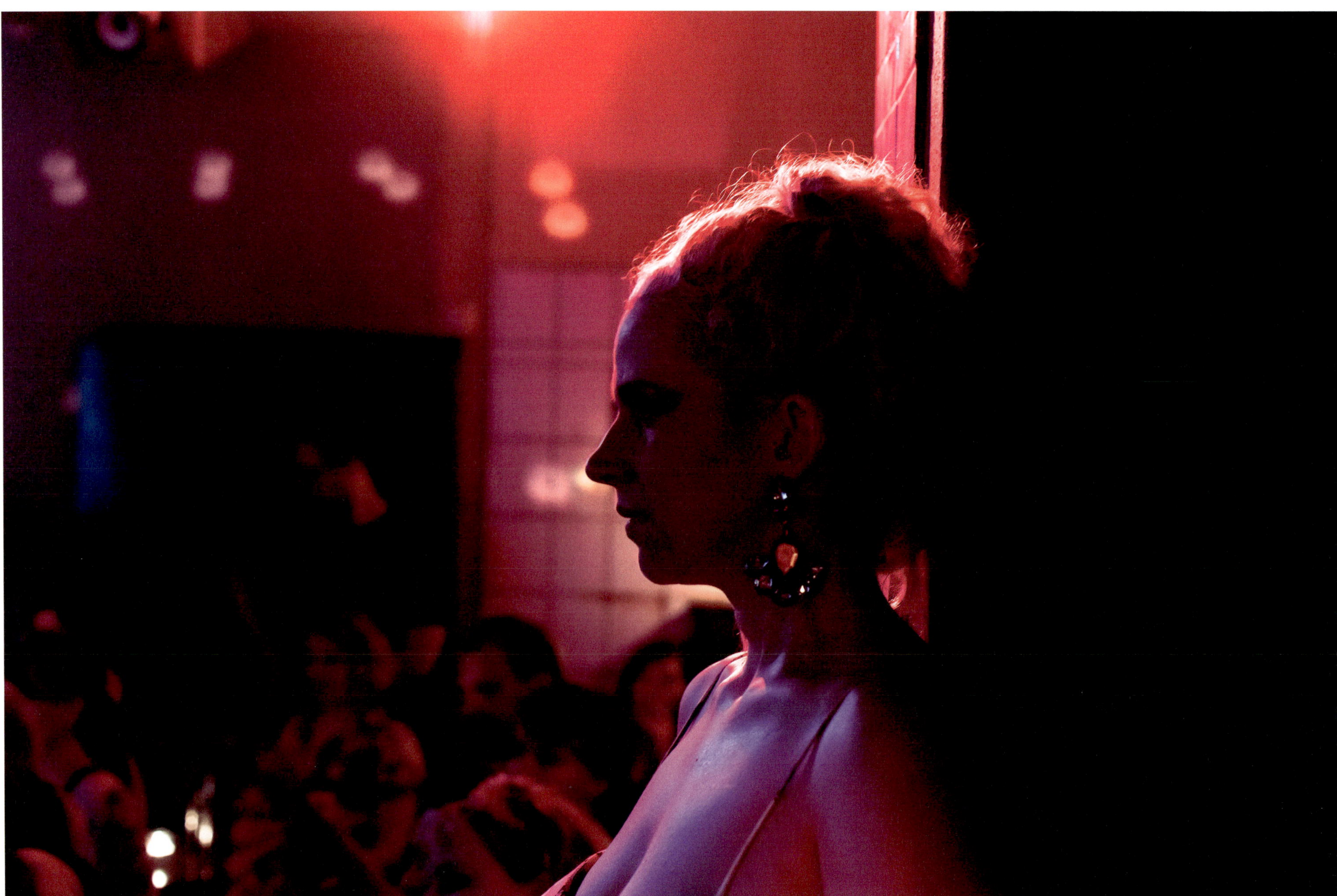

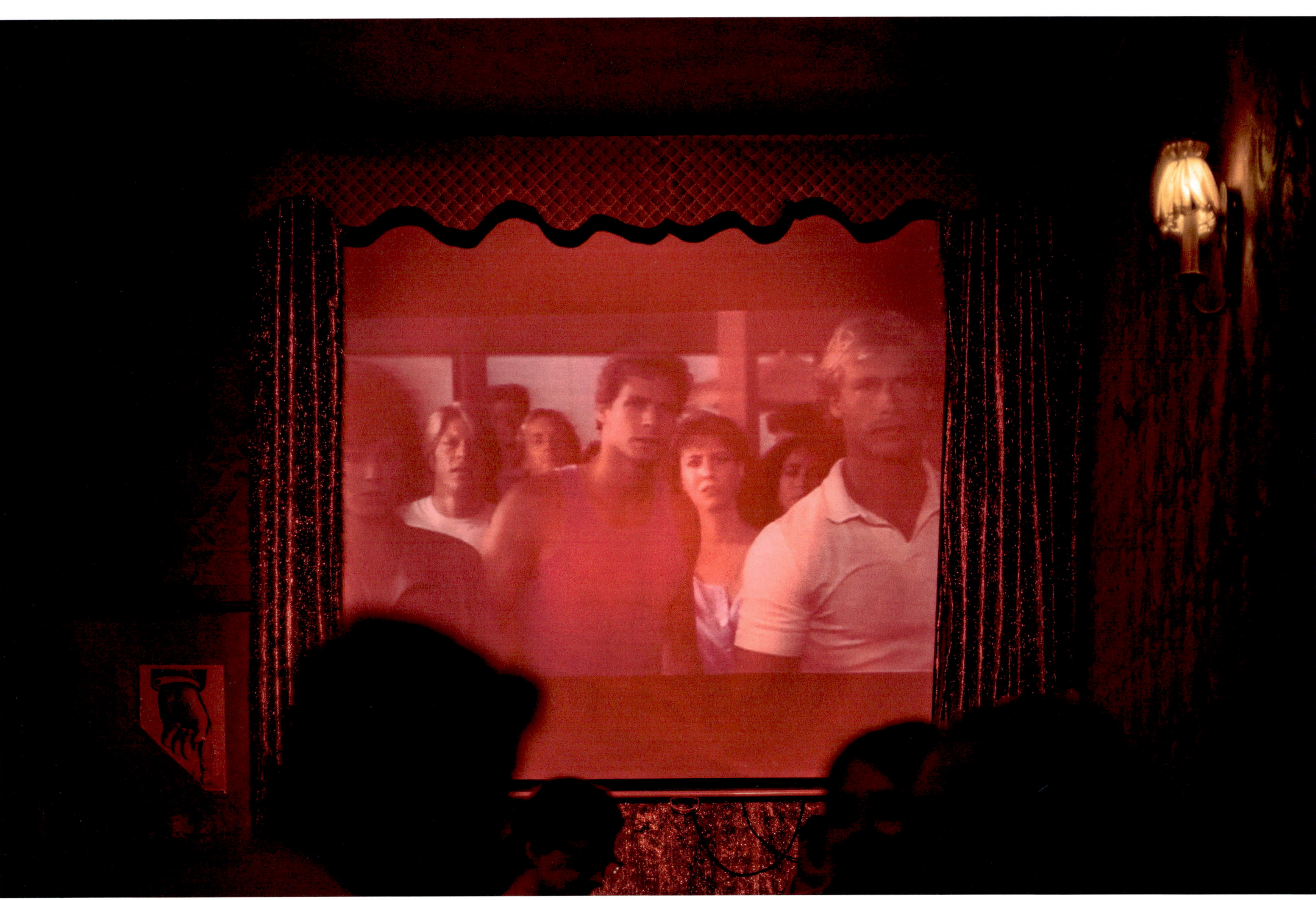

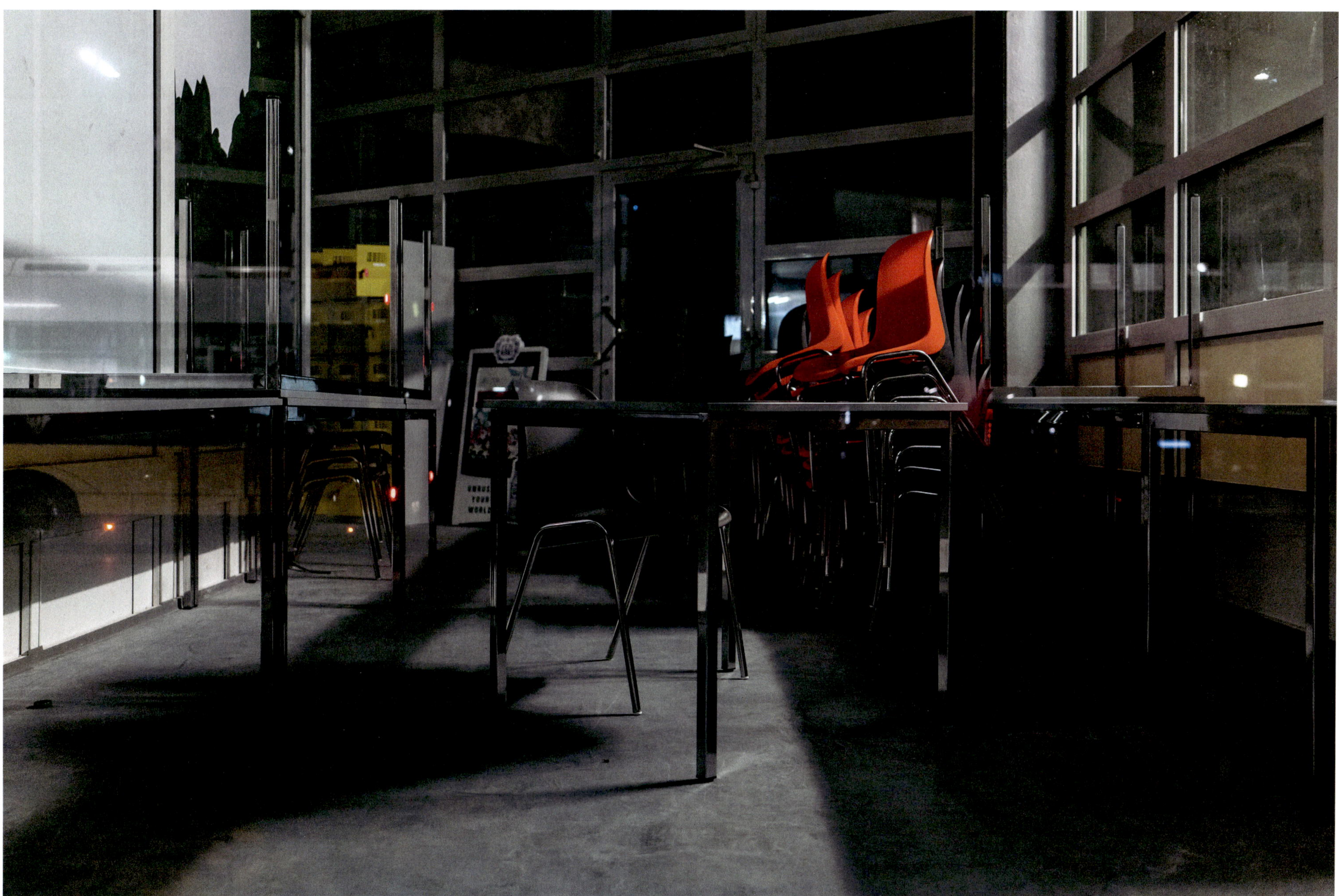

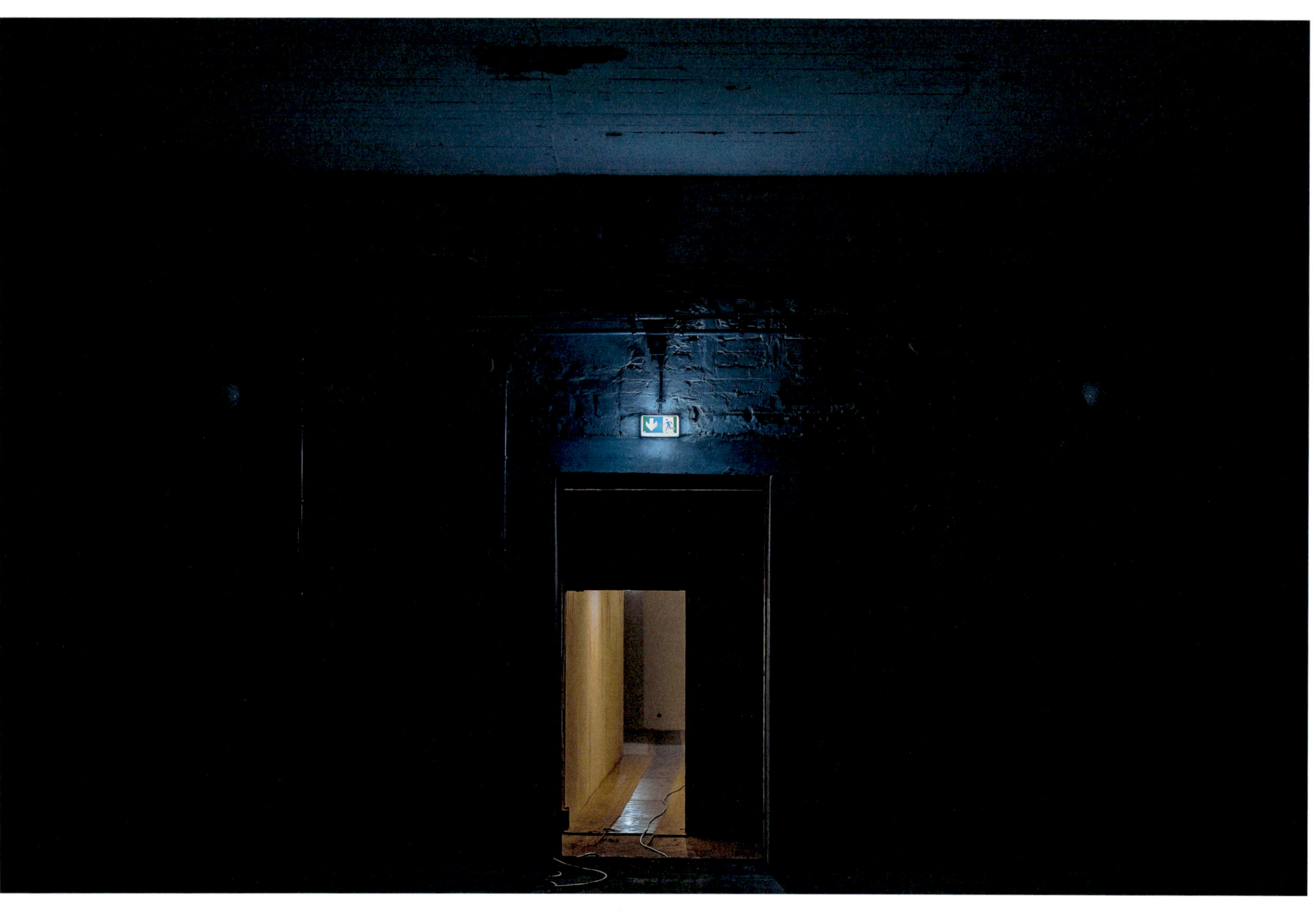

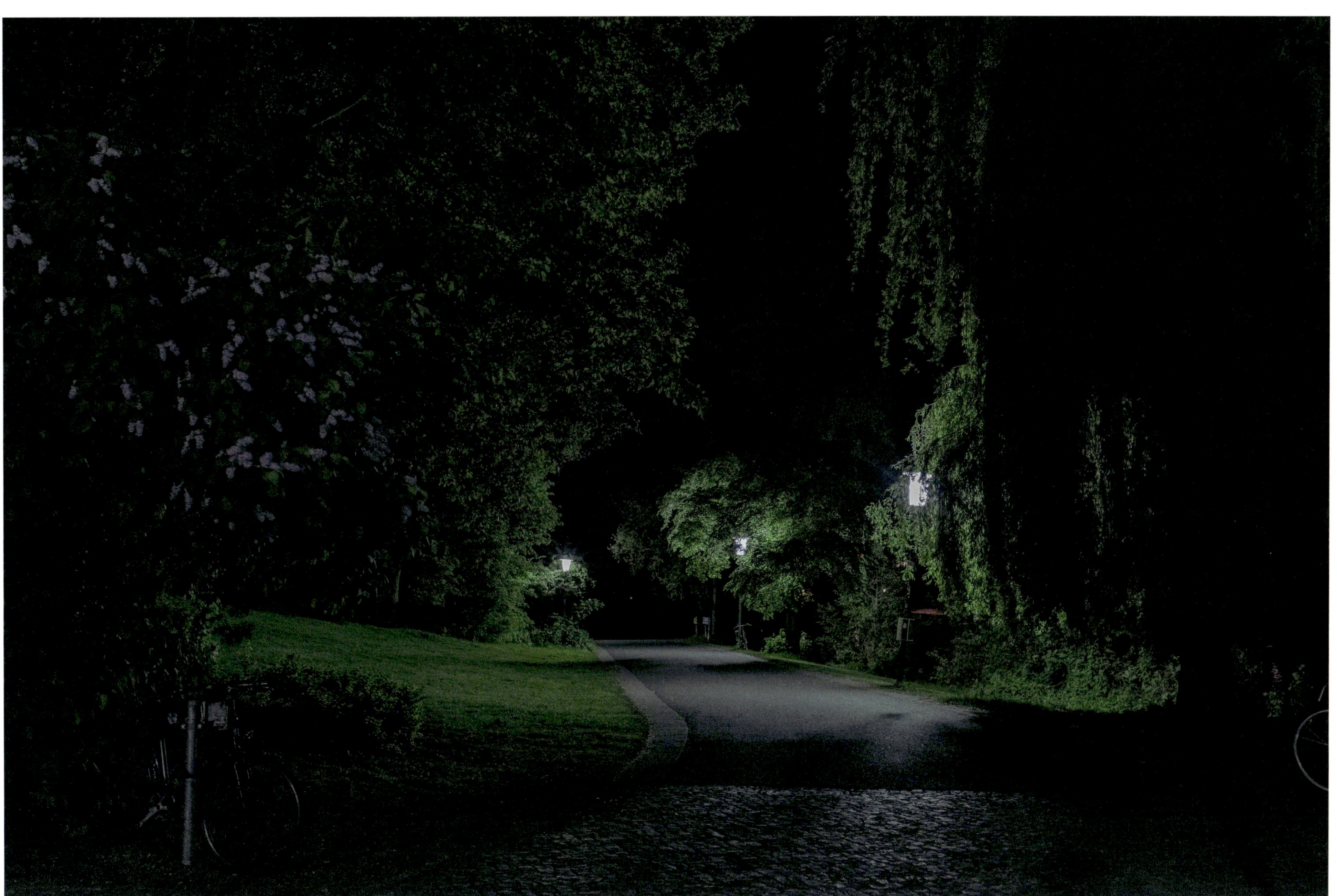

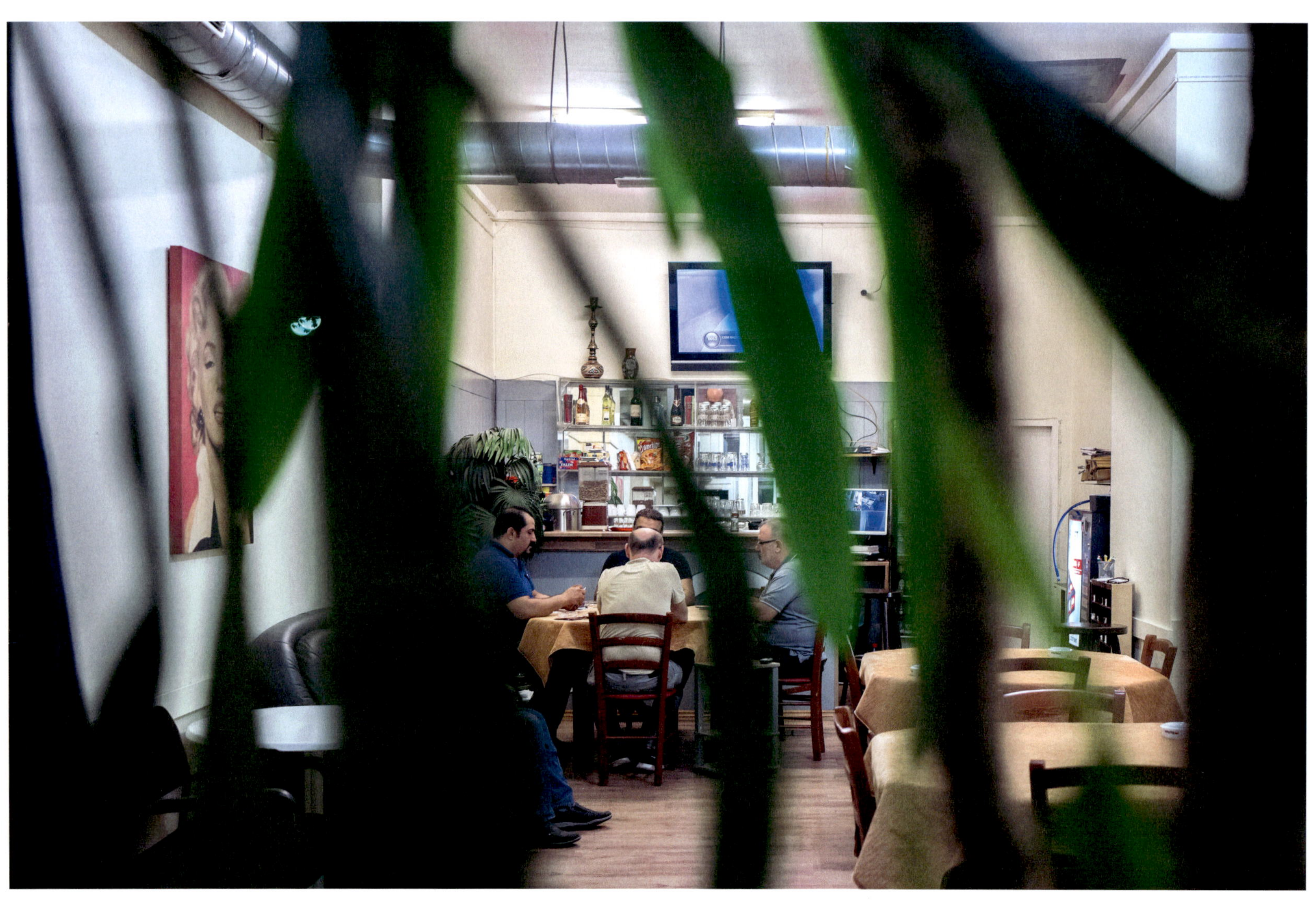

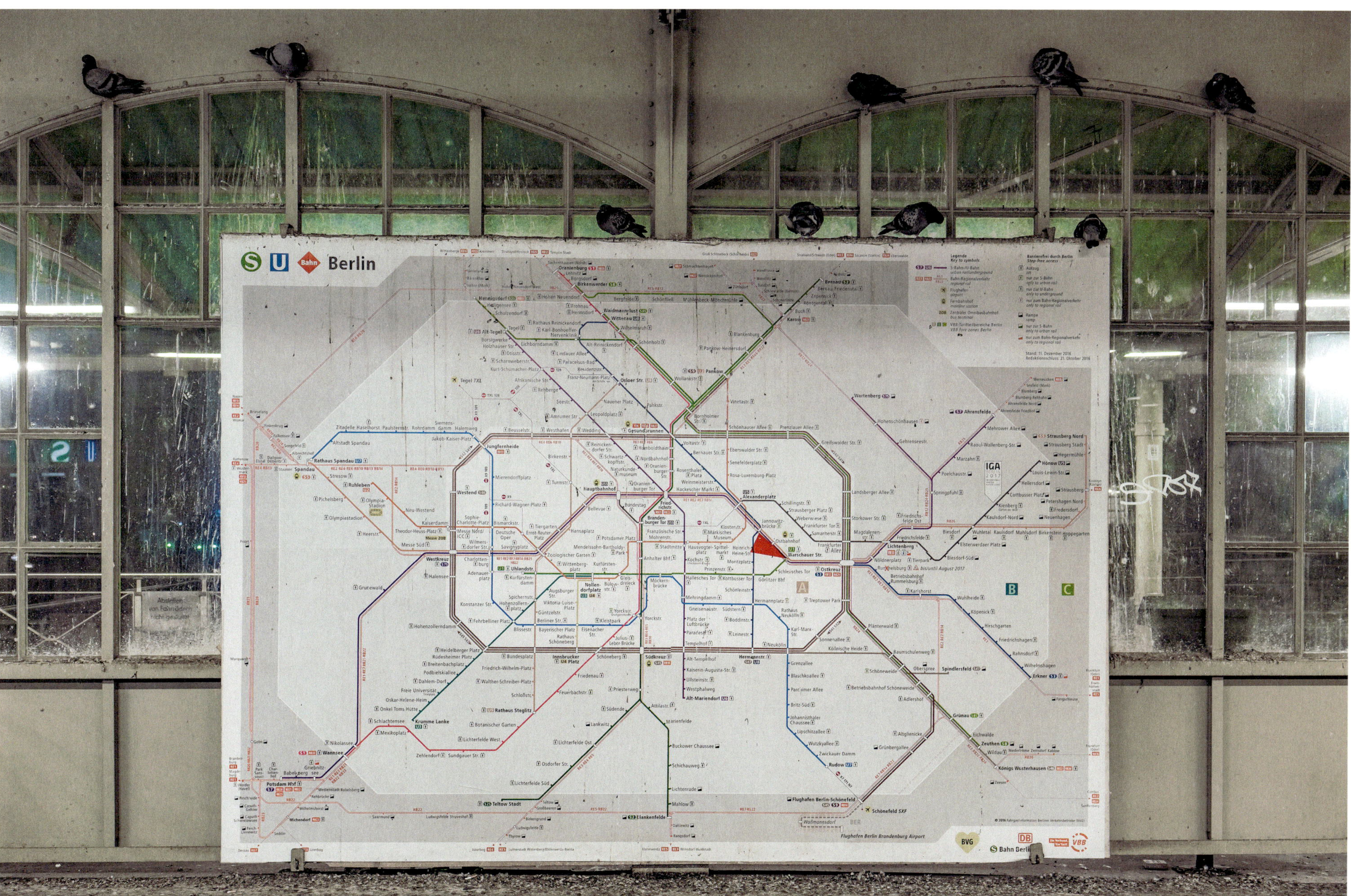

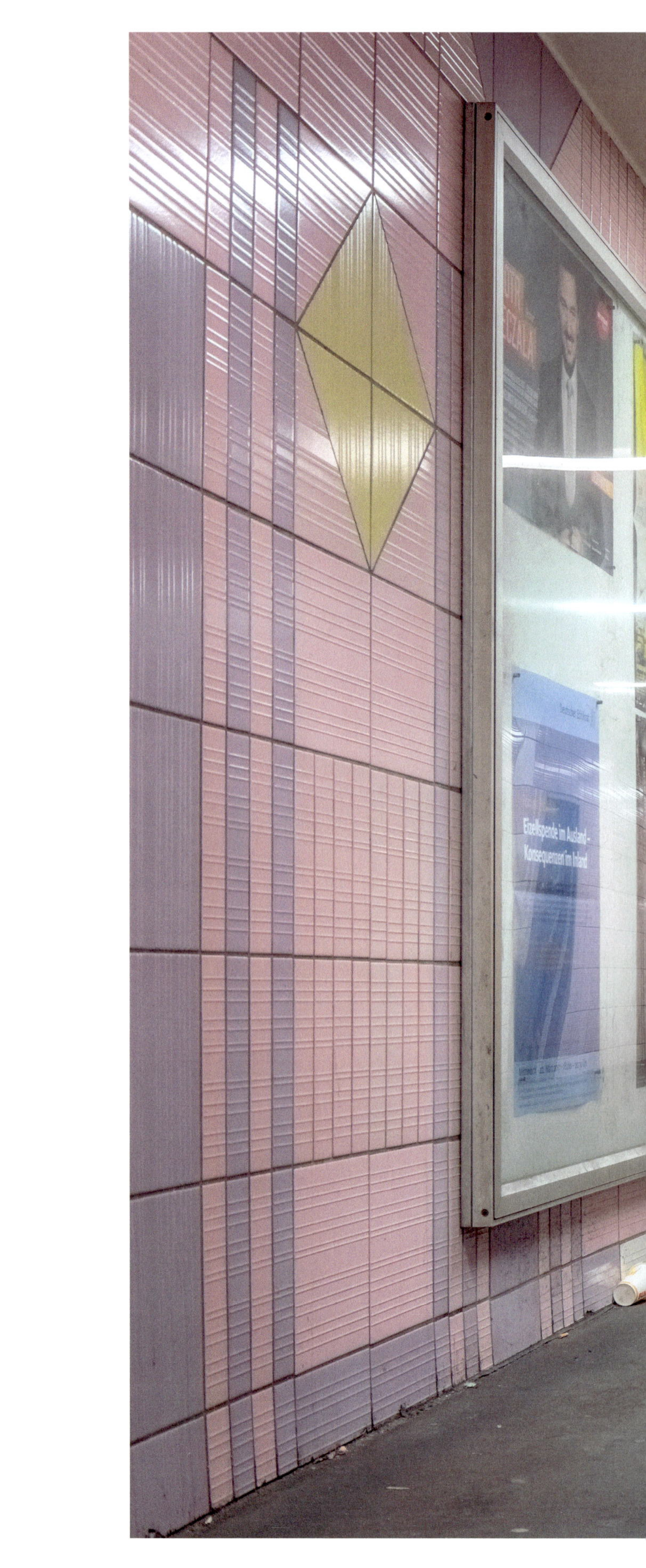
Einzelspende im Ausland –
Konsequenzen im Inland

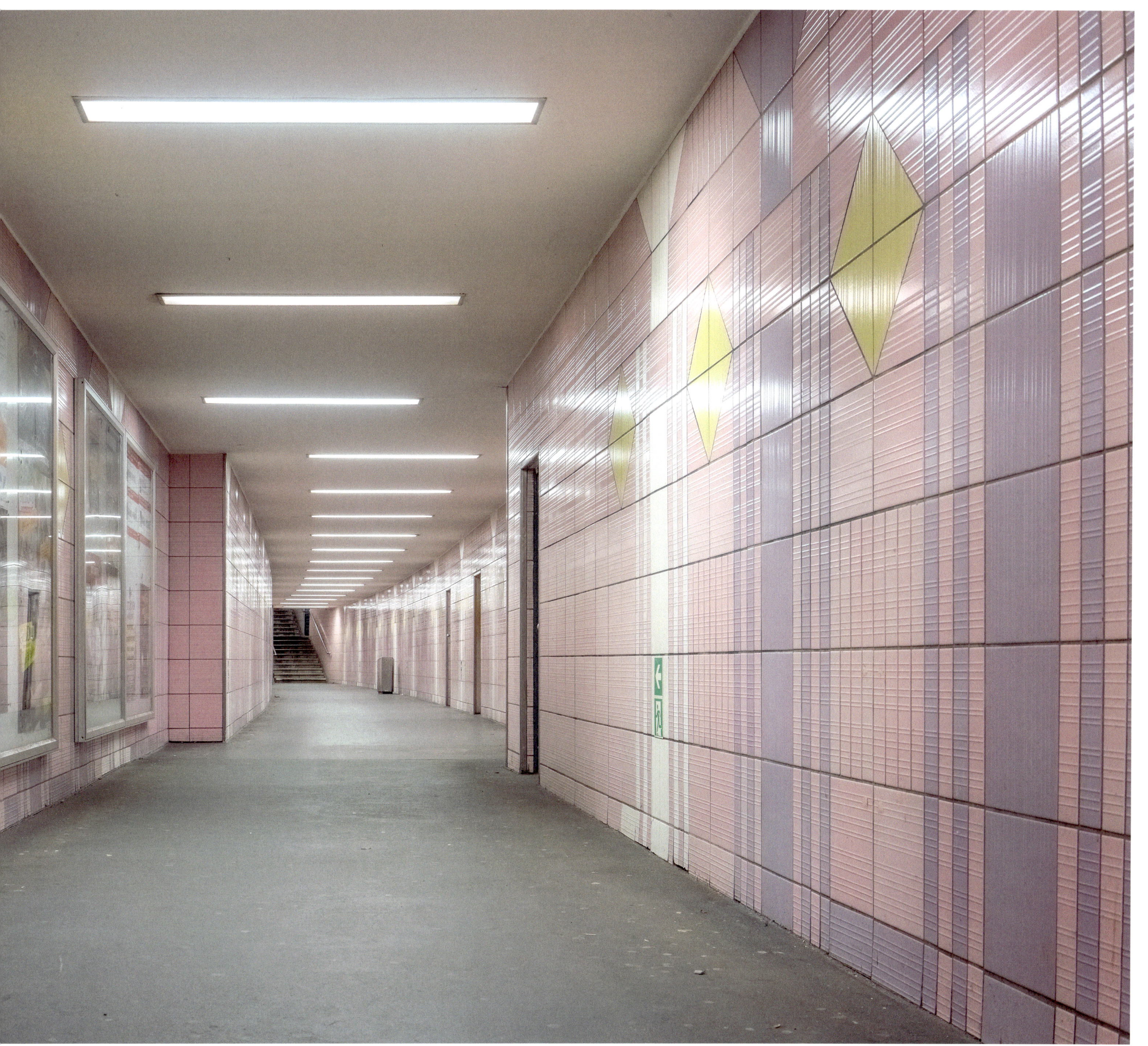

Contents

Romeo greets me every day. A small drawing in my bathroom, hung where a mirror over the sink would typically be placed, is one of the first things I see in the morning. The drawing, given to me as a gift by Romeo over a decade ago, depicts a goldfish—a rather fancy exemplar with willowy fins—looking deadpan and placid. The caption makes the drawing: "I'm afraid of dying," the goldfish admits, and with this reminder, I brush my teeth and venture into the day. As I stated in his 2011 book of animals, titled *I'll Be Dead by the Time You Read This*, "Romeo's anxious goldfish reminds me of the fullness of existence; for to be afraid of dying is not to lead a fearful life, but one so precious you don't want to lose it."

I find it suiting that my daily connection to Romeo Alaeff—whom I've known for nearly a quarter century—is one of existential panic; Romeo's work is about many things and takes many forms, but all of it is about some underlying psychological condition, a lingering feeling of unease, of alienation, of disconnect, of unknowing. The first film of his that I screened in 1998 in Berlin, entitled *Believe*, was a narrative of familial friction, maybe even dysfunction. It was Alaeff's own family story, which is significant because it was almost too strange to be true, were it not, in fact, true. In 2004, I included Alaeff's work in a group show I curated at Artists Space in New York called *Based on a True Story*. He presented the follow-up to *Believe*, titled *Goin' Down to Mexico*, which continued the story of Romeo's half-brother Gabriel, who at the time was living tenuously in a church in Mexico while considering the next steps in his life. The zaniness and youthful wisdom of the thirteen-year-old Gabriel in *Believe* was now supplanted by something more ominous, darker, more vulnerable; Gabriel is lost, and genuinely seeking.

While all of Romeo's projects since then could not be more different in style, material, and scale, the emotional punch remains the same. In his *Evolution of Despair* series of animal drawings—executed in ink, impeccably detailed, and masterfully drawn—Alaeff presents us with the breadth of the emotional lives of animals: a sheepish looking hamster gives us the side-eye and reveals that "things got weird"; a seal in a state of stupor informs us that "the pills aren't working"; my mortally afraid goldfish. In his animal portraits, as in his films, Alaeff is an astute observer of emotions, psychologies, and the invisible scars passed down through family, acquired in life, or simply present in one's psychological makeup.

Alaeff's next body of work, begun after he moved to Berlin, represents another shift in material, scale, and subject matter: monumental architectural drawings in charcoal, or translucent-gray watercolor on white gessoed ground, depict public sites and plazas, lobbies and other interiors, with large swaths blurred and erased, as if white-out had infected the drawing and obliterated its central motifs. If an architectural drawing can represent dread and tension, then these are just that; charged with the uncertainty of exposure to invisible dangers, the drawings represent—as the series title suggests—*Life During Wartime*.

The photographs that Alaeff has taken since then, a selection of which are collected in this volume, continue the exploration of psychological states hidden in our surroundings, or maybe the emotional states these sites trigger in him, or in us. I see my friend Romeo in every image: his diligence, his observational exactitudes, his jitters, his deeply personal and fundamental sense of displacement. They strike me as *true*.

"Perhaps home is not a place but simply an irrevocable condition."

— James Baldwin, *Giovanni's Room*

Ausländer
by Romeo Alaeff

Following its defeat in World War I, Germany ceded territory to the newly reconstructed state of Poland. The Free City of Danzig, however, an ethnically German city-state, retained its semi-autonomous status. It was there that my father's family was branded with the surname "Auslander," from the German, *Ausländer*, meaning "foreigner." The exact reason this name was affixed to them is not entirely clear, except that they were ethnically Polish, and Jewish; as most of the Auslander family perished in the Holocaust, this historical detail vanished with them. My grandfather, however, set off to study agriculture in the Netherlands before Hitler annexed Danzig and built the nearby Stutthof concentration camp. From there, he immigrated to the British Mandate for Palestine and cast off the Auslander name. A brother and two sisters soon followed, and in 1948, when Israel acquired statehood, the four siblings assumed new nationalities. The family members who remained in Danzig were separated into ghettos and concentration camps, and then systematically executed. One of the rationales for this brutality—according to the National Socialist Party anyway—was that *Danzig ist Deutsch*.[1] That is, Danzig is for Germans, *die Juden* (the Jews) not included.

> Today, the Free City of Danzig is the Polish city of Gdańsk. * Before the British assumed control and enacted the Mandate for Palestine, this area had been part of the Ottoman Empire. For thousands of years before that, the region had been conquered by Canaanites, Israelites, Philistines, Assyrians, Babylonians, Persians, Greeks, Romans, Arabs, Crusaders, Egyptians, and others. Today, the land area that made up the British Mandate for Palestine is divided into Israel, Jordan, and the Occupied Palestinian Territories. The varied peoples who call this land home are nationally identified as Israeli, Jordanian, Palestinian, or stateless, depending on whom you ask.

Having been misled about who my birth father was, I was ignorant of this family history until my mid-twenties. I mistakenly believed that my paternal identity traced back to Bukharan Jews[2] who escaped persecution under Stalin; this family decided to make India their new home, and it was there, in the ethnically cosmopolitan city of Karachi, that the man I believed to be my father was born. He and his family eventually migrated to Mandatory Palestine, but in the early 1960s, my "father," not feeling at home in what had by then become the state of Israel, sailed for New York City in pursuit of the American Dream. He became a US citizen and found success, first painting houses, then cutting diamonds, and then, when it was all the rage in the '70s, selling cocaine. Ultimately, he fled back to Israel to evade a prison sentence and, after many homesick years in the country he once repudiated, died there as a fugitive.

> Today, Karachi, India, is Karachi, Pakistan. * The part of the Soviet Union my father's family was originally from is now the Republic of Uzbekistan. * Before the European settlers became "Americans," the continent of North America was home to over five hundred indigenous tribes; over 90 percent of the native peoples who lived there were wiped out by European diseases, warfare, and mistreatment.

My mother's parents were refugees from Yemen, part of an exodus of Jews living as *dhimmi*[3] under Muslim rule. My grandmother was tortured[4] for resisting conversion to Islam under the Orphans' Decree, but the Jewish community secured her freedom through an arranged marriage. She fled Aden with her unacquainted, much older husband, arriving in Mandatory Palestine in 1933.

3   *Dhimmi* (protected person): a protected status under classical Sharia law that exempted Jews and Christians from forced conversion in exchange for payment of the Jizya tax, subordination, and second-class citizenship. For example, "*Dhimmis* were excluded from public office and armed service, and were forbidden to bear arms. They were not allowed to ride horses or camels, to build synagogues or churches taller than mosques, to construct houses higher than those of Muslims, or to drink wine in public.... A *dhimmi* had little legal recourse when harmed by a Muslim.... his oath was unacceptable to an Islamic court." Mitchell G. Bard, *Will Israel Survive?* (New York: Palgrave Macmillan, 2007), p. 40.

4   My *safta* (grandmother) was pricked with needles in sensitive parts of her body, and hot shish kebab skewers were applied to her legs, cheeks, neck, and buttocks. To educate them in the ways of Islam, the Shiite Zaydi took under their protection all orphaned *dhimmi* children. The decree, which mandated the forced conversion of Jewish orphans, was the primary driver of emigration for Yemeni Jews. Aharon Gaimani, "The 'Orphans' Decree' in Yemen: Two New Episodes," *Middle Eastern Studies* 40, no. 4 (July 2004), pp. 171–84.

1   This is a reference to a Nazi propaganda poster from 1939 depicting the city of Danzig under the emblem of the German Reich—a *Parteiadler* (Party's Eagle) clutching a swastika. At the bottom of the poster, in gold blackletter typeface, it states: *Danzig ist Deutsch* (Danzig Is German).

2   Bukharan Jews: a Jewish ethnoreligious group from central Asia who spoke a Tajik dialect of the Persian language called Bukhori.

In the early twentieth century, many Yemeni immigrants[5] to Mandatory Palestine were transferred to Rehovot, a Polish-Jewish settlement, to provide agricultural labor. The rapid integration of disparate Jewish ethnic groups across the nascent country of Israel, however, exposed cultural prejudices. Though spiritually bonded as diasporic Jews, some Ashkenazi Jews[6] felt superior to Sephardic and Mizrahi Jews (though prejudices could also run the other way). It was on the Ashkenazi side of this divide that my biological father was born, while my mother hailed from the Mizrahi side.

In the 1960s, when my mother was nineteen and madly in love with Elvis Presley, she traded her dirt-floor home in Rehovot for a basement apartment in New York City. It was there that she met and married the person I would erroneously come to know as my "Russian" or "Bukharan" father.

```
Before Rehovot became a Polish settlement, the area was
populated by Arabs for whom land ownership was not the norm.
The sale of this land by absentee landlords to Jewish settlers
displaced many Arabs who called it home. * Ancient Yemen
was once ruled by indigenous dynasties across various kingdoms.
In 1904, the country was split by its previous conquerors:
the Ottomans claimed the North, or the Ottoman Yemen Vilayet,
and the British claimed the South as part of the Protectorate
of South Arabia. In 1918, after the Ottomans were defeated
in World War I, North Yemen became an independent kingdom ruled
by imams; in 1962, the imams were overthrown, and the North
became the Yemen Arab Republic. In 1967, the British left South
Yemen, which became the People's Democratic Republic of
Yemen. Since 1990, Yemen has been reunified under one national
flag, though as of this writing, the country is embroiled
in a civil war that has displaced millions from their homes.
```

As a first-generation American, I often felt like an *Ausländer*. In Brooklyn, where I was born, I didn't much notice my "foreign-ness," but when my mother remarried an American[7] evangelical (my "cowboy" stepfather), who insisted on returning to his small Texas hometown, it was a distinction I couldn't escape. There were exactly two of us at my new elementary school—so-called "brownies"—me and a kid from India. The Indian kid's family had emigrated from New Delhi, but to the fairer kids, we were both conspicuously "Mexican." And though I didn't yet understand the slurs "spic" and "wetback," their intended effect was not diminished; I quickly learned that Mexicans (me and my Indian compatriot included) were not "real" Americans—according to the eight-year-olds in Lubbock, Texas, anyway.

```
The US State of Texas was taken by force from Mexico. Before
that, it was taken by force by the Spanish, and before that,
it was home to a variety of Mesoamerican tribes. * The city
of Delhi has seen a succession of rulers, from Hindu kings to
Muslim sultans to the British East India Company, followed
by direct British rule. In 1911, the capital of British India
shifted from Calcutta to New Delhi, and in 1947, following
India's independence from the British, New Delhi was officially
declared the capital of India.
```

In 1994, while a photography graduate student at the Rhode Island School of Design (RISD), I embarked on a documentary film about my family, titled *Believe*, discovering in the process that my presumed father—along with his Soviet-Bukharan extraction—bore no genetic or genealogical connection to me. The film (and later, a couple of strands of DNA) exposed the family secret that my biological folk actually traced back to the Auslanders—*Untermenschen*[8] as the Nazis saw them—from Danzig. It was then that I learned about my Polish grandfather (and my Lithuanian grandmother) and how he wound up in the culturally split town of Rehovot, one of the only places in the universe where his son, a Polish-Lithuanian-Israeli boy, could chance upon a Yemeni-Israeli girl. And just like that, like a close-up magic trick, I was no longer a Yemeni-Uzbeki-Bukhari-American-"Mexican" with a Soviet backstory. Now—*abracadabra*—I was a Yemeni-Polish-Lithuanian-American-"Mexican"—with a

---

5   From the perspective of Yemeni Jews, as for many diasporic Jews, they were not "immigrants" in the strict sense of the word. Rather, they saw their migration as a "return to Zion" (שִׁיבַת צִיּוֹן)—that is, they were returning home after millennia of exile. The consummation of Jewish longing for their ancestral homeland (the "promised land") was in conflict with the claims of Arabs who had for generations settled in the area, a conflict that still rages on today.

6   Generally, Ashkenazi Jews were from Germany, France, Eastern Europe, and Slavic countries; Sephardic Jews were from Spain, Portugal, and North Africa; Mizrahi Jews were from Asia and the Middle East. European Jews arriving in Israel/Palestine tended to have higher levels of formal education and, assuming it wasn't confiscated or abandoned, intergenerational wealth.

7   My stepfather's family immigrated to the United States from Germany, England, Scotland, Wales, and Ireland. His parents were devout Church of Christ parishioners. After my mother's remarriage and our move to Texas, we began attending a nondenominational church.

8   *Untermensch* (subhuman), plural *Untermenschen*: a term used by the Nazis to describe non-Aryans, including Jews, Romani, Slavs, Serbs, Russians, and people of color.

German backstory. As fate would have it, I had *three* fathers and a mother whose families had all emigrated from vastly different worlds, each for different reasons, each forced to redefine the meaning of home.

After graduating from RISD, I returned to New York City, but any semblance of home eluded me. Since 2012, I have lived in what was formerly East Berlin, in the same country that my biological grandfather was merely lucky to have left. Like many foreigners here, I've had to repeatedly trek to the *Ausländerbehörde* (foreigners' office) to plead for a visa extension. Like the Auslander name pinned to my grandfather's family, I was officially an *Ausländer* in Germany, and it was never clear for how long I'd be able to call Berlin home. I briefly explored obtaining permanent status via renaturalization,[9] but the inconvenient fact that I was born out of wedlock renders moot my historical ties to Germany[10]—according to the German government anyway.

A few decades ago, East Berlin was the capital of the Deutsche Demokratische Republik (DDR) and was controlled by the Soviet Union. Before that, Berlin was the capital of the Third Reich. Before that, it was the capital of the Weimar Republic. Before that, it was the capital of the German Empire. Before that, it was the capital of the Kingdom of Prussia, and before that, the capital of the Margraviate of Brandenburg. In 1990, East and West Berlin were reunited, making it the capital of the Federal Republic of Germany.

Berlin

Berliners often ask me why I would trade the "big city" for the "village" of Berlin. I struggle for a short answer but wind up resorting to a version of the following story: in 1998, I was invited by Joachim Abrell, Cay Sophie Rabinowitz, and Christian Rattemeyer to screen my family documentary *Believe* at OSMOS in Berlin. I stalled on accepting the offer, as well as one for an upcoming group show called *Home Screen Home* at Witte de With in Rotterdam, because I was flat broke—I resigned to skip them both. But, by a turn of luck, I was introduced to someone who had just seen one of my short films at the *New York Video Festival* at Lincoln Center. Hearing of my predicament, he offered to pay for the trip, but with one caveat: that he could tag along. My new benefactor-friend, at the ripe age of twenty-nine, had decided that he was finished with Wall Street and that he had reaped enough cash to burn it in his two-story penthouse fireplace if he so chose. He sought to style himself as a shabby-chic Lou Reed, perhaps with a dash of Nan Goldin and Marcel Proust (in fact, he was living in Lou Reed and Laurie Anderson's former West Village apartment). To that end, my new friend committed in earnest to living a "transgressive" life, and Berlin, a city that had long intrigued him with its mythic tales of techno-imbued debauchery, seemed like the perfect place to forget things past.

Once in Berlin, we sought out the hidden parties, but the abandoned buildings that sheltered them were impossible to find, especially during an exceptionally dark and bitter cold January (and when a copiously graffitied steel door finally opened, we were summarily dismissed). One night, we found our way to Delicious Doughnuts Research (DDR), a once-upon-a-time hot spot for electronic music. Still on the hunt for fabled bunker clubs and magic passwords, I approached a lanky, Bowie-esque Berliner who was leaning coolly against the DJ booth. That Berliner was Ben Klock, a local DJ who went on to become one of the original—and preeminent—residents of Berghain, arguably the most fabled techno club of them all. More importantly, he went on to become one of my best friends, and the reason I returned to Berlin over the years, each time empty-threatening to move there.

Fast-forward seven million hot New York minutes to 2012: despite a glorious rooftop view of the Empire State Building, when my rent doubled at the Garment District retail space where I was illegally living, I realized that New York City had become unlivable; worse, I had come to feel like a stranger anywhere else in my country of birth. I reasoned that it was time to make good on my threat of moving to Berlin. I boxed up my belongings, put them in a shipping container, and boarded a plane. I had no plan B, nor a plan A for that matter.

Eight years later, though I've settled in, a feeling of alienation still haunts me. I wander Berlin at night with a camera, photographing the city from a safe distance, (still) trying to find my footing in this *fremdes* (foreign) land. I'm not sure

---

9   Article 116 (2) of the German constitution (*Grundgesetz*) states: "former German citizens who between January 30, 1933, and May 8, 1945, were deprived of their citizenship on political, racial, or religious grounds, and their descendants, shall on application have their citizenship restored."

10   Though I had produced DNA results proving paternity, without a marriage certificate, my application for citizenship under Article 116 (2) of the German constitution could not proceed.

if documenting Berlin brings it closer or keeps it at bay, but as I get lost down dark, desolate streets, I ruminate on what seems to be a universal condition: that of being—literally or metaphorically—an *Ausländer.*

Personally, it's a familiar feeling, similar to the estrangement I felt as a first-generation American, the progeny of immigrants from what may as well have been distant planets. As I struggled to negotiate dueling nationalities, identities, and religions, no place I've ever drifted through truly felt like home. Now, as I attempt to connect to yet another city, this time by meandering through its vacant spaces, I consider the plight of my extended family, all of them emigrants from somewhere—Yemen, the Uzbek Soviet Socialist Republic, Poland, Lithuania, Germany, Israel, England, Scotland, Wales, Ireland—all compelled to trade *Heimat* (homeland) for *fremdes* land, all forced to contend with situations more perilous than mine. I don't take for granted that my musings are a distinct privilege. For untold others—migrants, refugees, and displaced persons the world over—these are not philosophical abstractions. Privilege notwithstanding, I chase the elusive feeling of home, camera in hand, even if I suspect I'll never find it.

Berlin: Imagine a City
by Rory MacLean

Imagine Berlin. Imagine a city of fragments and ghosts. Imagine a metropolis which inspired countless artists and witnessed uncountable murders. Imagine a laboratory of ideas, the fount of both the brightest and darkest designs of history's most bloody century. Imagine the most arrogant capital of Europe devastated by Allied bombs then divided. Imagine it reunited and reborn as one of the creative and tolerant centers of the world.

In my lifetime I have known three Berlins: West Berlin where I made movies with David Bowie, East Berlin where I researched my first book, and now the unified capital. Over the years I have visited so often that today, if the notion took me, I could find my younger self in almost any corner of the city.

If I waited long enough at Bahnhof Zoo, I would see myself aged nineteen fall from the Hoek van Holland train and into waiting arms. At night on Savignyplatz I would catch sight of myself, four years older, cycling home in the summer rain, soaked to the skin, my companion and I throwing off our clothes as we rode: shirts in the Tiergarten, skirt in the Spree. Along Friedrichstraße I'd watch myself—over thirty by 1989 and losing my hair—run between East German ministries, applying for travel permits for a country that might no longer exist (none of the bureaucrats knew for sure).

Later in the Grunewald, the dense urban forest which hugs the city's western fringe, I'd linger until I spotted myself—with notebook in hand—bow my head in the forest cemetery. In the black earth at my feet the stones were engraved *Unbekannter, Unbekannte, Unbekannt*. Unknown man, unknown woman, unknown. Some victims of the Allied bombing were so disfigured that their sex could not be determined.

Finally today I see myself lost in the memorial to the Jews murdered in the Second World War. The vast, undulating labyrinth of concrete plinths rises and falls away into the darkness of Gertrud-Kolmar-Straße. I stumble between its hard-edged, disorientating stelae, built on top of sealed Nazi bunkers, spooked by dusky sounds and shadows, moved by the echo of children's voices and footsteps.

Like so many others I inhabit Berlin, and it inhabits me. Our memories are not fixed and lifeless fragments to be retrieved like dusty books from a library shelf. Instead they impel an evolving dialogue between our past and present selves. All our histories—personal, collective—become imaginative reconstructions, the ever-changing stories into which we look to understand the chaotic tumble of new events.

Similarly Berlin's identity is not set in stone, or brick. Its story is also ongoing. Again and again the city reinvents itself, reconciling a mythic idea of itself with its bitter, bloody, buoyant past. The Berliner Schloss has risen again as Germany becomes paymaster of Europe. Mel Brooks's *The Producers* runs at the Admiralspalast, "Springtime for Hitler" ringing out in the theater where the Führer once kept a private box. After every performance of the Cold War musical *Hinterm Horizont*, the audience spills across the former death strip whistling "Mädchen aus Ost-Berlin." In the shadow of the Brandenburg Gate, out-of-work actors don Chinese-made East German uniforms to sell fake East Zone passes. Fat Tire Bicycles offers Nazi and Red Berlin tours every hour on the hour. Not so long ago one visitor even asked their tour guide, "Can you direct me please to the Third Reich?"

"Just walk down this street and turn right at 1933," the guide replied.

With *die Wende*, Berliners at last can come to terms with their history, and so are able to believe in something again. At the Potsdam Institute for Climate Impact Research, once the Albert Einstein Science Park, the environmental pioneer John Schellnhuber talks about accepting responsibility for tomorrow, drawing a direct line from the darkest memories. "We never again want to look the other way when we face wrong developments. It is a century-long exercise in responsibility."

In Berlin-Mitte, Internet crusaders champion the city as Europe's startup capital, a new generation of entrepreneurs creating wealth for the twenty-first century as industrialists Borsig and Rathenau did 100 years ago. At the Chancellery, the boss of Deutsche Bank celebrates his sixtieth birthday in the company of the country's political and corporate leaders while outside, beyond the rank of bullet-proof Mercedes, activists work to break up the party, to change the old ways, harnessing "big data" to expose abuses of power and privilege. Meanwhile at their own parties, the speeding tattooed tourists step onto the stage, the canvas, the film set that is modern Berlin, to play their role like movie extras, refashioning themselves—or being refashioned—as has happened here time and again, embracing the myth.

In this fractured capital, every citizen—whether perfectionist or revolutionary, collaborator or dissident, resident or visitor—can dare to imagine a place which no one else has ever seen. Its poets, scientists, performers, politicians, and digital natives conjure up visions as potent as its actuality. Ideas rather than evil now spiral out from the center, from all its neighborhoods, filling the absences, creating a city that, in its constant state of becoming, is as much a conceit as a reality.

Berlin is a living city, for all its ghosts. It is fresh and green because of its woods and lakes but especially because it is always reinventing itself. "Berlin ist eine Stadt, verdammt dazu, ewig zu werden, niemals zu sein," wrote author Karl Scheffler over a century ago. "It is a place doomed to forever become, never to be." In its streets, on its avenues, atop the Victory Column, the living walk alongside the dead, remembering, forgetting, and, together, imagining the world anew.

In *Speak, Memory*, Nabokov makes the poetic, or the playful,
speculation that Russian children before the Revolution—and his
exile—were blessed with a surfeit of sensual impressions to
compensate them for what was to come. Of course, fate doesn't
play such premonitory games, but memory can perform retrospective
maneuvers to compensate for fate. Loss is a magical preservative.
— From *Lost in Translation: A Life in a New Language* (1989)

"Therefore the Lord God sent him forth from the garden of Eden, to till the ground from whence he was taken. So he drove out the man; and he placed at the east of the garden of Eden Cherubims, and a flaming sword which turned every way, to keep the way of the tree of life." Thus Genesis, on humankind's first exiles. Since then, is there anyone who does not—in some way, on some level—feel that they are in exile? We feel ejected from our first homes and landscapes, from childhood, from our first family romance, from our authentic self. We feel there is an ideal sense of belonging, of community, of attunement with others and at-homeness with ourselves, that keeps eluding us. The tree of life is barred to us by a flaming sword, turning this way and that to confound us and make the task of approaching it harder.

On one level, exile is a universal experience. But, of course, exile also refers to a specific social and political condition— although even in that sense, it was never a unitary category, and we tend to compress too many situations under its heading. The different circumstances surrounding individual migration, and the wider political or cultural contexts within which it takes place, can have enormous practical and psychic repercussions, reflected in the various words we use for those who leave one country for another. There are refugees, émigrés, emigrants, and expatriates, designations that point to distinct kinds of social, but also internal, experience. It matters enormously, for starters, whether you choose to leave or are forced to; it matters also whether you're coming to a new land unprotected and unprovided for or whether you can expect, or transport, some kind of safety net. When my family came from Poland to Canada, we were immigrants, a term that has connotations of class—lower than émigrés, higher perhaps than refugees—and degree of choice—more than is given to refugees, less than to expatriates.

Historically, too, the symbolic meaning, and therefore the experience of exile, has changed. In medieval Europe, exile was the worst punishment that could be inflicted. This was because one's identity was defined by one's role and place in society; to lose that was to lose a large portion of one's self. After being banished from Florence, Dante lived less than a hundred miles from his city-state—and yet he felt that his expulsion was a kind of psychic and social death, and his dream was either of return or of revenge (which he certainly executed very effectively in the *Inferno*). Real life, for Dante, was in Florence; it could not exist fully anywhere else. Joseph Conrad's father wrote to his infant son, who had been born during a time when Poland was erased from the map, "Tell yourself that you are without land, without love, without Fatherland, without humanity—as long as Poland, our Mother, is enslaved." In other words, for a patriot of an occupied nation, it was possible to feel radically exiled within that country, as long as it did not possess the crucial aspect of national sovereignty.

All of these forms of exile implied a highly charged concept of home—although that home was not necessarily coeval with one's birthplace. For the medieval clerics and church functionaries who traveled from monastery to monastery, the center of gravity was the city that housed the papal seat. The Jews have had the most prolonged historical experience of collective exile; but they survived their Diaspora—in the sense of preserving and maintaining their identity—by nurturing a powerful idea of home. That home existed on two levels: there were the real communities that Jews inhabited in various countries; but on the symbolic and perhaps the more important plane, home consisted of the entity "Israel," which increasingly became less a geographic and more a spiritual territory, with Jerusalem at its heart. While living in dispersion, Jews oriented themselves toward this imaginative center of the world, from which they derived their essential identity.

In our own century, the two great totalitarianisms, Nazi and Soviet, produced the most potent forms of exile, although the Soviet expulsions proved more permanent. The refugees from Nazi Germany, with their bright galaxy of artists and intellectuals—Hannah Arendt, Bertolt Brecht, Theodor Adorno, Herbert Marcuse, and others—were pushed from their country by a vile regime, but once the war was over, they could go back, and some chose to do so. The exiles from Eastern Europe—Vladimir Nabokov, Czeslaw Milosz, Milan Kundera, Joseph Brodsky, and others—thought that their banishment was for life, though history reversed it for some of them in the end.

But in recent years, in Europe most markedly, great tectonic shifts in the political and social landscape have taken place, which I think are affecting the very notion of exile—and of home. For what is happening today is that cross-cultural movement has become the norm rather than the exception, which in turn means that leaving one's native country is simply not as dramatic or traumatic as it used to be. The ease of travel and communication, combined with the loosening of borders following the changes of 1989, give rise to endless crisscrossing streams of wanderers and guest workers, nomadic adventurers and international drifters. Many are driven by harsh circumstance, but the element of voluntarism, of choice, is there for most. The people who leave the former Soviet Union nowadays are likely to be economic migrants or mafia tax dodgers buying up elegant real estate in London rather than dissidents expelled by ruthless state power. In one Bengali village, for example, there is a tradition of long seasonal migration, or sojourning. Many of the village's men leave for several years or even decades, but always with the intention of returning. These are hardly privileged émigrés or expatriates, but neither are they powerless victims of globalization. Instead, they are people with agency and intentionality, playing the system. Smart young men choose different countries for the timely economic advantages they offer—better wages, better interest rates. Almost all go back, a bit richer and a bit more important in the eyes of their fellow villagers. Theirs are migrations divested of tragedy if not of adversity.

Of course, there are still parts of the world, South America or Southeast Asia, where political dissidents are expelled by demagogic dictatorships and cannot return while those dictatorships endure. There are still refugees from Bosnia whose return is barred by the sword of violence. I do not mean to underestimate for a moment their hardships, but I would think that even in their case, the vastly increased mobility and communicative possibilities of our world change the premises of their banishment: friends can visit or phone; they know that if the government of their country changes—and political arrangements, along with everything else, have become susceptible to quicker change—they can go back, or travel back and forth.

The *Herald Tribune* recently characterized the increasing numbers of American expatriates in Europe: "They are the Americans abroad, and their number is soaring in a time when travel is unblinkingly routine, communications easy and instant, and telecommuting a serious option. They are abroad in a world where they can watch the Super Bowl live from a Moscow sports bar or send an e-mail from an Internet cafe in Prague."

Well, exactly. We all recognize these basic features of our new, fast-changing social landscape. Whether we have left or not, we know how easy it is to leave. We know that we live in a global village, although the village is very virtual indeed—a village dependent not on locality or the soil but on what some theorists call deterritorialization—that is, the detachment of knowledge, action, information, and identity from specific place or physical source. We have become less space-bound, if not yet free of time.

Simultaneously there has grown up a vast body of commentary and theory that is rethinking and revising the concept of exile and the related contrapuntal concept of home. The basic revision has been to attach a positive sign to exile and the cluster of mental and emotional experiences associated with it. Exile used to be thought of as a difficult condition. It involves dislocation, disorientation, self-division. But today, at least within the framework of postmodern theory, we have come to value exactly those qualities of experience that exile demands—uncertainty, displacement, the fragmented identity. Within this conceptual framework, exile becomes, well, sexy, glamorous, interesting. Nomadism and diasporism have become fashionable terms in intellectual discourse. What is at stake is not only, or not even primarily, actual exile but our preferred psychic positioning, so to speak, how we situate ourselves in the world. And these days we think the exilic position has precisely the virtues of instability, marginality, absence, and outsiderness. This privileging of exile compresses two things: first, a real description of our world, which indeed has become more decentered, fragmented, and unstable, and second, an approbation of these qualities, which is more problematic, because it underestimates the sheer human cost of actual exile as well as some of its psychic implications, and perhaps even lessons. My emigration took place during the Cold War, though not in the worst Stalinist years. My parents chose to leave, though that choice was so overdetermined that it could hardly have been called "free." But I happened to be a young and unwilling emigrant, yanked from my childhood, which I had believed to be happy. Therefore, I felt the loss of my first homeland acutely, fueled by the sense (the certain knowledge, it seemed then) that this departure was irrevocable. Poland was abruptly sundered from me by an unbridgeable gap; it was suddenly elsewhere, unreachable, on the other side, and I felt, indeed, as if I were being taken out of life itself.

This kind of abrupt rupture breeds its own set of symptoms and syndromes. It is, first of all, a powerful narrative shaper; it creates chiaroscuro contrasts, a stark sense of biographical drama. The stories that emerged from the Cold War are legion, but one certain outcome of exile that takes place in a bipolar world is the creation of a bipolar personal world. Spatially, the world becomes riven into two parts, divided by an uncrossable barrier. Temporally, the past is all of a sudden on one side of a divide, the present on the other.

Flash-forward to 1994, and a rather ordinary trip I took to Kraków that year with an English friend. The Westernization of my native town was everywhere evident. Where previously there had been no market, there was now commerce. Where before there was the great Eastern European nada, now there were boutiques, Krups coffee machines, Armani suits. It was perhaps the presence of my Western friend, who kept saying that Kraków looked like any small European city with a well-preserved historical center, that made me realize palpably what I had known in principle: that the differences between East and West were blurring pretty completely and that simultaneously the various divisions and oppositions I had set up in my inner landscape were shifting and blurring, too. When I came

upon a lone shop window featuring a display familiar from the days of yore—a dry loaf of bread, an apple, and a desultory can of Coke—I pointed it out to my friend excitedly. Look! This was how it used to be! But this was not the way things were now. The dusty little vitrine was a trace, a remaining mark of a world that, for all its misery, had the appeal of familiarity and, most saliently, of clarity. Now I would have to live in a world in which the bipolar structure was gone, in which everything is intermingled, and no site is more privileged—either in its deprivation or in its pleasures—than anywhere else. I would have to change my narrative.

At this vanishing of contrasts, I confess that I felt not only relief but regret. It was a regret, undoubtedly perverse, for the waning of clarity. But I also felt the loss of the very sense of loss I had experienced on my emigration. For the paroxysm I experienced on leaving Poland was, for all the pain, an index of the significance I attached to what I left behind. Still, what had I mourned in 1959? What was it that stood for home? Though I was too young to know it, the fervor of my feelings was produced by the Cold War. And yet my response had nothing of geopolitics about it. As a bare adolescent, I was too politically innocent to be a budding nationalist; in any case, as a daughter of Jewish parents recently transplanted from the Ukraine and not fully engaged in the body politic, I was in a poor position to become a patriot. So it was not the nation I felt exiled from, not Conrad's father's Poland; my homeland was made of something much earlier, more primary than ideology. Landscapes, certainly, and cityscapes, a sense of place. I was lucky enough to grow up in a city that really is quite enchanting, and that escaped the ravages of the war. There was the webwork of friendships and other relationships, for example with my teachers. But there were also elements less palpable that nevertheless constituted my psychic home.

For the great first lessons of my uprooting were in the enormous importance of language and of culture. My first recognition, as I was prized out of familiar speech and social environment, was that these entities are not luxuries or even external necessities but the medium in which we live, the stuff of which we are made. In other words, they constitute us in a way of which we perhaps remain unconscious if we stay safely ensconced within one culture.

For a while, like so many emigrants, I was in effect without language, and from the bleakness of that condition, I understood how much our inner existence, our sense of self, depends on having a living speech within us. To lose an internal language is to subside into an inarticulate darkness in which we become alien to ourselves; to lose the ability to describe the world is to render that world a bit less vivid, a bit less lucid. And yet the richness of articulation gives the hues of subtlety and nuance to our perceptions and thought. To me, one of the most moving passages in Nabokov's writing is his invocation of Russian at the end of *Lolita*. There he summons not only the melodiousness or euphony of Russian sounds, compelling though these may be, but the depth and wholeness with which the original language exists within us. It is that relationship to language, rather than any more superficial mastery, that is so difficult to duplicate in languages one learns subsequently.

In more religious times, certain languages were considered sacred; that is, they were thought, in the words of a wonderful social historian, Benedict Anderson, to have "ontological reality inseparable from a single system of representation." Arabic, for example, was considered to be the only language in which the Koran could be written; the sacred texts could not be translated into any other language. So with Latin for the medieval Catholic church and Hebrew for Orthodox Jews. Some premodern people today still have the sense that their language is the true language, that it corresponds to reality in a way other languages don't. And it may be that one's first language has, for the child, this aura of sacrality. Because we learn it unconsciously, at the same time as we are learning the world, the words in one's first language seem to be equivalent to the things they name. They seem to express us and the world directly. When we learn a language in adulthood, we know that the words in it "stand for" the things they describe; that the signs on the page are only signs—arbitrary, replaceable by others. It takes time before a new language begins to inhabit us deeply, to enter the fabric of the psyche and express who we are.

As with language, so with culture: what the period of first, radical dislocation brought home was how much we are creatures of culture, how much we are constructed and shaped by it—and how much incoherence we risk if we fall out of its matrix. We know that cultures differ in customs, food, religions, social arrangements. What takes longer to understand is that each culture has subliminal values, predispositions, and beliefs that inform our most intimate assumptions and perceptions, our sense of beauty, for example, or of acceptable distances between people or notions of pleasure and pain. On that fundamental level, a culture does not exist independently of us but within us. It is inscribed in the psyche, and it gives form and focus to our mental and emotional lives. We could hardly acquire a human identity outside it, just as we could hardly think or perceive outside language. In a way, we are nothing more—or less—than an encoded memory of our heritage.

It is because these things go so deep, because they are not only passed on to us but *are* us, that one's original home is a potent structure and force and that being uprooted from it is so painful. Real dislocation, the loss of all familiar external and internal parameters, is not glamorous, and it is not cool. It is a matter not of willful psychic positioning but of an upheaval in the deep material of the self.

Is it then all pain and no gain? Of course not.

Being deframed, so to speak, from everything familiar, makes for a certain fertile detachment and gives one new ways of observing and seeing. It brings you up against certain questions that otherwise could easily remain unasked and quiescent, and brings to the fore fundamental problems that might otherwise simmer inaudibly in the background. This perhaps is the great advantage, for a writer, of exile, the compensation for the loss and the formal bonus—that it gives you a perspective, a vantage point.

The distancing from the past, combined with the sense of loss and yearning, can be a wonderful stimulus to writing. Joyce Carol Oates, in a striking formulation, has written that "for most novelists, the art of writing might be defined as the use to which we put our homesickness. So powerful is the instinct to memorialize in prose—one's region, one's family, one's past—that many writers, shorn of such subjects, would be rendered paralyzed and mute." In exile, the impulse to memorialize is magnified, and much glorious literature has emerged from it. *Native Realm* by Milosz or Nabokov's *Speak, Memory*, some of Brodsky's essays in *Less Than One*, or even Kundera's much cooler take on transplantation in *The Book of Laughter and Forgetting*—these are works of lyrical commemoration informed by a tenderness for what is lost and by the need, even the obligation, to remember.

But the perspective one gains from dislocation is, of course, not only retrospective but prospective. Exile places one at an oblique angle to one's new world and makes every emigrant, willy-nilly, into an anthropologist and relativist; for to have a deep experience of two cultures is to know that no culture is absolute—it is to discover that even the most interstitial and seemingly natural aspects of our identities and social reality are constructed rather than given and that they could be arranged, shaped, articulated in quite another way.

For this reason, too, exile can be a great impetus to thought and to creativity, which is why so many artists have actively chosen it: James Joyce, with his motto of "Silence, exile, and cunning"; Samuel Beckett with his decision to write in French rather than English, precisely for the advantages of defamiliarization. And for the nonwriter, too, biculturalism can have its bracing pleasures—the relish of sharpened insight, the savviness of skepticism—which can become positively addictive.

But I have come to believe that these virtues have their serious defects, that in the long term, the addiction may be too seductive, that as a psychological choice, the exilic position may become not only too arduous but too easy. Perhaps the chief risk of privileging the exilic narrative is a psychic split—living in a story in which one's past becomes radically different from the present and in which the lost homeland becomes sequestered in the imagination as a mythic, static realm. That realm can be idealized or demonized, but the past can all too easily become not only "another country" but a space of projections and fantasies. Some people decide to abandon the past, never to look back. For others, the great lure is nostalgia—an excess of memory. One of the most extreme examples of "living in the past" I've come across is the history of Polish refugee camps in England, which had been set up during World War II for people who had come there with the Polish army. These camps remained until the late 1950s, their inhabitants existing in virtual isolation, many never learning English and always hoping that the magic moment of redemption—the moment of return—was around the corner. But the actual Poland was no longer the one they remembered; it had changed in ways they would surely have found unpalatable, or at least highly perplexing, had they actually been able to go back.

For Jews in their long Diaspora, the need to preserve the symbolic center in an indifferent world—to keep intact a vision of a lost paradise and a promised land—often led them to insulate themselves from their surroundings, to retreat to their community as a place of refuge and spiritual fortress. I have written a

book about the history of a shtetl in Poland, a small town whose population was half-Jewish, half-Polish.[1] The shtetl, for Eastern European Jews, was home in its most secure—internally secure, that is—form. In these small, rural enclaves, everyone knew everyone else, and everyone followed the same rules of behavior and spiritual life. No one was allowed to fall out of the communal net; no one needed to suffer from the modern malaise of uncertainty and alienation. The shtetl was a highly resilient, highly organized microsociety, and for many of its members, its strict codes and protective arrangements provided the satisfactions of warmth, safety, and certainty. But for others, the regulation of everyday life became oppressive, the avoidance of the larger world stifling.

Even before World War II, the metaphoric walls of the shtetl were beginning to break down. Many of its inhabitants, for various reasons, chose to leave literally; others began to question the structures of belief, causing heated conflicts within the shtetl itself.

Of course, the insulation of the shtetl was not only self-inflicted. But my point is that exile, and the pain of radical change, do not necessarily lead to a more radical personality structure or greater openness to the world. On the contrary, upheaval and dislocation can sometimes produce some rather more conservative impulses of self-defense and self-preservation. My own tendency was certainly to nostalgia and idealization—perhaps because I was ejected before my loss of innocence, before I could develop more considered opinions and preferences or revise my feelings about the place I came from. And once you leave, such revisions become very difficult.

In the later phases, the potential rigidity of the exilic posture may inhere not so much in a fixation on the past as in habitual detachment from the present. Such detachment can of course be a psychic, or even moral, luxury—but it comes at a price. In his fascinating, provocative essay, "Exile as a Neurotic Solution,"[2] A. B. Yehoshua, a leading Israeli writer, makes the startling observation that during the eighteen hundred years of the Diaspora, there were many intervals

1   *Shtetl: The Life and Death of a Small Town and the World of Polish Jews* (Boston: Houghton Mifflin, 1998).

2   In Étan Levine, ed., *Diaspora: Exile and the Contemporary Jewish Condition* (New York: Steimatzky/Shapolsky, 1986).

when Jews could have settled in Palestine easily, or more easily, than in the countries where they chose to live, but that in fact, Palestine was the one place they consistently avoided. It was as if, he suggests, they were afraid precisely of reaching their promised land and the responsibilities and conflicts involved in turning the mythical Israel into an actual, ordinary home. Life in Diaspora had its enormous difficulties; but it offered the benefit of turning conflict outward, against a hostile or uncomprehending world, and thus avoiding the internal conflicts within the Jewish polity—conflicts that have certainly become evident since the founding of Israel (as they are in any functioning society). Whatever the historical accuracy of Yehoshua's thesis, it does remind us of certain hazardous syndromes of the exiled stance: that this posture, if maintained too long, allows people to conceive of themselves as perpetually Other, and therefore unimplicated in the mundane, compromised, conflict ridden locality that they inhabit; it allows them to imagine the sources and causes of predicaments as located outside, in a hostile or oppressive environment, rather than within.

In our current, habitually diasporic, habitually nomadic world, the oppositional, bipolar model no longer holds. The goalposts have shifted—indeed, the whole playing field has changed—in ways that remain elusive and hard to define. When all borders are crossable and all boundaries permeable, it is harder to project conflict outward, to imagine an idyllic realm or a permanent enemy. This is initially confusing, but it is surely to the good. Indeed, the merits of the new situation are easily discernible. They are the benefits available to those American expatriates who can leave America without ever really leaving. We move not only between places but between cultures with more grace and ease. We are less shocked by the varied assumptions prevailing among different peoples, less prone to absolutist assertions of our rightness. We have become tangibly aware of the plurality of values that such liberal thinkers as Isaiah Berlin have tried to teach us. In the political sphere, the ease of movement across borders should surely work to counter dogmatic or fanatical nationalism, although given the rise of national conflicts, this result may not be self-evident. But for those who move freely among countries and cultures, it becomes difficult to maintain the notion of any one nation's superiority or special destiny. The literature of this new nomadism or

diasporism, of which Salman Rushdie is perhaps the most prominent representative, is a transnational literature in which multiple cultural references collide and collude and in which their interplay is seen as exactly that—robust, vital play. This is a vision of exile, if it can still be called that, as comedy, rather than despair.

Is it then, in this blithe new world, all gain and no pain? I don't quite think so.

The new nomadism is different from other Diasporas. It exists in a decentered world, one in which the wanderers no longer trace and retrace a given territory or look to any one symbolic locus of meaning. If we take such radical decentering as a metaphor for a way of being and of selfhood, if we rewrite displacement as the favored position (which it holds in postmodern theory), then the model is not without its own, sometimes high, costs. In the Bengali village people have a suggestive way of talking about this: they say that their land has lost some of its strength because its inhabitants are dispersed—as if the land draws power from the loyalty and attachment of the humans who live on it. But I wonder if, in our world of easy come, easy go, of traveling light and sliding among places and meanings without alighting on any of them for long, we don't risk a dispersion of internal focus and perhaps even of certain strengths—strengths that come from the gathering of experiences so that they add up to memories, from the accumulation of understanding, from placing ourselves squarely where we are and living in a framework shared with others. I wonder if, in trying to exist in liminal spaces, or conceiving of experience as movement between discrete dots on a horizontal map, we don't risk what Kundera calls the "unbearable lightness of being," the illness that comes upon people unanchored in any place or structure, the Don Juans of experience who travel perpetually to new moments and sensations and to whom no internal site—of attachment, need, desire—is more important than any other.

In the "bipolar" mentality, the idea of home may become too dramatized or sentimentalized. In the "nomadic" configuration, exile loses its charge, since there is no place from which one can be expelled, no powerful notion of home. Indeed, these days we are wont to say not so much that all fiction is homesickness as that all homesickness is fiction—that home never was what it was cracked up to be, the haven of safety and affection we dream of and imagine. Instead, home is conceived of mostly as a conservative site of enclosure and closure, of narrow-mindedness, patriarchal attitudes, and dissemination of nationalism. And, indeed, the notion of "home" may have been, in recent times, peculiarly overcharged, as the concepts of "country" and "nation" have been superimposed on each other with a seeming inevitability. "France," for the French, is both *la belle France* and *la patrie*. Such overlapping is not a necessary one. We have seen, for example, in the unhappy case of the former Yugoslavia, that a geographic territory can abruptly change its national identity. But the nostalgia of exiles for their birthplace has undoubtedly often been augmented by this conjunction of geographic and patriotic longing.

The transports of patriotism, narrowness of provincial perspectives, and confinements of parochial traditions are not plausible solutions to the dilemmas of our time. And yet continual dislocation, or dispersion, is both facile and, in the long run, arid. Can anything be rescued from the notion of home, or at-homeness, that is sufficient to our condition? One of the most interesting and subtle meditations on home I know of is found in V. S. Naipaul's autobiographical novel *The Enigma of Arrival*. The place at which he was trying to arrive was a small cottage attached to a large house on a historic estate in England. For Naipaul, this entails multiple ironies; he grew up in an Indian community in Trinidad and understands all too well that his very presence on the estate is the end result of long imperial relations. He also knows that the cottage, the manor, the ancient plain, correspond for him to some fantasy of England that he developed precisely when growing up in Trinidad and that included some dream of permanence, dignity, beauty. It takes a while before Naipaul squares these preconceptions with the realities of the place where he lives—realities that include change, modernization, conflict. Slowly he begins to see the landscape before him through other eyes. He imagines how the estate looks to the temporary workers, to whom a cottage with a thatched roof is simply temporary shelter, not a home, "a place to which you could transfer (or risk transferring) emotion or hopes." He begins to imagine how the estate looks and feels to its owner, who suffers from accidie, a melancholic withdrawal from the world; Naipaul interprets this malaise as a symptom of the landlord's excessive at-homeness, a security that has become a stasis. He understands that the power relations of today are complex enough to confer on him some advantages unavailable

to his aristocratic landlord—the advantages of dynamism, of ambition, even of need. Slowly Naipaul learns to read the landscape in a less romantic and more complex way. He comes to love the place from the position not of fantasy but of knowledge.

The slowness of this process is crucial; in Naipaul's book, that ruminative leisureliness makes the act of creating a home akin to the process of writing. It is through gradual accretion of details, of knowledge, of relationships that he comes to imaginative possession of the place, as he comes to imaginative possession of his subject.

Naipaul's understated allegory suggests that there are two kinds of homes: the home of our childhood and origin, which is a given, a fate, for better or for worse, and the home of our adulthood, which is achieved only through an act of possession, hard-earned, patient, imbued with time, a possession made of our choice, agency, the labor of understanding, and gradual arrival.

The experience of enforced exile paradoxically accentuates the potency of what is given, of the forces that have shaped us before we could shape ourselves. This is what Brodsky says about the magnetic pull of one's parental home and the exile's dilemma of having wandered away—or having been forced to wander—too far:

> For a while, he is absorbed with new vistas, absorbed with building his own nest, with manufacturing his own reality. Then one day, when the new reality is mastered, when his own terms are implemented, he suddenly learns that his old nest is gone, that those who gave him life are dead. On that day he feels like an effect suddenly without a cause. . . . What he can't blame on nature is the discovery that his achievement, the reality of his own manufacture, is less valid than the reality of his abandoned nest. That if there ever was any-thing real in his life, it was precisely that nest, oppressive and suffocating, from which he so badly wanted to flee. He knows how willful, how intended and premeditated everything that he has manufactured is. How, in the end, all of it is provisional.[3]

I agree and sympathize, even empathize, with this almost entirely. The acute loss I felt on emigrating was commensurate with the depth of my attachment—and there is something about that that I don't want to disavow, and which can be a source of later per-

3   Joseph Brodsky, "A Room and a Half," in his *Less Than One: Selected Essays* (New York: Farrar, Straus & Giroux, 1986), end of section 18.

ceptions and affections. After leaving Russia, Nabokov wrote in several languages masterfully, but he was transposing the love of his first language to his subsequent ones. We need to develop a model in which the force of our first legacy can be transposed or brought into dialogue with our later experiences, in which we can build new meanings as valid as the first ones. This can be done only through a deepening investigation, through familiarization. It is fine, and illuminating, to see all the structures that construct us for what they are and to see through them; but we must acknowledge the need for frameworks that contain us, for sites that are more than temporary shelters. And we need to see that in our world it may be insufficient to define ourselves as Other in opposition to some archetypal oppressor or hypothetical insider. Our societies are too fragmented to have an easily discernible inside or permanent centers of power. At the same time, we need a conception of a shared world, a world in which we exist by virtue of shared interests rather than mutual alienation, to which we can bring our chosen commitments and hopes.

> There is a Hasidic parable about the Baal Shem Tov, the founder of the Hasidic movement. In the parable, thieves come to the Baal Shem Tov and tell him of a network of underground corridors and tunnels that leads directly from Poland to Palestine. They offer to take him there, and he agrees. They walk through the tunnels with great difficulty. At one point, they come to a murky bog, which almost stops them. But they persist. They get more than halfway to their destination. Then, suddenly, the Baal Shem Tov sees before him "a flaming sword, turning this way and that," and decides to go no farther. He turns back to the place from which he started.

The psychological or mythological meaning of this parable has had many interpretations. Perhaps on one level it says something about the Baal Shem Tov's ambivalence about going to Palestine, his own neurotic solution. But I think that the parable's unconscious, compressed message may be that you can't steal into paradise. You can't approach the tree of life by a shortcut. Of course, the parable also suggests something about the fearsomeness of approaching our object of desire and finding ourselves in paradise—which may then turn out to be an ordinary garden, needing weeding, tilling, and watering.

To be sure, in our human condition, it takes long, strenuous work to find the wished-for terrains of safety or significance or love. And it may often be easier to live in exile with a fantasy of paradise than to suffer the inevitable ambiguities and compromises of cultivating actual, earthly places. And yet, without some move of creating homing structures for ourselves, we risk a condition of exile that we do not even recognize as banishment. And paradoxically, if we do not acknowledge the possibility and the real pain of expulsion, then we will not know that somewhere there is a tree of life that, if we labor hard enough to approach it, can yield fruits of meaning after all.

Explorers
by Charles Simic

They arrive inside
The object at evening.
There's no one to greet them.

The lamps they carry
Cast their shadows
Back into their own minds.

They write in their journals:

The sky and the earth
Are of the same impenetrable color.
If there are rivers and lakes,
They must be under the ground.
Of the marvels we sought, no trace.
Of the strange new stars, nothing.
There's not even wind or dust,
So we must conclude that someone
Passed recently with a broom . . .

As they write, the new world
Gradually stitches
Its black thread into them.

Eventually nothing is left
Except a low whisper,
Which might belong
Either to one of them
Or to someone who came before.

It says: "I'm happy
We are finally all here . . .

Let's make this our home."

Refugees

by Charles Simic

Mine is an old, familiar story by now. So many people have been displaced in this century, their numbers so large, their collective and individual destinies so varied, it's impossible for me or anyone else, if we are honest, to claim any special status as a victim. Particularly since what happened to me fifty years ago is happening to someone else today. Rwanda, Bosnia, Afghanistan, Congo, the endlessly humiliated Kurds—and so it goes. Fifty years ago it was fascism and communism, now it's nationalism and religious fundamentalism that make life miserable in lots of places. Recently, for instance, I was translating the work of a woman poet from Sarajevo for an anthology, and its editors had great difficulty locating her. She had vanished. She was not a young woman, she had plenty of friends, but no one seemed to know what had happened to her in the confusion of the war. It took many months to find her sweeping floors in a restaurant in Germany.

"Displaced persons" is the name they had for us back in 1945, and that's what we truly were. As you sit watching bombs falling in some old documentary, or the armies advancing against each other, villages and towns going up in fire and smoke, you forget about the people huddled in the cellar. Mr. and Mrs. Innocent and their families paid dearly in this century for just being there. Condemned by history, as Marxists were fond of saying, perhaps belonging to a wrong class, wrong ethnic group, wrong religion—what have you—they were and continue to be an unpleasant reminder of all the philosophical and nationalist utopias gone wrong. With their rags and bundles and their general air of misery and despair, they came in droves from the East, fleeing evil with no idea where they were running to. No one had much to eat in Europe, and here were the starving refugees, hundreds of thousands of them in trains, camps, and prisons, dipping stale bread into watery soup, searching for lice on their children's heads, and squawking in dozens of languages about their awful fate.

My family, like so many others, got to see the world for free thanks to Hitler's wars and Stalin's takeover of Eastern Europe. We were not German collaborators or members of the aristocracy, nor were we, strictly speaking, political exiles. Small fry, we made no decisions ourselves. It was all arranged for us by the world leaders of the times. Like so many others who were displaced, we had no ambition to stray far beyond our neighborhood in Belgrade. We liked it fine. Deals were made about spheres of influence, borders were redrawn, the so-called Iron Curtain was lowered, and we were set adrift with our few possessions. Historians are still documenting all the treacheries and horrors that came our way as the result of Yalta and other such conferences, and the subject is far from finished.

As always, there were degrees of evil and degrees of tragedy. My family didn't fare as badly as others. Thousands of Russians whom the Germans forcibly brought to work in their factories and on their farms were returned to Stalin against their will by the Allies. Some were shot, and the rest packed off to the gulags so they would not contaminate the rest of the citizenry with newly acquired decadent capitalist notions. Our own prospects were rosier. We had hopes of ending up in the United States, Canada, or Australia. Not that this was guaranteed. Getting into the United States was especially difficult. Most Eastern European countries had very small quotas, unlike the Western European ones. In the eyes of the American genetic experts and immigration policymakers, South Slavs were not highly desirable ethnic material.

It's hard for people who have never experienced it to truly grasp what it means to lack proper documents. We read every day about our own immigration officers, using and misusing their recently acquired authority to turn back suspicious aliens from our borders. The pleasure of humiliating the powerless must not be underestimated. Even as a young boy, I could see that was the case. Everywhere there are bureaucrats, the police state is an ideal.

I remember standing in endless lines in Paris at police headquarters to receive or renew resident permits. It seems like that's all we ever did when we lived there. We'd wait all day only to discover that the rules had changed since the last time, that they now required, for instance, something as absurd as my mother's parents' marriage certificate or her grade school diploma, even though she was in possession of a French diploma since she did her post-graduate studies in Paris. As we'd stand there pondering the impossibility of what they were asking of us, we'd be listening to someone at the next window trying to convey in poor French how the family's house had burned, how they'd left in a hurry with only one small suitcase, and so on, to which the official would shrug his shoulders and proceed to inform them that unless the documents were produced promptly, the residence permit would be denied.

So what did we do? Well, if the weather was nice, we'd go and sit outside on a bench and watch the lucky Parisians stroll by carrying groceries, pushing baby carriages, walking their dogs, even whistling. Occasionally a couple would stop in front of us to smooch while we cursed the French and our rotten luck. In the end, we'd trudge back to our small hotel room and write home.

The mail didn't travel very swiftly, of course. We would go nuts every day for weeks waiting for the mailman, who couldn't stand the sight of us since we were always pestering him, and finally, somehow, the documents would arrive thanks to a distant relative. Then they had to be translated by an official translator who, of course, couldn't make heads or tails out of the dog-eared fifty-year-old entry in a provincial Balkan school or church registry. In any case, eventually we'd go back to the long line only to discover that they were not needed after all, but something else was. Every passport office, every police station, every consulate had a desk with a wary and bad-tempered official who suspected us of not being what we claimed to be. No one likes refugees. The ambiguous status of being called a DP made it even worse. The officials we met knew next to nothing about where we came from and why, but that did not prevent them from passing judgment on us. Having been driven out by the Nazis brought us a measure of sympathy, but having left because of the Communists was not as well received. If the officials were leftists, they told us bluntly that, ungrateful wretches that we were, we had left behind the most progressive, the most just society on the face of the earth. The others figured we were just riffraff with fake diplomas and a shady past. Even the smiling dummies in store windows on the elegant Avenue Victor Hugo regarded us as if we were out to steal something. It was actually all extremely simple: either we were going to get a foothold here or somewhere else, or we were going back to a refugee camp, prison, or, even worse, to "the embodiment of man's dearest longing for justice and happiness," as the communist world was described in certain quarters.

Immigration, exile, being uprooted and made a pariah may be the most effective way yet devised to impress on an individual the arbitrary nature of his or her own existence. Who needed a shrink or a guru when everyone we met asked us who we were the moment we opened our mouths and they heard the accent?

The truth is, we had no simple answers. Being rattled around in freight trains, open trucks, and ratty ocean-liners, we ended up being a puzzle even to ourselves. At first, that was hard to take; then we got used to the idea. We began to savor it, to enjoy it. Being nobody struck me personally as being far more interesting than being somebody. The streets were full of these "somebodys" putting on confident airs. Half the time I envied them; half the time I looked down on them with pity. I knew something they didn't, something hard to come by unless history gives you a good kick in the ass: how superfluous and insignificant in any grand scheme mere individuals are. And how pitiless are those who have no understanding that this could be their fate too.

I stepped off the boat in New York City on August 10, 1954, with my mother and my brother. The day was hot, the sky was cloudless, and the streets were full of people and cars. My father, who was already in the United States, put us up in a hotel just off Times Square. It was incredible, astonishing. The immigration officers didn't torment us and rip up our papers. They didn't send us back. Our being here and breathing was perfectly legal. Watching TV, ordering room service, and taking a shower broke no laws. Every half hour, we asked my father again if this was true. When he told us yes, we literally jumped for joy. No New Year's Eve, no birthday celebration, no party afterward ever gave me as much happiness. A fear had lifted.

"My love of the country follows from my love of its freedoms," Lewis Lapham said, and I know that's true. I felt that the first day I came to America, and I still feel the same.

I was sixteen, old enough to take walks by myself. The city, which I had seen in so many movies, felt strangely familiar. I'm a big city boy and all large cities resemble one another in a fundamental way. Walking around confirms what one already knows. Here's where the rich live, here the poor. Here is where business is conducted and the expensive stores are to be found. And finally, here is the neighborhood where one goes to have a good time. Nobody had to explain to me the difference between the young women I saw on Madison Avenue and the ones hanging around a candy store on Eighth Avenue. It was the same in Paris and in Belgrade. Of course, New York is also unlike any European city. Its bright colors were startling after the grayness of Europe. Guys in pink shirts, wearing neckties with palm trees on them, getting into yellow taxis on a street of huge neon signs and billboards showing smiling, rosy-cheeked faces drinking tea and puffing cigarettes. That was really something.

Architecturally, too, the city was full of surprises. A skyscraper in midtown next to a three-story building with a hot dog stand. Water towers, fire escapes, trash on the sidewalks, a street with a dozen movie houses all showing films twenty-four hours a day and then a building seemingly made entirely of glass and a park with carriages pulled by horses. The question a newcomer asks, inevitably, is, Where am I going to live? Is it going to be a tenement in Hell's Kitchen or one of the brownstones on some quiet side street on the Upper East Side?

Our initial needs and worries were few and basic. First, and most importantly, we wanted new clothes and an American haircut to take away that look of a hopeless loser that comes with being a DP. We spent the first few days in New York changing our disguises. Jeans, Hawaiian shirts, cowboy belts, colorful T-shirts, sneakers, and other such items, procured cheaply in the vicinity of Times Square, appeared to me to be the height of elegance. To my great surprise, the natives still gave me funny looks on the street. Unwittingly I had transformed myself from a European schoolboy to a country hick, the kind you often saw around the Port Authority Bus Terminal or outside a 42nd Street movie house showing westerns.

Then there was the problem of language. I had studied English, could read it more or less, but speaking it was a different matter. I remember asking for directions the second or third day in New York and not being understood. I wanted to know how many blocks to the Empire State Building. A simple question, except that instead of "blocks," I said "corners." The astonishment and the embarrassment of speaking and not being able to communicate are deeply humbling. Every day in America, I realized, I would have a fresh opportunity to make a complete fool of myself. Quickly, I learned to keep my mouth shut except when absolutely necessary. In the meantime, I read the movie marquees, I tried to follow the TV and radio programs. In secrecy I repeated words and phrases I overheard: Hey, smart aleck!

Crackerjack. Okeydokey. Chase butterflies. Hogwash. Hold the phone. Go to the dogs.

Then there was food. All these burgers, cherry Cokes, hot dogs, grilled cheese sandwiches, apple pies à la mode, and dozens of different candy bars had to be sampled. If you've grown up on thick soups and casseroles, American fast food has the advantage of being portable. It's hard to eat spaghetti or goulash in bed or in a car; it's much easier with a bag of chips or a can of peanuts. It's a perfect invention for someone hungry all the time, as I was. It sounds nice intellectually to claim that an expatriate can never feel at home anywhere again. It's definitely not true of a sixteen-year-old. I was more adaptable than a cat or a goldfish would have been. I was eager to see and taste everything.

Once, my father's rich boss invited us to his house for a Sunday meal. We expected a huge feast and were astonished by the canned vegetables and the thin, overcooked slices of roast beef served in small portions. No spices; no hot peppers; not even a proper amount of salt and pepper. We couldn't get over it. Whatever inferiority complexes we had about entering American homes were quickly cured by the poorly cooked food we were given to eat. Banana splits at some drugstore counter were nothing to sneer at; the tasteless, soggy white bread they served at home made no sense. When we wanted to eat well, we'd seek out a Hungarian or German restaurant in Yorkville or an Italian place down in the Village.

Of course, we always had the option of getting together with other Yugoslavs for some home-style food. However, there was a heavy price to pay. The talk made it difficult to enjoy the cuisine. Exiles usually imagine that theirs is a temporary situation. It was just a matter of days before communism collapsed and their homes and their lives would be restored to them just as they were. Nostalgia is big on the menu at such gatherings, and so is anger at how events turned out. My parents were tired of Balkan squabbles; they wanted a breather. Also, they didn't think there was a likelihood of ever going back. They turned out to be right. The Communists, thinly disguised as democrats, are still in charge at home and so is the old secret police.

To want to be an American, which I certainly desired, made us strangers even to our own kind. They eyed us suspiciously. Without the superiority one's own ethnic group readily provides, what do you have? It's terrible when collective sentiments one is born with begin to seem artificial, when one starts to suspect that one's exile is a great misfortune but also a terrific opportunity to get away from everything one has always secretly disliked about the people one grew up with. I now understand the big choice we made without quite realizing that we were making it. We stopped seeing our fellow Yugoslavs. Already in those early days, I realized that America gave me an opportunity to stop playing the assigned roles that I inevitably had to play around my fellow Serbs. All that deferring to tradition, clannishness, and machismo, with their accompanying vocabularies, I happily gave up. Nor did the role of the professional exile, forever homesick, forever misunderstood, attract me. Adventure lay elsewhere. America and the Americans were far more interesting to me, and so was the anonymity that came with full-scale assimilation.

Actually, that's not entirely accurate. Many of my early friends were Italian, Jewish, Irish, and other immigrants. One of the great experiences of a city like New York was the exposure to so many other ways of life. The ideal of the times was, of course, the melting pot. Still, what did I know about the Blacks, Chinese, Cubans, Lebanese, Hungarians, Russians, Sicilians, before I lived in New York? There is no school as good as the life that takes you one day from a Hungarian butcher on Second Avenue to an Irish bar in Chelsea, an Italian coffee shop on MacDougal Street, and a jazz club off Sheridan Square in the company of a young woman who hails from Texas. No wonder nationalists of all stripes hate cities. It's hard to remain the faithful and obedient son of your own clan when so many other attractive options offer themselves. One has to be a fool or a hypocrite to sing the praises of one's native customs to the exclusion of every other, after one has lived in New York City. The cities are, indeed, agreeably corrupting. They produce free individuals and that, as every state and religious institution the world over will tell you, is an unpardonable heresy.

If the choice, then, was between deepening my own displacement and trying to belong, I made my situation even more complicated by moving away from home when I was eighteen. In other words, exactly two years after I stepped off the 44th Street pier, I found myself again adrift. My parents were not getting along, and life at home was most unpleasant, so I had no alternative. I broke a few more ties I still had to my old identity. I had no other relatives or friends. I had no fixed address or purpose. There was no question of college because my parents were not able to support me, and my grades were not good enough to get me a scholarship anywhere. But if you think that I cried myself to sleep every night over my predicament, you're wrong. It was one of the happiest times of my life. Finding a job and making ends meet—as I discovered quickly—was very easy. Both in Chicago and New York, I could find decent work in a matter of hours. I did everything from being a mail clerk at a newspaper to selling shirts in a department store. I worked in several offices as a bookkeeper. I met all kinds of interesting men and women. Best of all, I felt safe in this country from the persecutions we were accustomed to, and that was more than enough to make a young man permanently cheerful.

In the meantime, there were Charlie Parker, Thelonious Monk, Billie Holiday, Bessie Smith, Duke Ellington, the Five Spot, Birdland, rhythm and blues, country music, film noir, Scott Fitzgerald, Wallace Stevens, William Carlos Williams and the entire New Directions list, the Gotham Book Mart, MoMA, Willem de Kooning, Jackson Pollock, *Partisan Review*, the Brooklyn Dodgers, the Yankees, boxing at Madison Square Garden, "The Honeymooners," Sid Caesar, "I Love Lucy," and literally hundreds of other things to learn about. I was astonished to encounter other recent arrivals who had little or no interest in any of this.

To fall in love with a country or another human being requires some gullibility, and I had plenty to spare. It took me at least fifteen years to appreciate the full extent of our political corruption and to see the problems and injustices this country is faced with. Early on, I was living a version of the American Dream, ignorant of the simple fact that a white boy with an accent is more readily employable than a person of color. There has always been a kind of see-no-evil, let's-pretend demeanor about this country. It needs fresh supplies of true believers to keep it going, and that's what I was. In addition, there was the generosity that I and so many others found here. Every cliché about getting a second chance and reinventing oneself turned out to be true. It gave one confidence—America did that. Who could resist that sudden burst of optimism? I could not.

The clearest proof I had that I've become "an American" came to me in 1962 when I found myself in the U.S. Army in Europe, first in Germany and then in France. The little towns and small cities with their closely knit, insular societies frightened me. It was very pleasant to dine in one of the fine restaurants in Nancy or Colmar, but the silence of the streets after eight o'clock in the evening gave me the creeps: closed shutters, locked doors, lights out almost everywhere. I could well imagine what being a refugee there would be like. More recently, during the break-up of Yugoslavia, I reexperienced my estrangement from the old world. I found myself, for example, incapable of taking sides or seeing any attraction in being a nationalist. The advantage of the melting pot is that it undermines tribalism. One gains a distance from one's own national folly. Fashionable present-day multiculturalism with its naive calls for ethnic pride sounds to me like an attempt to restore me to precisely that state of mind my parents ran away from in Europe. The American identity is a strange concoction of cultures, but at its best it is a concoction prepared and cooked by each individual in his or her own kitchen. It ought not to come in a package with a label and a fake list of wholesome, all-natural ingredients.

There's an old Soviet poster picturing Comrade Lenin standing on the planet earth holding a broom. He's sweeping off "undesirable elements," men and women easily identified by their clothes as belonging to the bourgeoisie. That was us. For that very reason, every project for betterment of humanity, every collectivist ideology, no matter how chaste it sounds, terrifies me. Barbarism, intolerance, and fanaticism have been the by-products of all utopian projects in this century. Infallible theories of history and human progress brought about the most repellent forms of repression. The noble-sounding attempt to make the whole of society accept a particular worldview always leads, sooner or later, to the slaughter of the innocents.

We, displaced persons, were caught between two rival intellectual projects: fascism and communism. Our persecution was justified because we lagged in our understanding of the laws of history. We stood in the way, and so our misfortune was unavoidable and not to be greatly regretted. This harsh view, as we know, had the enthusiastic support of many of the leading writers and intellectuals in Europe. The violence and injustice may have been regrettable, but were in the service of messianic hopes for future happiness. The political writings of the times—both on the left and the right—consist of endless justifications for inflicting death and suffering on the innocent.

If you think I'm exaggerating, consider this. While we stood in lines at the Prefecture, Sartre, Aragon, de Beauvoir, and their kind were dining in style or attending some gala at the Russian or Yugoslav embassy, celebrating Stalin's or Tito's birthday. In this century, the executioners' best friends have often turned out to be writers and intellectuals. The last remaining myth of our age is the myth of the intellectual's integrity and independence. The true enemy continues to be—to return to what I said at the very beginning—the innocent bystander. Or, more precisely, the antagonist has always been the individual conscience. It's that part of ourselves that remains stubbornly suspicious of mass enthusiasms, the one that makes us sleep badly at night. At 3 a.m., the proposed means that are justified by the lofty ends look pretty nasty. For the "lunatics of one idea," as Wallace Stevens called them, that has always been the supreme obstacle on the way to Utopia. Millions perished or lost everything while huge intellectual and military efforts were being made to obliterate and circumvent the conscience of countless human beings.

Speaking as one of the laboratory animals used in a series of famous historical experiments, I'd say I ended up, for better or for worse, with a clearer idea of how the world works—and that's no small matter. I prefer that solitary knowledge to the jubilation of the masses in Red Square or at some Nuremberg rally. I have a firm conviction that the ideologues on the left and on the right are interchangeable. I have a contempt for all shepherd-and-flock theories, all euphorias of thinking the same thought with hundreds of others, all preaching and moralizing in art and literature. Besides, I am a poet, the kind they call a lyric poet. A lyric poem is the voice of a single human being taking stock of his or her own existence. If it works, we speak of its "originality," meaning it is without precedent, it doesn't fit preconceived notions. The poem is both a part of history and outside its domain. That is its beauty and its hope. A poet is a member of that minority that refuses to be part of any official minority, because a poet knows what it is to belong among those walking in broad daylight, as well as among those hiding behind closed shutters.

Second Country
by Joseph Kertes

When the Hungarians surprised the Russians by rising up against them in the fall of 1956, the borders opened and my family fled. I was almost five. We left behind us our relatives and friends, our comfortable home in Budapest, our possessions (except for what we could carry), our language, our culture, a thousand years of history, and these last memories. I saw a Hungarian soldier hanging from a lamppost, and he was staring right at me, as I was at him, but he could no longer see. He would remain a constant reminder that we still had our lives. And a chance for freedom lay ahead.

We ran like mad, hundreds of us. We ran by foot by night across the frontier into Austria. Bombs kept going off, and my brother and I would stop to look up, but there were no planes dropping them. My brother kept asking what was going on, and no one answered. It was not until we'd crossed the border that we found out we'd been running across a minefield. But my father kept urging us on in the darkness, and he kept telling us we were the lucky ones, but I was young. I kept looking behind me and wondering who the unlucky ones might have been and hoping, possibly, that we still might go home to join them. But then the vision of the hanging soldier loomed up over me, kept me running onward.

We arrived at last at a single lamppost, shining brightly in the darkness, and my father told us, "This is Austria." I remember thinking what a crappy country we'd come to. We left home for this? This solitary lamppost?

We were uncertain as to where we were headed ultimately, so my grandmother had taken opera records with her, not knowing when she would hear her favorite music again. (My father was so angry with his mother on account of the weight of her bag that he broke a couple of her records on the pedestal of that Austrian lamppost.) My mother had taken old photographs and a few recent ones of my brother and me as babies, plus a few memorabilia. We might as well have been anticipating Tim O'Brien's *The Things They Carried*. My father had taken only valuables: gold jewelry and gold coins. My older brother (two and a half years older) carried fighting toys: spurs and a gun in a holster, both of which looked real, and a bullet belt with what looked like real bullets, in case we made it all the way to the Wild West. I had a chocolate marzipan bar, some tin soldiers which my brother also liked, and a sheriff's badge my brother said I could carry and keep.

Though harried and apprehensive, we nevertheless felt safe outside our homeland. For us, our homeland had a sad history. My mother had lost both her parents and six of her siblings in World War II. My father had lost his only sibling, his only brother. And now what we hadn't lost to the Germans during World War II, we lost or left behind for the Russians. The idea of "ownership" became fluid. The Russians had liberated Hungary from the Germans, but they never left. They squatted on Hungary, and the West left them to it, as they had with Poland and Czechoslovakia. Stalin had shrewdly allied himself with the West to defeat Hitler, and now he quietly and unobtrusively gobbled up the nations he had liberated—unobtrusively at least until this brief revolution in Hungary. When the larger-than-life statue of Papa Stalin that had stood in Heroes' Square in Budapest came crashing down at the hands of the rebels in 1956, all the ironies came crashing down with it. (Stalin was larger-than-life in every respect—demonic at the best of times—but smaller-than-life in actual stature. Like Hitler. Like Napoleon.)

Standing at the Austrian lamppost, we were now free, free from the clutches of our conquerors and oppressors. So now what? We made our way by bus to Vienna, the bus loaded with Hungarian refugees like us, and we were taken to a large army barracks, which the Austrians had set up for us. We were tested for illness, inoculated and disinfected with sprays and ointments. We were given a good meal, plus chocolates. Then the big question to follow on "So now what?" was "So where to?"

This decision was critical for my family, and we appreciated that we had a choice at all. My Jewish family had no such options during World War II. And famously, or infamously, Jews trying to flee Europe in 1939 aboard the German liner the St. Louis, from Hamburg, Germany, were turned away in Cuba, then Miami, and sailed back to Europe where most perished. In another instance, Rudolf Kastner, a Jewish Hungarian lawyer, had arranged with Adolf Eichmann that, for a certain amount of money, the German commander would allow 1,600 Jews to escape to Switzerland. The selection process was ruthless in that the determining factor was money and money alone. Most who couldn't afford to pay perished. (Some 600,000 Hungarian Jews perished.)

Then along came the Soviets, deftly swallowing one country after another the way the Third Reich had wanted to. The West must have felt guilty, so they opened their doors to us. At the grand bus station in Vienna, Hungarians got free tickets to anywhere they wanted to go in Europe. Each bus was labeled with a different capital—take your choice: Paris, Rome, Bonn, Madrid, Amsterdam, Brussels, Lisbon and beyond—London, Stockholm, Copenhagen …

My mother's aunt from the Bronx, "the Tante," met us in Vienna and took us out to a radiant café for lunch, a café to rival any in Budapest (and that's saying a lot). She gave my parents a thousand American dollars to do with as we pleased. She then offered to set us up in New York. She told us that she and her husband owned three kosher butcher shops in the Bronx, and we would be well fed and well looked after in America. My father's first cousin from Toronto offered to set us up in Canada. He had escaped ten years before and had opened a successful radio shop. He let us know in a telegram that we could stay with him and his family until we found our footing. It was great to have the choice, but refugee agencies and Western countries in general were generous with relocation subsidies and possibilities, and like us many had relatives who had preceded them to the free world.

> That night my parents had a colossal argument. I'll never forget the screaming. Helpers in the army barracks shooed them outside. My grandmother hugged me and clamped my ears shut when she found me crying in my cot.

My father said he was not going to America to become a butcher. He had not been able to become a lawyer because of the anti-Jewish laws instituted in 1939 (when he turned eighteen). He'd become a tool and die maker and felt he could do better on his own in Canada. He badly wanted to make it on his own. He had been born into wealth, and it was all gone, so he had a chance to prove he could do it. But not as a butcher. My father's cousin said he could get him a job as a skilled worker at General Motors just outside Toronto.

> My parents agreed to meet the Tante the next day and to flip a coin. Tails was Canada. Heads was the Bronx. Tails it was. So Canada it became.

What an astonishing fate awaited us in the New World, in Toronto. My father always said he'd brought us to a country "without issues," which of course wasn't true. For one, what had we Europeans done to the First Nations people we had pushed aside, then tried to "cleanse" of their "savagery"?

> But what was true was that in the New World people from many countries, people like us, had to live together and had to make it work, had to do so in harmony. Heterogeneity seemed to be the key. As cultures in Europe and everywhere else, it seemed, remained homogeneous, they often viewed outsiders as Other, as different and therefore to be looked upon with suspicion. The other memorable thing my father used to say, after years in Canada, was that "Europe is a failed experiment. It should be paved over and turned into a parking lot."

So most of the dark events of my life occurred before I started school. Most of my history, too, was loaded with dark events. The darkness followed us to the New World where, if it didn't dissipate, certainly it faded.

> It is a natural defensive impulse to worry that others might represent some kind of threat. The Otherness problem is a serious one because it implies division and is therefore— what else?—divisive.

Just by chance we came to a land that was struggling to find its identity. It had evolved away from Britain. It had not risen up against it the way America had. It had sidled up to the world's greatest power just to the south of us, a power that was to dominate culture and language and modern thinking for more than a century, spreading its character over the face of the planet, some people adoring it and some abhorring it in equal measure.

> The Canada of my childhood was sandwiched between the UK and the US, Janus-like, not knowing which way we were facing much of the time and not certain who we were, quite. In fact, if I can extend the metaphor, we were facing both ways at once and only rarely glancing straight ahead into the mirror.

If Chicago is the Second City, Canada is the Second Country. Rich, vast, free, broad-minded, tolerant, liberal, but Outside. We are outsiders. No Canadian Prime Minister would ever pronounce herself or himself to be the "leader of the free world," except in a comedy routine. We are good at comedy because we are ever the outsider, looking in on the earth-shaking power we have next door. Outsiders, ever-observant, are the best at comedy: Jews, Irish, blacks, homosexuals, minorities of all kinds.

> And what a cool power the United States has been. For too long, I desperately wanted to be American. I majored in American Lit. I was stirred by the bold songs, especially "The Star-Spangled Banner," the bold spirit of independence. Just crossing the border from Ontario into New York thrilled

me. It was the Great Magnet, which pulled all eyes toward it with such force that no one could look away. Billions of people watch the Oscars. Think of how significant that is. Think of how preposterous it is. It is because all eyes are on America. (Now more than ever.)

Quebec is almost the proof of what I'm saying. In Quebec, one of Canada's biggest provinces, people speak French. They have revolted against the dominance of English Canada for centuries, but it is not English Canada that has propagated English culture and language, nor even the old oppressor Britain. It has been America. Quebecers are Canadians. And if Canada is the Second Country, Quebecers feel as if they live in the Third Country. (Never mind Mexico. Who knows what place they think they occupy—or some Americans think Mexicans occupy—on this continent?)

And so we differ somewhat in the way we view refugees. It's the greatest thing about Canada, a thing we stumbled on quite by accident, and that has become part of our nature. Unlike America, refugees here searched for a national identity. The United States has been the proverbial melting pot. Canada is a salad. Some call it a mosaic. We retain our original identities somewhat. The hyphen is harder, more obdurate. I remain a Hungarian-Jewish-Canadian. (The hyphen might be hardening in America too, as populist sentiments darken against newcomers.)

Another remarkable difference is that, in my lifetime, Canada has moved from a pre-national state to a post-national state without ever stopping at national. We Canadians love Canada, but we are anti-nationalist at the same time. We didn't break away from Mother England in a revolution, as I said. We drifted away. We believe in "peace, order, and good government" more than "the pursuit of happiness," though the two aims are not mutually exclusive. Then there is Hungary, the place we left, still caught up in its vain nationalism to the exclusion of minorities. Nationalism is connected with ego and connected with intolerance because it again implies that others are "Other," people with different aspirations, different values.

The overwhelming majority of people fleeing oppressive regimes, like Syria, the way we did from the Soviets, want what we wanted: freedom, security, peace, quiet, shelter, food, decent work, education, a new language, a new way of seeing things, and hope, hope, hope. There are exceptions, of course: extremists and radical thinkers. But most—almost all—are not bursting to commit crimes. They want a future and are willing, for the most part, to relinquish their past, except for the richness it can add to the fabric of the New World, the new tapestry, illuminated and enriched by them. By us.

Moving Beyond Nationalism
Three Global Problems Create a Need for Loyalty to Humankind and to Planet Earth
by Yuval Noah Harari

For several generations the world has been governed by what today we call "the global liberal order." Behind these lofty words is the idea that all humans share some core experiences, values, and interests, and that no human group is inherently superior to all others. Co-operation is therefore more sensible than conflict. All humans should work together to protect their common values and advance their common interests. And the best way to foster such co-operation is to ease the movement of ideas, goods, money, and people across the globe.

> Though the global liberal order has many faults and problems, it has proved superior to all alternatives. The liberal world of the early twenty-first century is more prosperous, healthy, and peaceful than ever before. For the first time in human history, starvation kills fewer people than obesity; plagues kill fewer people than old age; and violence kills fewer people than accidents. If you think we should go back to some pre-liberal golden age, please name the year in which humankind was in better shape than in the early twenty-first century. Was it 1918? 1718? 1218?

Nevertheless, people are losing faith in the liberal order. Governments throughout the world are increasingly restricting immigration, imposing high tariffs, censoring foreign ideas, and turning their countries into walled fortresses. If this continues, the global liberal order will collapse. What might replace it? While nationalism has many good ideas about how to run a particular nation, unfortunately it has no viable plan for running the world as a whole.

> Some nationalists hope the world will become a network of walled-but-friendly fortresses. Each national fortress will protect its unique identity and interests, but all the fortresses could nevertheless co-operate and trade peacefully. There will be no immigration, no multiculturalism, no global elites—but also no global war. The problem with this vision is that walled fortresses are seldom friendly. In the past, all attempts to divide the world into clear-cut nations have resulted in war. Without some universal values and global organizations, rival nations cannot agree on any common rules.

Other nationalists adopt an even more extreme position, saying that we don't need any global co-operation whatsoever. Each nation should care only about its own interests, and should have no obligations towards the rest of the world. The fortress should just raise its drawbridge and man its walls—and the rest of the world can then go to hell.

Balancing Nationalism with Globalism
This nihilistic position is nonsensical. No modern economy can survive without a global trade network. And, like it or not, humankind today faces three common problems that make a mockery of all national borders, and that can be solved only through global co-operation. These are nuclear war, climate change, and technological disruption.

> You cannot build a wall against nuclear winter or against global warming, and no nation can regulate artificial intelligence or bioengineering single-handedly. It won't be enough if only the European Union forbids producing killer robots or only the United States bans genetically engineering human babies. If even one country decides to pursue these high-risk, high-gain paths, other countries will be forced to follow its dangerous lead for fear of being left behind. So whenever a politician says "My Country First," we should ask him or her: How can your country by itself prevent nuclear war, stop climate change, and regulate disruptive technologies?

To successfully confront these three problems we need more, rather than less, global co-operation. We need to create a global identity and encourage people to be loyal to humankind and to planet Earth in addition to their particular nation. Nationalism need not prove an impossible barrier to creating such a global identity. Human identities are quite adaptable.

> Today's nation-states are not an eternal part of human biology or psychology. There were no Italians, Russians, or Turks 5,000 years ago. True, humans are social animals through and through, with group loyalty imprinted in our genes. However, for millions of years humans lived in small, intimate communities rather than in large nation-states. Homo sapiens eventually learned to use culture as a basis for large-scale cooperation, which is the key to our success as a species. But cultures are flexible. Unlike ants or chimpanzees, Sapiens can organize themselves in many different ways, none of which is "the natural way." City-states are not more natural than empires, and nation-states are not more natural than tribes. They are different options on the Sapiens menu, and the choice between them depends on changing circumstances.

Large nations appeared only in the past few thousand years—yesterday morning, on the timetable of evolution—and they developed in order to deal with large-scale problems that small tribes could not solve by themselves. In the twenty-first century we face global problems that even large nations cannot solve by themselves. Hence it makes sense to switch at least some of our loyalties to a global identity.

It does not mean establishing a global government or abolishing all cultural, religious, and national differences. I can be loyal at one and the same time to several identities—to my family, my village, my profession, my country, and also to my planet and the whole human species. It is true that sometimes different loyalties might collide, and then it is not easy to decide what to do. But who said life was easy? Life is difficult. Deal with it. Sometimes we put work before family, sometimes family before work. Similarly, sometimes we need to put the national interest first, but there are occasions when we need to privilege the global interests of humankind.

"Heim kommt man nie," sagte sie freundlich. "Aber wo befreundete Wege zusammenlaufen,
da sieht die ganze Welt für eine Stunde wie Heimat aus."

— Hermann Hesse, *Demian: Die Geschichte von Emil Sinclairs Jugend*

Romeo Alaeff was born in Brooklyn, New York, in 1970. Initially studying biomedical engineering, he received his BA in photography from Tulane University in 1993 and his MFA in photography from the Rhode Island School of Design in 1996.

His work, expressed through a range of mediums, including film/video, drawing, printmaking, and writing, converges on epistemological, psychological, or sociological concerns. He has exhibited internationally in major museums, galleries, and film festivals including: Lyon Biennale, France; Artists Space, NYC; International Print Center, NYC; Dundee Contemporary Arts Center, Scotland; Brooklyn Academy of Music, NYC; State Hermitage Museum, St. Petersburg, Russia; Chelsea Art Museum, NYC; NY Video Festival, Lincoln Center; Witte de With, in conjunction with the International Film Festival, Rotterdam; National Museum, Madrid; Museum of Contemporary Art, Barcelona; Dallas Museum of Art; and Cartier Foundation, Paris.

His work has also been included in university curriculums such as Emory University's "The Displaced Person, Literature Beyond the Canon," The University of Texas at Austin's "American Studies: Religion and Society in American Literature," and Georgia State University's "Graduate Educational Psychology Seminar." In addition, Alaeff has been a guest artist at the Rhode Island School of Design, Brown University, Pratt, Parsons, The University of Georgia, and Georgia State University. He was also a photography instructor at the Rhode Island School of Design.

Romeo is the author of *I'll be Dead by the Time You Read This: The Existential Life of Animals*, a "humor/philosophy" book of drawings (Penguin/Plume, 2011). His stickers appear in *Stickers: Stuck-Up Piece of Crap; From Punk Rock to Contemporary Art* (Rizzoli, 2010).

Alaeff is also the founder and editor-in-chief of *Lines & Marks*, an online publication dedicated to the role and practice of drawing across the arts and sciences.

Yuval Noah Harari is a historian, philosopher, and the bestselling author of *Sapiens: A Brief History of Humankind*, *Homo Deus: A Brief History of Tomorrow*, and *21 Lessons for the 21st Century*. Born in Haifa, Israel, in 1976, Harari received his PhD from the University of Oxford in 2002 and is currently a lecturer in the Department of History at the Hebrew University of Jerusalem. His books have sold over 25 million copies worldwide. Prof. Harari originally specialized in world history, medieval history, and military history. In 2018 and in 2020, Yuval Noah Harari gave keynote speeches on the future of humanity on the Congress Hall stage of the World Economic Forum annual meeting in Davos. Harari regularly discusses global issues with heads of state, lectures around the world on the topics explored in his books and articles, and has written for publications such as *The Guardian*, *Financial Times*, *The New York Times*, *The Times*, *The Economist*, and *Nature*.

Eva Hoffman grew up in Cracow, Poland, before emigrating in her teens to Canada and then to the United States. After receiving her PhD in literature from Harvard University, she worked as a senior editor and literary critic at *The New York Times* and has taught at various British and American universities. Her books, which have been translated widely, include *Lost in Translation*, *Exit Into History*, *After Such Knowledge and Time*, and two novels, *The Secret* and *Illuminations*. She has written and presented programs for BBC Radio and has lectured internationally on the subjects of exile, historical memory, human rights, and other contemporary issues. She is a Fellow of the Royal Society of Literature and was awarded an honorary DLitt from Warwick University. She is currently a visiting professor at the Institute of Advanced Studies at University College London. She lives in London.

Joseph Kertes founded Humber College's creative writing and comedy programs and has been the recipient of numerous awards for teaching and innovation. He was for many years Humber's Dean of Creative and Performing Arts. His first novel, *Winter Tulips*, won the Stephen Leacock Medal for Humour. His third novel, *Gratitude*, won a Canadian National Jewish Book Award and the U.S. National Jewish Book Award for Fiction. His novel *The Afterlife of Stars* was a New York Times Book Review "Editor's Choice." His latest novel is called *Last Impressions*.

Rory MacLean is one of Britain's most innovative non-fiction writers. His books, which have been translated into a dozen languages, include UK Top Tens *Stalin's Nose* and *Under the Dragon*, as well as *Pravda Ha Ha* and *Berlin: Imagine a City*, "the most extraordinary work of history I've ever read," according to *The Washington Post*, which named it a Book of the Year. He has won awards from the Canada Council and the Arts Council of England and was nominated for the International Dublin Literary Award. He has worked on movies with Marlene Dietrich and David Bowie as well as humanitarian projects for the UN, EU, and ICRC. He divides his time between Berlin, Toronto, and the UK. rorymaclean.com

Christian Rattemeyer is the director of SculptureCenter in New York. From 2007 to 2019, he served as associate curator for drawings and prints at the Museum of Modern Art in New York. At MoMA, Rattemeyer's exhibitions include: *SURROUNDS: 12 Installations* (2019), *Transmissions: Art in Eastern Europe and Latin America, 1960–1980* (2016), *Alighiero Boetti: Game Plan* (2012), *Projects 95: Runa Islam* (2011). From 2003 to 2007, Rattemeyer was the curator at Artists Space in New York, where he oversaw and curated over sixty projects. Prior to that, Rattemeyer worked for Documenta 11 in Kassel as communication editor. He also co-founded and co-directed OSMOS, an independent project space in Berlin (1997–98). Rattemeyer has published widely on contemporary art, and his most recent book is *Exhibiting the New Art: "Op Losse Schroeven" and "When Attitudes Become Form" 1969* (Afterall Publishers, 2010). Rattemeyer holds an MA in art history and film studies from the Freie Universität Berlin and an MPhil in art history from Columbia University.

Charles Simic was born in former Yugoslavia in 1938. During World War II, when he was fifteen, he emigrated with his family from war-torn Belgrade to Paris and then to New York City. He is one of the most regarded—and prolific—writers of poetry, essays, and translations living today. A former US poet laureate and co-poetry editor of *The Paris Review*, his work has won numerous awards, including the 1990 Pulitzer Prize and the MacArthur Genius Grant. He has also worked as an editorial assistant for the photography magazine *Aperture*. Simic received the Frost Medal for "Lifetime Achievement in Poetry" and was elected to the American Academy of Arts and Letters in 1995, receiving the Academy Fellowship in 1998. Simic is professor emeritus of creative writing and literature at the University of New Hampshire, where he has taught since 1973.

Acknowledgments

178

Special Thanks
Sonja Altmeppen, anschlaege.de, Sa'ed Atshan, Bemi Aviel & Family, Christopher Baer, Nadine Barth, Anne Bertrand, Priscilla Briggs,
Peter Cairns, Charles Cohen, Jerry William Cullum, Lisa K. Dallos, Dawn d'Atri, Jessica Dimmock, Ines Dobosic, Gabriel Gibson,
Nathalie Grolimund, Tania Haddad, Anja Haering, Yuval Noah Harari, Hatje Cantz, Björn Hegardt, Eva Hoffman, Allen Houston,
Sandra Keller, Joseph Kertes, Justin Kimball, Ben Klock, Gintarė Kunigonytė, Le Pustra (p. 47), Rena Levi, Yardena Levi, Agata Lisiak,
Rory MacLean, Fadi Mohem, Christian Rattemeyer, Jason Ressler, Ashley Rindsberg, Signe Rossbach, Jens Rudolph, Anna Russ,
Marian Ryan, Monica Salazar, Charles Simic, Beth Solin, Stiftung Kunstfonds, Evan Strome, John von Bergen, Rik Watkinson,
Steven Weber, Isabel González Whitaker, Lisa Witter, Sue Wrbican, Nik Zajewski, Birte Zellentin

Special Edition Donors
Lillian Aviles, Chris & Elizabeth Baer, Danielle Black, Robin Blum, Mark & Shosh Blum, Marian Masters Cohen, Lance Esgard,
Ayana & Moshe Fishman, Gabriel Gibson, Celerie Kemble, Ben Klock, Julian Lauzzana, Rena Levi, Cebastian Martinez, Christopher Meadors,
Julie Mehretu, Paul & Avigail Noble, Fehmi Özkan, Natalie Papageorgiadis, Nathan Rao, Astrid Reischwitz, Christopher J. Slajus,
Alfredo Sosa, Isabel González Whitaker

for Ines

Colophon

Editor: Nadine Barth
Managing editor: Romeo Alaeff
Project management: Sonja Altmeppen
Copyediting: Dawn Michelle d'Atri
Graphic design and typesetting: anschlaege.de
Typefaces: GT Sectra, GT America
Production: Anja Haering, Hatje Cantz
Reproductions: anschlaege.de
Printing and binding: Livonia Print Ltd.
Paper: Magno Volume, 170 g/m², Munken Pure, 80 g/m²

© 2020 Hatje Cantz Verlag, Berlin, and authors
© 2020 for the reproduced works by Romeo Alaeff: the artist

Published by
Hatje Cantz Verlag GmbH
Mommsenstraße 27
10629 Berlin
Germany
www.hatjecantz.de
A Ganske Publishing Group Company

ISBN 978-3-7757-4820-9

Printed in Europe

Supported by Stiftung Kunstfonds

STIFTUNG**KUNSTFONDS**